THE LEGACY LEADER

2nd Edition

ANTHONY LOPEZ

Author of Breakthrough Thinking
and The Leader's Lobotomy

D1304715

Tate Publishing & Enterprises

Published by Tate Publishing & Enterprises, LLC
127 E. Trade Center Terrace | Mustang, Oklahoma 73064 USA
1.888.361.9473 | www.tatepublishing.com

Tate Publishing is committed to excellence in the publishing industry. The company reflects the philosophy established by the founders, based on Psalm 68:11,
"The Lord gave the word and great was the company of those who published it."

Book design copyright © 2010 by Tate Publishing, LLC. All rights reserved.
Cover design by Blake Brasor
Interior design by Nathan Harmony

Published in the United States of America

ISBN: 978-1-61663-614-2
1. Business & Economics / Leadership
2. Business & Economics / Management
10.07.12

DEDICATION

To Yvette, Cristina, and Marisa. You define my life. I love you.

To my dad, Hector Luis Lopez. You are a good man and a great father. I'm proud to be your son. I love you.

To my big brother, Hector Luis Lopez, Jr. You have always been my advisor and advocate. I love you.

To Mom. You inspired me to write the first book. Your memory has motivated me to keep going. I love you and I miss you.

ACKNOWLEDGMENTS

Over the years, there have been many people who have influenced and shaped my thinking and leadership philosophy. To them I am indebted. I have been blessed with great friends from whom I have learned much, and I have had the fortune to observe great leaders up close. I have even had the chance to work for a few. I am especially grateful to Colonel Dan Murray (USAF, Retired), who taught me to place the needs of my followers first. To Mr. Jesse Penn, from whom I've learned some of the most fundamental leadership lessons, and whose leadership style I strive to emulate, I owe you a debt of gratitude. I am especially thankful for Pastor Rick Hawks of The Chapel in Fort Wayne, Indiana—a leader with an enormous heart who taught me the power of humble communications. From my brothers and sisters of PRIMER—an organization that redefines the concept of network and creates more of an extended family than simply a professional organization—I have learned first-hand what servant leadership is all about. I am deeply appreciative of my friends, Raymond Arroyo, Daniel Gutierrez, Dan Guadalupe, Charlie Garcia, and so many others at PRIMER who freely give of their leadership talent. Thank you to Carol Zilm for the opportunity you gave me to lead a great organization in CareFusion. Finally, to all those with whom I have had the privilege of leading and collaborating over the years: thank you. I learned more from each of you than I can ever repay.

CONTENTS

FOREWORD

My leadership journey began in my early formative years, long before I was a cadet at the U.S. Air Force Academy, when I discovered that I had a passion for the subject—the art—of leadership. Through my service as Chairman of the Cadet Wing Honor Committee, and later when I moved up the ranks from cadet to officer, I saw how strong, decisive, and ethical leadership can motivate hearts and minds in a profound way. Years later, as a White House Fellow, I had the privilege of observing first hand as some of the nation's most distinguished leaders went about conducting the business of governing our country. During that period it became clear to me that leadership qualities and traits are as varied as the people who embody them. I also came to believe, however, that there are some important non-negotiable qualities that all individuals must possess if they are ever to fulfill their true potential as great leaders.

The most successful leaders understand and live by fundamental principles that keep them centered and focused. They understand that they must have clarity of mission, a principled character, a strong sense of duty, and a dedication to people that is unequalled.

They must act with a balanced sense of urgency, passion, and persistence. The greatest leaders are effective and inspirational communicators. They are people of great courage who are willing to risk personal failure for the privilege of leading a team through transformational change.

If experts were discouraged from writing a leadership book because "it's been done," we would never see another book on leadership published. Three thousand years ago, Sun Tzu wrote *The Art of War*, and since then there have been thousands of books written on the subject of leadership. Yet historically, there has never been a greater need for sound and effective leadership than there is today. Our world has shrunk around us, and the challenges that we face—not just as a nation, but as a human race—are daunting.

Global economic issues have created business crisis at a scale that we could not have imagined just fifty years ago. Yet within the crisis lie the seeds of opportunity for prosperity. Strong and decisive leadership is needed to uncover and exploit those opportunities. Technology is accelerating at a rate that outpaces even our current ability to find applications for it. It will take innovative leadership to drive discovery and exploration of these new areas. Our world is threatened by war, medical epidemics, and, in some cases, human suffering. We need courageous and committed leadership to inspire all of us to rise up and work towards solutions. The need for principle-centered, emotionally intelligent, and well-prepared leaders is increasing. Across all sectors—business, government, and the faith community—we need leaders today, and we will need leaders tomorrow, who have as an end goal the desire to create value and leave the world a better place than they found it.

Thus the need for leadership education continues. In this book, my friend Tony Lopez presents a profoundly important topic in an uncomplicated and practical way. Tony gets to the heart and essence of leadership, boils it down to its fundamental elements, and creates an outline for daily application that simply makes sense. His writing provides us with evidence that leadership need not be complicated. Rather, he reminds us that grounded on the fundamental non-negotiable requirements of character, integrity, and credibility, leadership is about creating something of lasting value and worth. With that as the foundation, Tony presents compelling arguments for what he calls "the mechanics of leadership," and outlines specific ways that leaders must behave in order to reach their full potential.

The greatest measure of a book is whether or not it makes a lasting impression on the reader. *The Legacy Leader* has made a lasting impression on me. I agree with Tony that all leaders must stay centered on and committed to creating a legacy that they can be proud of. The principles outlined in this book serve as an enduring guide and a strong reminder of what we must all strive for as leaders.

—Charles P. Garcia

About Charles P. Garcia

Charles Garcia is the bestselling author of *A Message from Garcia* and *Leadership Lessons of the White House Fellows*. He is a former White House Fellow, a graduate of the U.S. Air Force Academy, and Columbia Law School. In 2006, he sold his investment banking firm, which grew from three people to sixty offices in seven countries. Inc Magazine identified it as one of the top ten fastest-growing privately held companies in the United States. Garcia was named entrepreneur of the year by three national organizations. He is on the board of Fortune 500 companies and serves as the Chairman of the Board of Visitors of the U.S. Air Force Academy. For five years, he served as one of seven board members on the Florida State Board of Education, responsible for all education policy in the state. For more information about him, go to www.charlespgarcia.com.

PART 1

THE LEADER'S LEGACY AND THE MECHANICS OF LEADERSHIP

PREFACE

It was a sunny spring day in May 1985 when I attended my college graduation and was commissioned as a 2nd Lieutenant in the United States Air Force. As a brand new butter bar (a nickname for second lieutenants), I, like probably most twenty two-year-olds, thought that I knew exactly what I was going to accomplish with my life. I was going to be a general in the Air Force one day! I set out to get there by being the best officer that I could be and by planning career moves that would help me achieve my goal. The day I started wearing a flight suit was like Christmas morning for a five-year-old child. Life was good. This was the time when the movie *Top Gun* was still new, and every guy wanted to be Maverick, the hot-shot naval aviator played by actor Tom Cruise. After a few promotions and a few medals to decorate the left breast pocket of my uniform, I knew that I was on my way. At least I thought I did.

Looking back and reflecting on that period of my life, it seems so naïve and innocent. But life has a way of happening, and of taking us in directions and on adventures we never even imagined. That's exactly what happened for me on July 20, 1989. On that day, after my wife had suffered more than thirty hours of labor, I stood over her and tried to "coach" her on breathing between contractions. Comedian Bill Cosby captured this moment best when he described the futile attempt of men to "coach" their partners through the process of child birth. He says the only way for a man to understand the pain of childbirth is to take his bottom lip and pull it over his head! Almost twenty years later, my hand still hurts from Yvette squeezing it as she pushed through the contractions. I was smart enough then, and I still am today, not to complain about that given how trivial it is compared to what she endured.

Finally, our first daughter, Cristina Yvette, came screaming into the world. In an instant my priorities changed. Suddenly, being a general in the Air Force did not seem too important anymore. Now being a daddy became everything. The awesome responsibility of having a child sunk in overnight. I left my wife and newborn at the hospital that first night and went home to try and get some sleep. That was pointless.

I realized that life had changed. The hospital would force us to take the child home with us! My mind was filled with what I wanted for her. I considered the ways that I could impart to her important lifelong values that would help her become the best that she could be. For the first time, I gave serious thought to how I want to be thought of by someone else. What would I want her to say about daddy after he was gone? Here she was just a few hours old, and she had already caused me to reconsider all of my goals and objectives. I asked myself, "What do I want my legacy to be?" And so began what has become a lifelong passion for me: understanding what makes up a good legacy and trying to live up to it.

There is an old saying that the only two things in life that are certain are death and taxes ... and you don't really have to pay taxes. Well, there is one other certainty in life: *you will have a legacy.* That is not a choice we get to make. The only choice we have is what that legacy will be. Not all legacies will be good or long lasting ones.

Some of us will be remembered only as long as people who knew us are here to keep our memory alive. Others will be recorded in history to be remembered as long as there is a civilized world inhabiting this planet. A few will be immortalized by certain acts that defined their lives and others for the way they lived their lives in pursuit of a noble goal. For example, people like Mother Teresa and Martin Luther King, Jr., will forever be remembered as passionate and peaceful leaders who made the world a better place.

Considering the question of what my legacy would be led me to begin studying the subject of leadership. Whether you are leading a nation, a corporation, a church, a Boy Scout troop, or a family, you have a great opportunity to create a legacy that has significant impact.

Over the years I have read many contemporary books on the subject of leadership, and it became clear that most authors concerned themselves with the mechanics of leadership. Volumes have been written about how to lead—about what to do and when to do it. However, few have given serious consideration to the true purpose of leadership.

Many of these books glazed over the subject of purpose and called it "having a vision" or "sound objectives." In some cases, they simply said the purpose of leadership is to lead. That is either too deep in its philosophical significance for my simple brain to comprehend, or it completely misses the mark as to the true purpose of leadership. I suspect it is the latter. Leaders have a unique opportunity—indeed, an awesome responsibility—to do something of lasting value and worth that transcends more than just their immediate surroundings. Otherwise, what's the point?

I don't mean to imply that the mechanics of leadership are not important. They are very important. Leaders can and must learn how to be effective. They need to know how to develop strategies based on a well-developed vision. They must understand the principles of communication, empowerment, delegation, diversity, and other fundamental principles of good leadership. These are all important skills for leaders to have in their tool bags if they are to be successful. However, what they must always keep in the forefront of their thinking is *why* they lead. What is their purpose in leading?

Leadership is a noble duty. Those given the opportunity to lead must look beyond themselves and their personal interest. They should consider the reasons why they lead, and the short- and long-term impact on the lives of those they lead.

I have come to believe that regardless of a person's style of leadership, there are some fundamental constants that more than anything else define a leader's legacy. More than what they accomplish, how they go about accomplishing it will determine how they are remembered. These fundamentals are *character, integrity,* and *ethics.* I believe that when these are compromised, the leader will never achieve all that they potentially could have.

In this book, I, like other authors, present my ideas for how to learn some of the mechanics of leadership. I present my ideas of the types of behaviors a leader must exhibit to be a good leader, including his or her role as mentor, communicator, motivator, and designer of organizations. I outline my thinking on credibility and its important role in the leader's effectiveness. However, my focus is to present these concepts while illustrating the direct correlation between the leader's character and integrity and his or her effectiveness as a leader. My goal is, to help leaders understand how to go about creating a legacy that they can be proud of.

While I use many stories from my own experiences, successes, and failures to illustrate points in the book, I do so only in the spirit of relating stories of which I have first-hand knowledge and can write about with confidence. I do not use my personal stories as a proclamation of my abilities as a leader. Quite the contrary, I am humbled by the many great leaders who have led with purpose in the past, and by those who today are creating legacies that others, including myself, will envy. I can only hope to be as good as them one day.

Many of us have had the great fortune of being exposed to great and not-so-great leaders. Much can be learned from both types.

Knowing how not to behave as a leader is equally as important as learning the best leadership behaviors. I've been lucky to have the opportunity to lead groups as small as two people and as large as thousands. I have had successes as a leader and I have experienced some failure. Above all, I have learned that if your purpose is sound, your character intact, your heart in the right place, and if you care more about your followers than yourself, your battle to be an effective leader is ninety-nine percent won.

From time to time, we all need a reminder to take a step back and focus on what's important. Sadly, it often takes a life-altering event, such as losing someone or something of value to us, or some catastrophic event in the world, like the attack on the World Trade Center and the Pentagon that occurred on September 11, 2001, in the United States. Only then do we stop and take note. It is at times like those that we reflect upon what is important. We realize then that making or having money is nice, but it's not everything. We decide that many of the arguments or discussions we wasted energy on in recent times are fruitless. We recognize that our actions, whatever they were, may have affected our immediate circle of control for a short time, but they lacked any real significance in the long term. And we resolve to change. I hope this book will serve as a reminder that as leaders, we, more than any one else, can make a difference. I hope it reminds us that our leadership must have a fundamentally good purpose, and that we must labor to create a legacy we can be proud of.

—Anthony López

ONE

THE LEADER'S LEGACY

At one point or another in our lives we grapple with the question of purpose. The eternal question of "Who are we and why are we here?" has been asked since man first walked on the planet. There comes a time in our lives when we ask ourselves, "What am I here for?" and, "What will people remember about me when I am gone?"

We are here for a relatively short period of time. Those of us in our forties look at the eighteen year olds and say, "Don't blink, you will soon be me." How true that statement is. Life moves fast, and the clock is relentless in its march forward. As I was doing some research for this chapter of the book, I listened to a radio commentator who was talking on leadership and the legacy they leave behind. He began saying this:

> *"People think that fifty is middle age. How many people you know live to one hundred? No my friends, middle age is thirty to forty. Most people live to be between sixty and eighty years of age..."*

Ouch! Reality just hit many of you reading this, as it did me when I heard him say it. Down deep, we all know it, but we just don't want to think about it. So, since we are here for a relatively short period of time, it's never too early to start thinking about what the purpose of our lives really is. We ought not to delay in considering what our legacy will be. Perhaps better stated, it's never too early to start thinking about what *we want* our legacy to be.

In their book, *A Leader's Legacy*, James M. Kouzes and Barry Posner explore the question of leadership and legacy. They examine the critical questions all leaders must ask themselves on how they are behaving if they want to leave a lasting impact. In the book, the authors consider thorny and often ambiguous issues with which today's leaders must grapple. Kouzes and Posner captured the essence of legacy in the book. They summarize it this way: "The legacy you leave is the life you lead." Read that sentence again. Then read it again.

If you consider the legacy you want to leave behind, you quickly discover what your purpose in life is. They are one and the same! The reality, however, is that most people never really give this much serious thought. They move through life rather than living their life.

Over the years, I have thought of what the purpose of my life is and how I hope my wife, children, family, and friends will remember me when I'm gone. I have come to the conclusion that more than anything else, I will be remembered for who I was as a person, a friend, a father, and a husband. Nothing will define my legacy more than that; not the number of books I write or the number of companies I run. It certainly will not be for the amount of money I leave in the bank.

Consider this: there are a few words you will never see on a tombstone. You will never see "CEO" on a tombstone. You will never see the word "Director" or "Entrepreneur" or "Millionaire" on a tombstone. You may not even see the words "Nobel Prize Winner" despite the level of importance society places on these types of accolades. What you will see most often is "Loyal Husband," "Good Son," "Father," or "Friend." Thus, we should carefully consider what we spend our time on and what we want our legacy to be.

I have also come to the conclusion that two personal traits, more than any other, will impact my legacy. These two traits are my character and integrity. These two traits must form the foundation on which we build and, when necessary, rebuild our legacy. The same is true for all leaders.

Recent events in our society and history provide unarguable evidence of the decline in many people's expectation and requirements for their leaders to be persons of undeniable integrity and character. These words, in fact, have all but lost their meaning when used to describe those who are in positions of leadership. Where integrity and character at one time, now long gone, defined the very essence—indeed the core—of who a leader was, most now accept a flawed character as normal and of no real consequence to the leader's ability to be effective.

In 2003, when I first published the 1st Edition of *The Legacy Leader*, I began with the premise that character and integrity are the only two non-negotiable traits a leader must possess in order to be the most successful that they could ever be. Six years later, as I pen the 2nd Edition of the book, I am ever more certain that that premise is indeed the correct one.

In order to make my point back in 2003, I used an example of a contemporary leader who everyone would be able to relate to. Today, although several years later, the example I used then is still very relevant. This is especially the case given the visibility, media coverage, and notoriety that this individual continues to get even now. Without engaging in a political argument, perhaps one of the most visible and classic contemporary examples of the levels to which our expectations have fallen as it relates to the character and integrity of the leaders we choose to follow is former president William J. Clinton.

There can be lively debate as to whether President Clinton's policies on the economy led to a time of great expansion and wealth generation for many. We could argue whether his policies on the environment, foreign affairs, health care, and taxes were effective and the right policies for our nation during his years as president.

The political analysts of today, and the historians of tomorrow, will no doubt pass judgment on this and other political aspects of Clinton's presidency.

There is little debate, however, on what the character and integrity of the man are. Even his most avid supporters agree that he is a man of flawed moral character. They confirm that the many scandals generated as a result of his reckless personal behaviors left Bill Clinton with a legacy that will forever be tarnished; he leaves the memory of a president impeached as a direct result of being less than honest under oath about improper relations with a young intern. However, argue those same supporters, none of this affected his ability to be a good president and leader. They point to economic and other socio-political indicators and claim victory. Bill Clinton is by no means alone in the category of leaders who have fallen victim to their own lack of character and integrity. None of us are perfect, that's for sure! The fact remains, however, that President Clinton is a glaring example, and a loud warning to the rest of what goes wrong with a leader when character and integrity are compromised.

Once again, without engaging in a moral or political debate, would a fair question to ask be: "If President Clinton would not have had to spend so much of his eight years in office defending personal behaviors, many of which have been proven to be complete fact by his own admission, could he have been an even more effective president and leader? Could he have accomplished much more of his vision for America?"

Such a rhetorical question has, of course, no real answer. How could we ever know? Yet logic would seem to lead to the conclusion that he would have. It seems more than reasonable to think that the time and effort he spent on defending his actions could have been spent more productively pushing his agenda, communicating his ideas, motivating his followers, and directing his core group of leaders to drive results. Ultimately, it would have meant more time dedicated to being a leader. Amazingly, former president Clinton is more popular now than ever. He is still very much in the limelight of our political process in the United States, and has huge celebrity status! This only provides more evidence as to how our standards of what we expect from our leaders has degraded to dangerously low levels.

Unfortunately, the example of President Clinton is not unique. Recent events in the United States have fueled my thinking on the importance of character and integrity as the two non-negotiable fundamental traits of effective leaders, and as to how far we have fallen from that standard. Even in my own recent personal experience as a leader, I have come face to face with the dilemma of character and integrity, and have discovered how fragile a leader's reputation can be when these two standards are not held as absolute values. I am also convinced that a leader can redefine or reshape his or her legacy; that a leader can indeed recover from mistakes that tarnish his or her legacy and thereby redefine how he or she will be remembered.

In recent months, we have seen the complete meltdown of the financial industry in the US, indeed in the world, in the midst of reports of corruption and greed among the industry leaders in that area. We are angered, although not surprised, as the mismanagement by senior leaders in organizations such as AIG, Fanny May, and Freddie Mac, who have sought and received US government bailouts for their failed companies while they have personally lined their pockets with millions of dollars in salary and bonuses.

We roll our eyes in disgust as the executives of the US automobile industry travel via private corporate jets to attend a meeting with Congressional leaders to ask for billions of dollars in a government bailout of their sinking companies. Can you picture the board meeting where the decision was made by these disconnected leaders? How could they think it wise to travel the most expensive way possible to attend a meeting where they were basically asking for a handout? Wow! What where they thinking?

We have seen a rash of political leaders, one after the next, fall from grace because of corruption, sexual scandals, and abuse of their power.

Even John Edwards, who from 2007 to 2008 was a viable presidential candidate for the Democratic Party, was recently exposed as having had affair with a woman and fathering her child. The governor of New York, Eliot Spitzer, recently resigned when he was exposed for, on several occasions, soliciting the services of a high price prostitute and even using government funds to pay for her services!

On December 10, 2008, the breaking news story was the arrest of Illinois governor Rod R. Blagojevich on numerous corruption charges. The New York Times' headline read: "Governor Accused in Scheme to Sell Obama's Senate Seat." The governor's chief of staff, John Harris, was also arrested on corruption charges. The list goes on and on. Sadly, these are not the first, and will likely not be the last. Moreover, whether Democrats or Republicans, politicians, corporate officers, or church leaders, we find many examples of failed leadership stemming first and foremost not from their lack of education, intelligence, or skill, but from their failed ethical and moral character and integrity.

The subject of leadership has been covered in thousands of books and articles; from the early writings of Sun Tzu and the *Art of War*, to Druker's *Leader of the Future*, Kotter's *A Force for Change*, and Hershey's *The Situational Leader* to countless of other titles and authors. Some of these have revealed something fresh and new, while most have repackaged well-understood and practiced principles and presented them as revolutionary. Books on leadership seemed to have evolved, mutated in fact, to a set of rules on how to coach or manage resources. Whether people, money, or other forms of resources, it seems most books today start out talking about leadership and end up talking about business management practices.

Interestingly, books on leadership are found in the "Management" section of today's mega-bookstores such Amazon, Barnes and Noble, or Borders. Clearly, there is a need for books that deal with the mechanics of leadership. There are concepts and skills that can be learned and practiced in order to become a better leader. But, it seems, most have avoided delving into one of the elements of leadership that this author believes to be at the core of good and effective leadership, purposeful leadership with a legacy. This fundamental element is that of character.

Does character matter? Do the elements that define ones character also determine the level of effectiveness that a leader can achieve? In the past, such a question would be absurd. Could anyone doubt that men like George Washington, Abraham Lincoln, General George S. Patton, Ike Eisenhower, and Martin Luther King, Jr., valued and respected people of character? And that their own character was considered paramount when it came to their reputations as leaders?

Long gone, it seems, are the days when our leaders inspired our trust and loyalty. When leaders where expected to be people of the highest integrity, high morals, ethical, and of unblemished character. We long for leaders who put the interest of the followers before their own. The heroes of our past—those who history books have preserved for all time—seem suspended, as if frozen, waiting for someone to pick-up where they have left off, and inspire the same spirit among their followers. How we admire these historical figures! And often we are impressed by how our better-known contemporary leaders of today pale in comparison.

Arguably, these are different times than those depicted in our history. No doubt, Washington, Lincoln, Martin Luther King Jr., and the others had their flaws. It is true that they did not have to contend with the world of immediate and global news via satellite and the internet. Leaders today do have to live in the reality that when they make one slight misstep or say just two words that seem to someone inappropriate, they are instantly available to millions of people across the globe. Nevertheless, there are few that would question the integrity of people like Lincoln, Washington and King. Few would be willing to engage in a debate about whether or not they had high standards of personal behavior and ethics. Fewer still are those who would debate their effectiveness as leaders; their legacy as leaders.

Leadership theories and instruction manuals all share very many of the same ideas of what the traits and skills are that a person must possess to be an effective leader. Regrettably, in many cases today that definition is tainted to mean effective in the economic sense. Nevertheless, the books agree on the key elements that make up the leader and their role. It seems many, indeed perhaps most, neglect to account for, and factor in, the tremendous effect that the leader's character can have on the organization that they lead.

It is a person's character that defines who they are. Their core values and beliefs are buried deep within the programming that determines this character and drives their behavior. A person can no more betray their character, than they could alter their DNA. It is a part of each of us. Developed from a combination of everything we have been exposed to through formal and informal education, sociological conditions describing the person's early and formative years, family and other community settings, and life experiences in general. However, because character is formed primarily by external factors, unlike our DNA, it can be altered either through continuing life experiences, education, and conditioning or learned and practiced behavior, or other significant forms of influence.

The debate about character today seems to be a shallow one. It is typically reserved for political debates and company credos. But one hardly ever truly measured, valued, taught, and expected of today's leaders. Certainly, there are not many courses at the top MBA schools that focus on the subject of character and its profound effects on leadership. No course is given to first line supervisors, let alone top executive management, on why a person's character influences how they can achieve their vision for the organization.

In this text, we will explore how character is woven into the very fabric of leadership. It is my position that a leader, no matter how good he or she is, and regardless of what level of success he or she would personally and organizationally achieve, will never achieve their highest level of effectiveness as a leader if they are not people of strong character. Not strong in the sense of stubborn or tough. But rather, strong and respected as people who exemplify and model the behavior that society and the culture (organizational or geographical) in which they lead, has set as expected and accepted.

Can a leader be effective if they are of flawed character? I believe that the answer very much depends on the definition of success. Most would agree that if a leader is to be successful, they should have the following traits: strong communication skills, intelligence, visionary, be a good motivator, and be able to direct his or her followers. There are many other traits that can be listed for a good leader. But boiled down to their essence, it comes down to what Professor Kotter so simply states in his book *A Force for Change*: a leader's role is to align, motivate and direct their followers. The question that countless books try to address is not what a leader should do, but how they should do it.

In John C. Maxwell's excellent book *The 21 Irrefutable Laws of Leadership*, he does a terrific job of outlining many concepts of leadership in action. The application of these basic principles are what in essence, make a person become more effective in aligning, motivating and directing.

So, again we ask, does character matter? Does the legacy of a leader matter? Can it affect the organization's present and future? How about its past? I believe the answer to all of these questions to be yes. While the "how to" is critically important as to the success of the leader and ultimately the organization, the "why" can be equally as important. A leader of high integrity and character will by definition have a vision that is supported long term by the values and beliefs in the society in which they live.

Ultimately, followers will judge their leaders according to a standard predetermined by their own sense of values and ethics. For most people there are some shared values despite differences in cultures. Cheating, lying, stealing, and other unethical or immoral behavior are considered unacceptable for our leaders, albeit in some societies it is seems it is less reprehensible than others. That is not to say that in those instances, followers are not impacted by these leader traits. It may only indicate their level of resignation and acceptance to the behavior, and perhaps even by default and lack of action, it may represent their condoning such behavior.

However, given the choice, would followers not be more inclined to be motivated following someone they could implicitly trust? Would followers not prefer someone who, time after time, spoke honestly and truthfully? A person who consistently demonstrated concern for their well-being? The answer to these would be yes, with the following condition: the person would also need to have all the other required skills of a leader! We expect and need our leader to be a person with a vision and a passion for that vision. Of course we prefer a person who has the communication skills and charisma necessary to rally followers to succeed. No doubt we want a leader with the technical skills and intelligence to create and direct the proper organization.

Therefore, we seem to be back to the basics. It still is, to some degree, about learning to lead. It still is about the mechanics of leadership. But it is also fundamentally about having a person of character who can lead. It is about weaving the leader's character into the inner workings of the organizational culture. It's about creating a legacy as a leader that others would be proud of and want to emulate; for there is no stronger motivator than loyalty. Well directed, loyal followers are the most valuable resource a leader can have.

Sir Arthur Conan Doyle once said, "It has long been an axiom of mine that the little things are infinitely the most important." And so it goes with leadership. It is usually the small things that make all the difference in the world to the followers. It is a leader's day in and day out consistent behavior that motivates and drives an organization. It is the knowledge that whatever may come, difficulties and complicated situations, a leader's steadiness can be counted on.

Thus, if people are to follow, a leader must:

- Be of impeccable character and integrity
- Inspire loyalty among the followers
- Inspire trust among the followers
- Sincerely care about his or her followers
- Put the interest of the organization before their own

In his famous "I have a Dream" speech, Martin Luther King, Jr., said "I have a dream that my four children will one day live in a nation where they will not be judged by the color of their skins, but by the content of their character." Dr. King understood how important character is. And while he was, of course, speaking about civil rights, and I would not for a second attempt to diminish his purpose, this statement is fundamentally the belief that I hold to be true for leaders. They must be people of character. More specifically, they must be people of character who learn to lead. People who apply principles that will be expanded in this text, and that have been presented in many other books and articles, integrate them into their personal styles, and apply them on a daily basis.

TWO

THE LEGACY LEADER'S CHARACTER AND INTEGRITY

The inevitable question that all leaders will have to face is: "How will I be remembered?" Leaders need not try to create a legacy. They will have one, whether they like it or not. The only question that truly is within their control to answer is: what will that legacy be? Every action, every decision made by a leader contributes to their long-term legacy. There are, of course, decisions and actions taken, that more than any other will indeed define that legacy.

Abraham Lincoln will always have as part of his legacy the Civil War and the emancipation of the slaves. Patton will always be remembered as a strong, dynamic, and relentless leader who set objectives and achieved them, even at tremendous cost. The Reverend Billy Graham will have the legacy of a strong, evangelical leader who dedicated his entire adult life to preaching the Christian faith. John F. Kennedy will be remembered for the Bay of Pigs, the Cuban Missile Crisis, his famous, "Ask not what your country can do for you, ask what you can do for your country..." speech, and for Marilyn Monroe.

Gandhi will be remembered for his pursuit of change and resistance to tyranny through mass civil disobedience; Castro for being a ruthless dictator, Lee Iaccocca for saving Chrysler Corporation from bankruptcy, and General Johnson for creating one of the world's most respected companies, Johnson & Johnson. Walt Disney will forever live in history as a man of incredible vision and leadership who forged an empire based on a mouse. The Reverend Jesse Jackson would have been solely remembered for his life long pursuit of Civil Rights for black Americans, until his adulterous affair was revealed. Now, unfortunately, his legacy has been undeniably altered. In contrast, Martin Luther King, Jr., has his birth date honored as a holiday in this nation, in celebration and remembrance of his lifelong work in the Civil Rights Movement during the turbulent 1960s. It's not whether leaders will have a legacy, it's what will that legacy be.

Barack Obama will be remembered for being the first African American elected to the office of President of The United States. More importantly, however, he will be remembered for what he has not yet even done. If he chooses his daily actions wisely, he will create a legacy that he, his family, and all Americans can be proud of. I for one hope he will be incredibly successful in this pursuit!

From the moment that a leader is appointed, promoted, or in some other way elevated to that position, the record book is opened, the pen is dipped in ink, and the creation of a legacy is begun. Why is having a good legacy important? Why would it matter? Isn't it more important what the leader achieves rather than how they are remembered? The answer is that they are one in the same. How the leader will be remembered is defined by how they behave, which defines what they will accomplish while they are the leader and how long lasting the results will be.

If Walt Disney had not been a man of vision and passion for that vision, how could he have accomplished all that he did? His legacy is clearly a reflection of how he acted while he was the leader. That translated to his everyday actions, to the way in which he talked to his followers, and the way he motivated them and pushed them to greater highs of achievement. Moreover, had his vision been the wrong one, would there be a Disney World today? If Disney's legacy was that he was a mediocre businessman with little creativity, would the people who followed him been inspired to create the empire that exist today?

Lee Iaccocca could have used his excellent leadership and management skills to successfully close down Chrysler. After all, managing a bankruptcy takes an inordinate amount of talent if a manager is to reduce the loss to the investors while divesting the company. Instead he chose to lead through tough times by going back to basics, driving down cost, increasing the quality of the product, and creating a renewed sense of pride in the company by the employees. He put himself on the line. The rest is history. However, recent events in Chrysler and their downfall along with the rest of the automobile industry in the United States is a clear indication to all of us that leadership is not a fad or temporary requirement. It is clear that we need our leaders to be ever vigilant in their post. Sadly, that is not always the case.

A leader's legacy, which is created day in and day out during their tenure as leaders, affects the organization, group, and followers while they are the leader and in some cases long after they are gone. Whether positive or negative, the effect of the leader's legacy will be an integral part of the very fiber that makes up the organization, and that for an enduring term, defines its culture. Only after the new leader's legacy is well established and dominant will the predecessor's legacy be less impactful.

By default, then, if the legacy left behind by one leader is negative, the new leader's job is made much more difficult. They will have to work hard to overcome the organizational culture; to change the norms and expected behaviors before they can inject a new way of thinking and doing things. If, on the other hand, the new leader enters on the heels of a leader who leaves behind a positive legacy, they can quickly, albeit carefully and strategically, infuse their style into the organization and move it quickly to the next level of achievement.

A leader who carefully considers what they want their legacy to be can plan for it and work towards achieving it by behaving in ways that are consistent with their vision of their legacy. The question becomes, what really defines a Legacy Leader? Is it who they are? Is it what they do and how they do it? Is it their personality? Is it their character? Thus, before we can dive into the mechanics of leadership, we should begin with truly understanding the character of a leader. The best way to understand this is to begin with a clear definition of that often misused and misunderstood word: *character*.

> *Char-ac-ter (kar`ek ter)*: the distinguishing qualities of a person; moral excellence and strength. From the middle French caractere; from Latin character "mark, distinctive quality"; the attributes or features that make-up and distinguish the individual moral excellence and firmness.

Webster's definition of the word gives us a level starting point from which we can begin to better understand what a Legacy Leader must have. It leaves us, however, with many questions and possible interpretations. After all, what is moral excellence? What is meant by distinctive quality? Or "individual moral excellence and firmness"?

Who defines the moral standard? These are difficult questions to answer with certainty in today's diverse and global environment. Culturally, there are significant differences between what is acceptable from one group to another, from one nation to another, or from one part of the world to the other. What in one place would be construed as immoral behavior may indeed be expected, or at a minimum, accepted, in another.

Therefore, if we are to gain some consensus as to the meaning of the word character as it relates to leadership, we must define other related terms that would better frame the issues related to the leader. As is often the case when we seek a definition of one word, it becomes necessary to research the definition of several other words in order to gain a full understanding of not just the word, but of the concept of the word. Such is the case with the word character. The definition of character ends with the word firmness. Let us begin there.

What is meant by this word in this context? I believe the answer is found in the definition of the word *integrity*.

> *In-teg-ri-ty (in teg're te)*: 1. Firm adherence to a code of normal or artistic values. 2. Completeness; wholeness 3. Unimpaired condition; soundness 4. Honesty, sincerity, etc.

Firmness as it relates to character means standing steadfast on a belief or a set a beliefs. These would be non-changing or non-negotiable attributes. If a person is to be a person of character, they must be a person of integrity. By definition, a person of integrity is one that is honest and sincere. We can search for the meaning of these, but it is debatable as to whether there are levels of honesty and sincerity. However, at the risk of highlighting this author's bias, I would propose that the meaning is crystal clear and universally accepted. Honest means just that–telling the truth. Sincere means saying what we mean and meaning what we say. Arguably, these traits in a person would be rather universally understood regardless of diversity consideration around cultural norms.

The next term that must be explored in the search for a complete understanding of character is *moral*.

> *Mor-al (mor'al):* Relating to the principles of right and wrong; conforming to a standard of right behavior; ethical, virtuous, righteous, noble; implies conformity to established sanctioned code or accepted notions of right and wrong.

This definition makes it very clear that a moral person behaves in a way that is widely accepted by the culture in which they live and operate, as right. By default, they understand the difference between that which is socially acceptable and that which is seen as the wrong way to behave.

Clearly, morality would be difficult to generalize in terms of what is sanctioned behavior as this is very much driven by sociological and even historical events that define a group. Although, one could argue that there are some universally accepted practices around what is right and wrong. Behaviors such as stealing, killing, and lying could, with some degree of confidence, be placed in this category. Further analysis of this definition begs the question as to what is meant by *ethics*.

> *E-thics (e'tics):* the principles of conduct governing an individual or a group–*e-thi-cal*: conforming to professional standards of conduct. Suggest the involvement of more difficult or suitable questions of rightness, fairness, or equity. Virtuous implies the possession or manifestation or moral excellence in character. Righteous stresses noble, implies moral eminence and freedom from anything petty, mean or dubious in conduct and character.

This definition elegantly ties together the elements of morality and integrity back to the fundamental character. It declares an ethical person to be one who conforms to professional standards of conduct, which by definition means an ethical person is acting in a moral manner. It goes further to add the element of judgment. To act ethically a person would need to make some decision as to the rightness or fairness of an issue, and they must do so without the implication of self indulgence as indicated by the warning to be clear of petty, mean or dubious conduct. That is, to keep whole and true to the values and beliefs we expose.

With these definitions as background, we conclude then that a person of character therefore:

1. Makes a judgment as to what is right and wrong

2. Behaves in ways that are consistent with what is right

3. Remains faithful and steadfast to core values and beliefs consistent with the standards

4. Is not self indulgent or driven by selfish motivations

Thus, we say that it is a person's morals, ethics, and integrity that define who they are. Taken to the next logical level, we conclude that it is a group's or organization's morals, ethics, and integrity that define who they are. In fact, these terms are used liberally in company credos, mission statements, and mottoes. There are few performance appraisal systems used by companies to evaluate their employees that don't include some section for indicating the person's character.

Imagine for a moment a leader who exhibits all the traits we listed above for a person of character. Think of the power they could command. Of course, just because a person is of impeccable character, it does not mean that they will be a good leader. There are other qualities that must be present for a person to be an effective leader.

However, there can be no doubt that a person with a less-than-impeccable character will not, indeed cannot, achieve the very highest level of performance that they could and should, had they not been anchored by some character flaw or had they been people of unimpeachable character. We can list numerous examples where the legacy of a leader has been tarnished by a character flaw. Clearly, the energy they expended defending and explaining themselves, and the time and energy wasted by critics and followers alike, dealing with the character issue, could have been put to better use towards achieving the organizational vision and goals.

General Norman Schwarzkopf once said this about character: "Leadership is a potent combination of strategy and character. But if you must be without one, be without strategy." I don't think he could have said it any better than this!

For someone to become a true Legacy Leader, they must first be a person of the highest character. This may be the hardest of all traits to develop because it is usually established in a person early on in their lives by many external factors such as: family upbringing, schooling, church teachings, societal norms, economic status, and life experiences. These environmental conditions are not things that most people can control, particularly early on in life. Yet, they can be changed and attitudes altered. Thus, good character can be learned. Moreover, so can the other traits of being an effective leader.

In his book, *The West Point Way of Leadership*, Colonel Larry Donnithorne writes,

> "Leader of Character is the phrase the Academy uses to describe the kind of leader it wants its cadets to become. A leader of character has all of the qualities we normally associate with leaders—ambition, confidence, courage, intelligence, eloquence, responsibility, creativity, compassion—and one thing more which we unfortunately overlook too frequently among civilian leaders: A leader of character is absolutely trust worthy, even in times of great stress, and can be depended upon to put the needs of others—the organization, the community—above personal considerations not now and then, or when it the spirit moves him, or when it will look good on his resume—but in every instance."

In addition to being a person of high character, a Legacy Leader must also be credible and trustworthy, be an effective communicator, and be respected, although not necessarily liked. They must be a motivator, a change agent, and a mentor. They must deal with their own personal failures and character flaws. They must know how to empower their followers, and they must take accountability for the results of the organization they lead. Finally, a Legacy Leader understands that they are completely responsible for developing the leaders who would follow them.

In the final analysis, it is the leader's character that will ultimately define their legacy.

THREE

THE LEGACY LEADER
USES HEART

Having established the importance and non-negotiable requirement of character and integrity for a leader, we can tackle the mechanics of leadership. Some, myself included, would argue that this is the easy part. Certainly, it is at least easy to write them down, and even to teach them. Success, however, comes only to those leaders who apply these principles consistently.

Every once in a while a book comes along that has something fresh and new to say. The kind of book that literally changes the way we think and act. For me one of those books is *Managing from the Heart*, by Bracey, Rosenblum, Sanford, and Trueblood. First released in 1990, this short fictional novel relates the story of Harry Hartwell's transformation from someone known as a tyrant manager, to a caring compassionate leader.

In the book, Harry was pictured as a boss feared by his employees. When Harry has a near-death experience, he meets an angel, who gives him a choice: die, or learn to manage from the heart. In a short and entertaining story, the reader follows Harry as he stumbles his way through learning the principles embedded in the acronym H.E.A.R.T. Harry learns what each of the letters stands for:

H = Hear and Understand Me

E = Even if you disagree, don't make me wrong

A = Acknowledge the greatness in me

R = Remember to look for my loving intentions

T = Tell me the truth with compassion

What the authors made clear in their story is that these five concepts, when put to work, can help a manager get the most out of their employees. I for one am a firm believer in these five concepts, and have been trying to put them into practice each day since I first read the book. I am convinced they work.

Without minimizing their work, the concepts translate to basic ideas and fundamental behaviors. First, to manage people well, a manager must listen to his or her followers. Listen to their opinions. Listen to ideas they put forth. Even listen to their personal problems. They should, as Steven Covey would say, "Seek first to understand and then to be understood."

Second, in the event that managers don't like the actions of an employee, managers should seek to attack the behavior and not the person. Third, managers should always seek ways to acknowledge the positive traits and skills of their employees, and they should recognize these often and publicly.

Fourth, before passing judgment on an employee and coming down on them for not having performed in a way that would have met with the manager's approval, the manager should completely understand the circumstances under which the employee made the decisions he or she made. The manager should assume that the employee did not get out of bed that morning and say to themselves, "Let me see how I can go to work today and screw up." Rather, managers should assume that the employees had the best intentions in mind when they acted the way they did.

Finally, managers must learn the fine art of giving feedback to employees in a constructive way. While sometimes managers must deliver bad news as it relates to an employee's performance, most people don't need a ton of bricks to fall on them before they get the point. So, managers should find effective ways to communicate both positive and not-so-positive feedback to employees.

These simple yet profound concepts of people management completely revolutionized the way I managed people. While I was still an Air Force cadet, and later as a commissioned officer, we practiced what can best be described as an autocratic style of leadership. With few exceptions, what the commander said, we did. There was little thought given to the feelings or emotions that followers had about the orders given. Rank ruled. The highest-ranking person had the final say. He or she may ask for opinions prior to making the final decision on the course of action, but once decided, the order was given and executed by the followers.

Barring an order being of poor moral judgment or illegal in nature, there was no debate. We simply followed orders. In a military setting, this system works well. When people's lives may be on the balance and hinging on decisions made by a leader, it would hardly seem like the appropriate time to worry about looking for loving intentions, or telling someone the truth with compassion. Certainly, acknowledging the greatness in someone can wait until the mission is done. As to the first two concepts, there is little room for them in the militant way of management.

It took me about thirty seconds of being in Corporate America to realize that, while effective in the military, this management style would not serve me well in my new position as Manager of a Corporate Engineering Department in Johnson & Johnson. For me that meant a complete change in approach and style. Fortunately, I joined this foreign corporate world fresh out of my military career right around the time that *Managing from the Heart* was published. So, I practiced the concepts in H.E.A.R.T, and found that they do indeed work!

I discovered the power of these five basic rules while managing an organization of three hundred and fifty people in a twenty-four hour a day, seven days a week, medical device manufacturing operation. I was the Business Unit Manager for this organization and as such was completely responsible for all aspects of this business. I was ultimately accountable for everything from manufacturing planning to hiring and firing; from supply chain issues to quality issues; from employee evaluations to recognition and disciplinary action when necessary.

With a staff of fifteen professionals (line supervisors and middle managers) directly reporting to me, and a large contingent of dotted line support staff professionals (such as engineers, QA engineers, finance, materials management associates, production planners, and human resources experts), people-management made up the vast majority of what I did on a daily basis. I certainly believe that practicing the principles of H.E.A.R.T. contributed to whatever success I enjoyed as the Business Unit Manager for that organization. Yet, as good as these principles are for managing people, they do very little to help a leader do his or her job!

Like many other texts, the book *Managing from the Heart* blurs the lines between what it means to be a good manager and what it means to be a good leader. Almost every author on either of these subjects would agree that they are vastly different. Yet time after time, the two subjects are somehow joined and in many cases used as interchangeable concepts and ideas. Nothing could be further from reality.

Many of us have heard and even quoted people like Covey and Kotter on what it means to be a leader. Phrases such as, "A manager does things right." and "A leader does the right thing," have become almost cliché, albeit in this case it is one cliché that I believe to be true. In his book, *A Force for Change—How Leadership Differs from Management*, John Kotter puts forth the simplest and, in this author's opinion, one of most brilliant definitions of leadership. In his book, he states:

> "What constitutes good leadership has been a subject of debate for centuries. In general, we usually label leadership "good" or "effective" when it moves people to a place in which both they and those who depend upon them are genuinely better off, and when it does so without trampling on the rights of others. The function implicit in this belief is constructive or adaptive to change. Leadership within a complex organization achieves this function through three sub-processes, which, as we will see in further detail later on in this book, can briefly be described as such:
>
> - Establishing direction–developing a vision of the future, often the distant future, along with strategies for producing the changes needed to achieve that vision
>
> - Aligning people–communicating the direction to those whose cooperation may be needed so as to create coalitions that understand the vision and that are committed to its achievement
>
> - Motivating and inspiring–keeping people moving in the right direction despite major political, bureaucratic, and resource barriers to change by appealing to the very basic, but often untapped, human needs, values, and emotions"

How simple is that? A leader directs, aligns, and motivates. Period. Brilliant! But this is dramatically different from the job of a manager. That is not to say that a manager should not strive to motivate his or her people. But it is the leader's job to establish direction; it is the manager's job to work effectively with his staff drive towards the direction set by the leader.

One of the best analogies I've heard about the differences between a leader and a manager is this:

If the job calls for an organization to make their way through a jungle, a manager works hard to make sure that her team can cut through the jungle effectively. She concerns herself with making sure that the staff has the right tools to do the job. She worries that they have ample supplies to keep moving through the thick vines and grass of this hostile environment. She ensures that the staff is allocated effectively, in shifts, thereby making sure that followers are well rested and in good health as they continue to work cutting through the jungle. The manager may even, from time to time, take the lead, and with machete in-hand, slice across the brush leading the way. The leader on the other hand, searches for the tallest tree, climbs this tree and determines if the group is even in the "right jungle." The difference is one of perspective and vision. The leader must have both of these in very clear focus at all times.

Thus, while the H.E.A.R.T. principles do a great job defining the expectations of a manager, they fall short of defining behaviors that a leader must exhibit to be effective and become a Legacy Leader. The heart of a leader must be different from the heart of a manager. To a leader H.E.A.R.T must mean:

H = Have a vision

E = Empower your followers

A = Act consistently

R = Respect your followers

T = Take accountability for Results

Let's take each of these in turn, beginning with *Vision*.

"H = Have a Vision"

Without a clear, focused, well-defined vision, a leader will never achieve the highest levels of organizational performance possible. What they may indeed achieve however is many other less desirable results. Without a clear vision, leaders may frustrate their followers. Without a focused and defined vision, a leader may waste resources and time chasing the "wrong" strategies. Finally, without a well thought out vision, a leader may repeat mistakes others have made before; even worst, he may repeat mistakes he has made before!

Many books have been written on the "art of vision." The art of vision? Can it be as simple as "here's where I want to go and here's why I want to go there?" Why not make it that simple? If a leader sits for a while, contemplates their purpose and where they want to end up, and they can formulate the reasons why going where they want to go is worthwhile, half the battle is won!

Unfortunately, most today spend more time acting rather than thinking. They ascribe to the old adage, "Don't just sit there, do something!" More leaders need to work on the reverse: "Don't just do something, sit there!" Sit there and think. Think about what you want to do when you grow up. What you want your organization to be. What you want your followers to achieve. What you want your legacy to be!

If you start with these questions answered—particularly, the last one—you are staying true to one of Covey's Seven Habits of Highly Effective People: start with the end in mind. The problem with this, it seems, is that it is too simple. It makes too much sense. It's not complicated. In today's highly technical, sophisticated business world, if it does not have complicated scheme developed by a highly paid consultant, a fancy decision tree, a three-dimensional model, and modeling theory behind it (or at a minimum some pie charts and other graphics), a new concept of how to do something may not meet with the approval of "the experts." Can any of the "experts" refute that having a vision starts with simply sitting and thinking about it?

Some years ago, I attended a church retreat for the weekend. Just prior to that weekend, I had spent many hours working on a seminar presentation that I was scheduled to deliver to a group of professionals from a major Fortune 100 company. The subject was goal-setting and achieving your goals. I was getting ready to charge them up! To move them to action and to convey my passion to them about why having goals is so critically important and how to go about achieving them. I was going to motivate them towards making it all happen for themselves. I had toiled over the slides I would use. I had completed hours of research so that I could quote great achievers of the past. I was ready. But something happened at the very opening of that weekend retreat that threw the proverbial "monkey wrench" into my plans.

Our teacher for the weekend was a minister from Kentucky. He was a small, humble looking man, who, if appearances meant anything, could not hurt a fly. Our host introduced him, and the first words out of his mouth were, "Goals mean absolutely nothing!" He said it with conviction. He said it with strength. He said it as though he knew it was fact. This short, balding, white-bearded guy had, with just four words, destroyed countless hours of work for me—or at least that was my first thought.

Needless to say, the minister from Kentucky had my undivided attention. He went on to explain how goals mean nothing, unless you first have a purpose in life. A vision. You can work on goals all of your life. You can even accomplish most of the goals you set for yourself, but it they are not aligned and directing you towards what you really want to accomplish, of what lasting value are they? So, I went back at the end of the weekend, satisfied that my work had not been in vain. I did have to make a major modification to my presentation however. It started with a definition of purpose and vision. On so it goes with a leader. It starts with vision.

The harder part of vision is how to articulate it. The leader has to determine how to communicate it clearly and with passion so that others will not just follow, but they will believe in the vision with the same passion as the he or she does. A leader needs to have the followers take on the cause as if it where their own, because ultimately the success or failure - and the legacy - of the leader and the organization will depend on it. Thus the Legacy Leader must not only have a vision, but they must be great at communicating it. We will spend more time on communication later in the text.

"E = Empower your followers"

The Legacy Leader must embrace and practice the concept of empowerment. Most people pay it good lip service, but do nothing to truly create an environment where empowerment can take place; an environment where empowerment is nurtured and can grow. In the early 1990s, empowerment was *the* buzzword in corporate America. Every manager used the word at least three times a day. Consultants made small fortunes writing books and teaching courses on the subject. Today, just a few years later, the word is rarely used, except by leaders and managers once in a while when they are making speeches. It's gone the way of other buzzwords such as "re-engineering," "TQM" (total quality management), "intrapernurship," and, sadly, "diversity."

Most people who were a part of corporate America in the early 1990s can remember the energy and dollars spent around each of these, and many other "revolutionary concepts," to train all employees from the very highest levels of management to the shop floor employee. They were woven into the fabric of many vision and mission statements. Managers were measured against it. It was a good thing that they were measured against results in these areas, because each of these ideas has merit. Each helped organizations get better at what they do. In the case of ETHICON, Johnson & Johnson, the company I worked for at the time, it helped us create an organization that has since doubled in revenues.

Arguably, however, it is the concept of empowerment that in this author's experience and opinion surpasses the others in importance because without it, the others can't happen. By definition, the word *empowerment* means to give power. It means to authorize; to enable. A few things become clear immediately. To give power, you must have power. To authorize, you must be in a position to do so. So, if the people in charge of an organization, the leaders and the managers, do not "empower," nothing can happen. If leaders don't want a "diversity" process to take place, it won't. If they don't want to "re-engineer" their business, it will not happen. If they are not serious about quality, then neither will their employees be serious about it. Empowerment must begin with the leader. The leader must set the pace and the example. She must be willing to allow it to happen. She must create and environment where people can be empowered.

However, while leaders need to give power, part of the definition of empowerment included "enabling." That is something that the leaders and managers can do, but it is also something that employees must do. It is often the followers who have the skills and expertise to actually enable something to happen. The leader sets the direction, but the leader often is not the best person to make it actually happen. John Kennedy had the vision of landing a man on the moon and returning him safely home. But John Kennedy had no clue on how to technically get that done. He left that to the enablers: the scientist and technical experts. Thus, while Kennedy empowered NASA to do it, it was the experts at NASA who enabled it to happen.

Followers must therefore want to be empowered. Empowerment is not given, it's taken. The leader makes it available, but the follower must take it. So the leader or manager who says, "*I empower my people*" (emphasis on the "I"), really has not grasped the concept of empowerment. You can't really empower people. Just because the leader pronounces a person or group empowered, it does not mean that magically these people become energized, motivated and suddenly dedicated to the fulfillment of the leader's vision. People empower themselves. A leader's job is to create the right conditions for people to want to be empowered. To create a culture in which there is a hunger, recognition, and rewards for those who want to be empowered.

The legacy leader understands his role in creating this environment and practices some very basic, yet fundamental behaviors. Essentially, it comes down to this the following things that the empowering leader must do:

1. Foster, encourage, and practice open, complete, honest and transparent communications

2. Have a contagious positive attitude

3. Accept mistakes as lessons learned

4. Stay close to the action, but not in the way

5. Trust their followers, give people responsibility, listen well, praise people, have flexible controls, make resources readily available, and have a clear vision

Empowerment is a relatively simple concept, but the leader that does not embrace it does so at his or her own peril. More importantly, they do so at the peril of their legacy.

"A = Act Consistently"

There is nothing that destroys trust more than acting in inconsistent ways. There is nothing that debilitates a leader more than if he or she is not trusted. Therefore, a Legacy Leader must act consistently! It's as simple as that. A leader who acts inconsistently gives his followers cause to doubt their intent and motivation. If they doubt those two elements, they basically question the vision. If they question the vision, they will have trouble supporting it. If they have trouble supporting the vision, it will not be achieved.

For the Legacy Leader, the issue of trust is also directly related to that of character. To build trust a leader must be a person of character. Followers are very forgiving of leader's mistakes, particularly when they see that the leader learns and grows from these mistakes.

I'm reminded of the story of an executive who worked for a major US auto company. While in charge of one of their major divisions, there were some mistakes made that cost the company millions of dollars. When the executive, thinking they could save themselves and their boss some embarrassment, tendered his resignation, but his boss refused it saying, "I've just invested millions of dollars in you, you can't quit now!" There is a leader who understands that mistakes may be costly, but they can be great lessons as well.

Mistakes will be made, and can be forgiven and forgotten. However, people will have difficulty trusting in someone who stumbles or makes mistakes because of character flaws. In her essay included in the book *The Leader of the Future*, Judith M. Bardwick writes:

> "Without integrity, trust is never achieved. The best leaders are transparent: they do what they say; they 'walk the walk.' People believe them because they act in line with the values they espouse. They do not play Machiavallian games of manipulation and duplicity. In that sense, they are simple."

She's right. Legacy Leaders act consistently.

"R = Respect your followers"

In his book, *The 21 Irrefutable Laws of Leadership*, John C. Maxwell writes:

> "When you don't have the strength within, you can't earn respect without. And respect is absolutely essential for lasting leadership. How do leaders earn respect? By making sound decisions, admitting their mistakes, and putting what is best for their followers and the organization ahead of their personal agendas."

This statement brilliantly and simply captures what a Legacy Leader must do to earn respect: first he must give it! If a leader puts the followers' needs first—certainly ahead of their own—and they do everything possible to take care of the followers' needs, they will quickly gain trust and respect from their followers.

One experience that made the power of respecting my followers very real for me was when I was in charge of a team composed of both civilian and military members. I was a 1ˢᵗ Lieutenant at the time, and my team was on TDY (Temporary Duty) to Kirkland Air Force Base, New Mexico.

When we arrived at the base, our first stop was to check in and get keys to our assigned quarters. According to military rules, officers are assigned their own rooms in the Visiting Officers Quarters (VOQs). Civilian government workers (at least those of certain service level) also were assigned their own private rooms. On the other hand, non-commissioned officers of the rank of Technical Sergeant and below were typically (and by regulation) assigned a roommate rather than a private room, even in the event that there were rooms available for each person. I always found this rule troublesome.

When we arrived at the front desk of this "military hotel," I checked in first and got the key to my mini-suite (private bathroom, small living area, and TV). Next, the civilian team members got their private room assignments. When it was time for the four sergeants who were traveling with us to get their rooms, sure enough, they were paired up and assigned two rooms for the four of them. As I overheard the airman behind the counter indicate to them their room assignments, I stepped in and asked that each of them be assigned a private room.

"Sorry sir," explained the airman, "regulations are that E-6 and under are assigned two to a room."

"I understand," I replied. "Are the quarters filled to capacity?"

"No sir," he replied

"Well, then please assign them each a private room," I insisted.

"Sir, I can't approve that, I would have to check with my boss."

"I understand. Where is he?" I asked.

"I'll get him sir, he's in the office."

While the airman went in search of his boss, all four enlisted members of my team starting telling me that it was "okay," that they understood the regulations, and that they were used to having this be the case whenever they traveled on TDY. They told me, "Don't worry about it sir. It's not worth getting called on the carpet for it." Getting called on the carpet meant getting chewed out by your superior officer while standing at attention in front of his desk.

"There are rooms available, and you guys are adults just like me and the other guys here," I said, pointing to the civilian members of my team. "So, why shouldn't you have some privacy like us?"

At that point the airman's boss, a Technical Sergeant (E-6) himself, came out to the desk. "How can I help sir?" he asked me.

"I'd like to have private rooms for the sergeants please."

"I'd have to have approval from the person in charge of the unit sir."

"That would be me," I said.

He looked at me, looked at the airman, and said, "Give them each a room."

"Thank you," I said.

"No problem sir. I hate sharing rooms when I go TDY. I wish my commanding officer cared enough to get me a private room."

Then, in unison, came a sincere, "Thank you sir," from the four team members.

"No sweat guys. I'll see you guys for dinner in about 30 minutes." I grabbed my bags and walked off.

From that moment on, I had the most motivated and loyal team members a leader could want. I made many mistakes with them. They forgave them. I made many demands of them. They delivered. More importantly, they protected me. All because I took care of their basic and simple needs. I cared enough about them. I've never forgotten the lesson I learned that day of the power of putting your followers first! For anyone who has been a lieutenant in the military and has had a team of enlisted men and women supporting them, they know well that if they don't protect you, you are dead!

That simple act of respect for their privacy, followed by a consistent behavior of respect for them, led them to trust and respect me in turn. The Legacy Leader respects his followers.

"T = Take accountability for results"

"The buck stops here." Enough said. Legacy Leaders are responsible for results.

FOUR

THE LEGACY LEADER IS CREDIBLE AND TRUSTWORTHY

The Story of Hand Innovations, LLC

On January 18, 2006, I met with members of the Hand Innovations, LLC, management staff for the first time. DePuy Orthopaedics, a Johnson & Johnson company and the organization I was working for at the time, had just closed a deal to acquire this Miami-based orthopedic company. Hand Innovations (HI) had grown to nearly $50 million in annual sales in a matter of a few short years, on the back of innovative technology for the repair of distal radius (wrist) fractures. The company also owed its success to the engineering genius of a few individuals, including Dr. Jorge Orbay, a hand surgeon and the founder of the company, and Javier Castaneda, one of the finest engineers in the business that I have ever had the pleasure of working with.

Acquiring this small but growing company was an important move for DePuy in its quest to be a leading player in the world-wide trauma segment within orthopedics. HI was composed of great engineers, a strong professional education group, and a good marketing team. They also counted on a very hungry sales organization that was quickly driving increased revenues, competing with the largest trauma companies in the United States, and winning! HI had an operations group based in Miami that did the packaging and shipping. They also had a very strong collections department. This small team of people made it its sole function in life to keep the money coming in. This is a lifeline for any small company where cash flow is the difference between paying the bills and having to borrow to pay the bills.

HI was a team that had, and still has, a culture of "get-it-done." Because of its location (a town called Kendall just south of Miami), not surprisingly, it was a company where ninety five percent of its Miami-based employees were of Hispanic descent. In fact, for most, Spanish was their native language. There was a culture of family and friendship. There was a genuine feeling of mutual respect and caring between members of this team that led to a spirit of achievement. The entrepreneurial spirit soared in this small company. People saw what needed to get done, and they did it.

In Hand Innovations, emotions ran high, and they still do. They are healthy emotions of passion towards achievement and success. This was a proud group of people! And not surprisingly, it was also a very grateful group. For many of these individuals working for a company like HI was part of the golden opportunity that they were searching for when they left their homelands. For some that homeland was Cuba, and for others Venezuela. Yet others called their home country El Salvador or Honduras. Wherever they hailed from, coming to Miami was a search for a better life for themselves and their families. A search for the quintessential American dream! So for many, the job at HI was a part of making that dream a reality.

The people of HI were also very grateful to Dr. Orbay, whom they saw as the person who had created this great small company and gave them the opportunity. They respected Dr. Orbay because of his position, both in the company and the community. The person replacing Dr. Orbay would have a tough challenge to overcome in order to gain the trust and credibility with this team.

In November 2005, the day before Thanksgiving, my boss gave me a call and offered me an opportunity to lead Hand Innovations immediately after the acquisition. After careful consideration with my family, I accepted the challenge. It was one of the best decisions I have ever made. For the next six weeks, I had the opportunity to get up to speed on HI, our products, and the people. I learned all that I could about the key members of the staff. All of this was done under a veil of great confidentiality because the deal had not yet been finalized between Johnson & Johnson and Hand Innovations, so it was important to maintain secrecy. That did not make the job any easier.

As part of the preparation for our taking over the company, I did a good deal of homework. I made sure to speak with several leaders who had led integrations of two companies before. Their advice on what to do and what not to do was as varied as the companies they had led. Nevertheless, I paid close attention to the lessons learned that they each shared with me.

There was one thing all these integration leaders agreed on was how important their credibility as leaders was. One of the most important keys to the success of any integration of two companies is the credibility that the leader will be able to garner from the very first time he or she is introduced to the team.

To that end, I would need the support of all of the DePuy staff that would be involved with the integration, so we met to discuss a few standards of behaviors that I thought would be important. First, we would be humble in our approach. We were stepping into a company that was very successful and had grown quickly to $50 million in annual sales. Clearly this meant that the people who had made that happen were quite good. Our goal was to make sure they understood that we valued them, and I for one was looking forward to learning from them and what had helped them be so successful.

Secondly, we would be transparent in our communications.

Being completely and consistently honest in all that we said and did. As it turned out, this was the single most important factor in the ultimate success of the integration. There is simply nothing more important for a leader to do than to be transparent and honest in all of their communications. Finally, we agreed that we would strive to learn from this team of people that had generated such great success in a very short period of time, and try to incorporate some of those lessons learned back into the parent company. Armed with not much more than these three tenets, on January 18, 2006, I scheduled a meeting with my new staff in Hand Innovations.

I invited the HI management staff to join me in the Johnson & Johnson offices in Miami, which were about twenty minutes away from the HI offices. No doubt they all knew what the meeting was about, as the rumors of the acquisition were everywhere. Since we were going to formally announce the acquisition the next day, I felt it was important to reach out to the entire management staff. My goals were simple: first, I wanted to meet them and have them meet me in neutral environment. Second, I wanted them to be the first to hear what my objectives were. Third, I wanted them to hear me say how impressed I was with this powerful team, and how humbled I was feeling to have the opportunity to lead this group. Finally, I needed to ask for their help!

After sharing a bit about myself, our DePuy staff, and the overriding objectives that we were embarking on as a new combined team, what I would need most was their support, and their trust. So I asked for both! I knew I was asking much of this group of strangers. They did not know me, other than what they had heard about me, or what they had found out about me by Googling my name—something I was amused to find out later a few of them had done. They had no reason to believe what I was saying. Quite the contrary, in fact they had more reasons not to trust me! After all, historically acquisitions and company integrations are not pleasant experiences especially for those being acquired. Many of the individuals in the room had been through acquisitions before, and they knew from experience how painful they can be. They understood that no matter how civil things can appear, when one company takes over another, there will be changes made. Often times, those changes impact people's jobs and therefore, their lives as well.

Here I was talking about how humbled and fortunate I felt to be leading the company and yet there was no doubt in my mind that despite how true this statement was, to some it must have felt like an "act." I talked about us wanting to learn from them, and to protect and maintain their entrepreneur spirit, but I would guess that some heard those words and were skeptical. I can't say that I blamed them for that.

But what they had not heard before was a leader who asked for their support and their trust, and who in return offered them only that he would be one hundred percent honest and transparent with all communications. I promised that decisions would be made with the full understanding of the ramifications to the business and to the people impacted. What perhaps was new to them was a leader who acknowledges that the path that that lies ahead would be a tough one to hoe. I assured them that I understood that even some of the people in the room may not be a part of the organization once it was restructured and integrated to DePuy. Yet, I was asking for their support and trust. What right did I have to ask for these things? None. So I offered the only thing I thought was worth as much as the trust I was asking for them to give me: my trust in return.

Consider this: what did they have to lose? As a leader I had made myself vulnerable. I had asked for help, and I had offered something that leaders almost always do: honesty, truth, and my trust. Sadly however, all too often, leaders don't deliver on these. Therein lays the secret to the success in this strategy: do what you say you will do! There is no more powerful way for the leader to gain and maintain credibility.

Fast forward three years, and I am more convinced now than ever that the success of Hand Innovation's integration to DePuy, and the success that the organization has continued to enjoy since, is in great part due to the fact that we have held to the principle of complete, transparent, frequent, and honest communications. They knew what I knew when I knew it. Of course, there are times when confidential information needs to remain that way. But leaders hide behind the shroud of confidentiality all too often. Information should be deemed confidential and for limited distribution as a matter of exception, rather that a general rule.

The more information a leader can share, the higher his or her credibility will soar, and the more he or she will be trusted by the organization. It's really that simple. In fact, experience shows that even when information can't be shared, explaining the reasons for the information being kept confidential also goes a long way towards helping leaders build their credibility. Over time the organization will trust the leader even more, and will respect the need for confidentiality on particular issues.

I had the privilege of leading Hand Innovations until June 2008. During the two and a half years after the acquisition, we restructured the organization, implemented numerous new policies that apply to all J&J companies, moved the company to a new location, completely restructured the sales distribution channel, and managed to grow the company sales to nearly $100 million. The process of integration caused us to downsize the organization by more than 100 people. Yet with all the turmoil, the downsize, the constant change, and the restructuring, we had no regrettable losses of any employees in that period. Moreover, the annual employee surveys indicated that the team's motivation and engagement level remained at the very highest levels.

I am convinced that one of the main reasons we've enjoyed this success is because of the credibility that I enjoyed as a leader. I've learned a clear lesson that leaders must work hard to gain and keep their credibility and trust with their teams. Without it, they will fall short of achieving their vision for the organization.

The level of loyalty that some leaders can command from their followers has always amazed me. At the core of loyalty is credibility. You can not have one without the other. Thus credibility is one of the most important qualities of a leader.

At the root of the word *credibility*, we find the Latin word *credo*, which means, "I believe." When a leader has followers who "believe" in them, they can be certain that their vision will be fulfilled! The power that is unleashed when followers connect with the leader's vision because they are bought into them as a credible, trustworthy, person of character, cannot be contained, and is expressed in the ultimate success—or failure—of the organization. Thus, leaders need to focus on gaining and keeping their credibility. In this chapter, we will explore a few ways that a leader can do this.

Not surprisingly, as with most of the fundamental concepts of leadership, earning and keeping credibility is not hard to do. It's as simple as exhibiting and consistently demonstrating integrity, respect for others, honesty, ethical and moral behavior, and trust. A great place to start is applying the H.E.A.R.T. principles previously discussed!

Additionally, there are a few more things a leader must do to gain and keep credibility:

1. Stay true to their vision. He or she must act in ways that are completely consistent with the vision in public as well as in private

2. Spend a significant amount of time communicating. Listening, talking, and evaluating and exchanging ideas, and sharing their vision

3. They must always tell the truth

4. They must remove obstacles (including persons) that would stand in the way of the organization reaching its goals and vision

5. Be true to their values and beliefs

6. Have the capacity and ability to make the organization succeed

Credibility and its organizational impact

There is no doubt that the leader's credibility has a huge impact on the organization. The only question is how that impact will manifest. Can the leader's credibility affect the present organization? How about its future? Can it affect the organization's past? Let's explore these questions with the end in mind of understanding what the Legacy Leader must do in order to create and lead an "Achieving Organization."

On January 18, 2001, the national media was focused on the breaking story detailing the illegitimate son of the Reverend Jesse Jackson who had been born twenty months earlier. Ironically, that would mean that the Reverend was advising President Bill Clinton on how to handle the scandal of the extra marital affair between he (the president) and Monica Lewinsky, the White House intern, at the same time that he was involved in his own illicit relationship. How unfortunate!

Reverend Jackson's opponents and critics cried out about the hypocrisy of it all, and quickly questioned the man's (Jackson's) integrity, character, and his credibility. Frankly, they had every right to. What is most unfortunate however is the effect that this single act of lapse in judgment had on Reverend Jackson and the organization he led at the time. It had a profound, negative impact, on the man's life long work. This single act cast a large shadow of doubt over the work of the organization he led. Is that fair? That's debatable. But fairness is not the issue; facts are. And the fact is that his credibility and character are forever tarnished. So his message and impact are reduced. That's undeniable. No matter what, some will always now have cause to doubt him in the future.

Let me be perfectly clear: it is not my intent to denigrate or judge Reverend Jackson, his character, or his organization. I have long admired Reverend Jackson and the work that he has done his entire life. I certainly do not question his motive as a life long advocate for civil rights. I do, however, consider it unfortunate that all of that was virtually washed away by his lack of judgment as it relates to his personal affair. Nevertheless, that stands as an example and a blaring warning siren to other leaders who wonder how much their character and credibility matters. Fortunately, it is also possible for a leader to recover from such blunders. In the years since, Reverend Jackson has continued to be a strong leader in the community and a wonderful advocate for civil rights around the world. Other leaders have not been as successful in recovering after having a fall from grace.

Credibility and its impact on the leader

Let's start with the immediate impact to the leader. The leader's behavior is now known to be hypocritical, untrustworthy, deceitful, not forthcoming, of poor moral and professional judgment, and to a certain degree selfish. Additionally, in the case of Reverend Jackson, some would consider his behavior to have been disrespectful and disloyal to his followers. Realize that we are referring to one event! This does not imply that we should assume that all of his acts are characterized in this manner. But, and this is a huge but, it means that we may always wonder if what he has said in the past, is now saying, or what he will say in the future, is indeed the truth.

In other words, his credibility is questionable. If his credibility is questionable, so is the trust we are willing to give as followers; and frankly that is exactly the way it should be. When followers do not expect a higher standard from their leaders and are too quick to rationalize away the behavior, they may be blinded to accepting the reality. Once again, we can name countless of examples where followers ignored (or were unable to recognize) the flaws in their leader and followed them even at their own peril.

In cases such as these, the leader's credibility is reduced to zero in an instant. No longer can this person be given full trust. All the statements made, all decisions and actions taken may be questioned by some of the loyal followers, and certainly by those who were never completely loyal or who are indeed critics of the leader. The legacy of the leader is now forever re-defined! Lastly, his character has forever been tarnished and probably forever damaged. Is that too harsh? Perhaps. But to leaders much is the reward, so much should be expected. No, it's not too harsh. Legacy Leaders can't afford this kind of lapse in judgment.

The Leader's credibility impacts the organization's past, present and future

Next, let's consider the impact of the leader's credibility on the organization. We need to look at the impact on the organization from three dimensions: past, present, and future. First, the past: how can a leader's currently disclosed improper behavior affect the organization's past? The answer is because that improper behavior casts a shadow of doubt over the group's integrity as it is categorically defined by the leader. This can mean that all those somehow associated with the organization (employees, volunteers, customers, users, suppliers, stockholders) now scratch their heads in wonderment and ask themselves, "Have I been treated fairly all along?" Have I made commitments or agreements with an organization that has foundations on sandy rather than rocky soil?

For example, when the leader is found to have been involved in an improper business relationship, it may beg the question, what else has been going on? Indeed, there may be absolutely nothing wrong or improper going on. Sadly, however, the leader's behavior can cast an overbearing shadow over the organization. That shadow can have positive as well as negative connotations.

What about the impact on the organization in the present? The organization suffers much more than a black eye; it's injured by a one-two punch combination that brings the organization to its proverbial knees and possibly puts them down for the knockout count. At a minimum, it rattles the very foundation of the organization, its people, vision, and purpose for existence. It puts everything that the followers of that leader worked for, at risk. It forces those people to re-evaluate their core values.

In fact, people may begin asking themselves, "Do I remain loyal to the leader?" To do so, they must first re-think, and perhaps alter, their beliefs and replaced them with a new set of values. Undoubtedly, as proven time and time again, some followers will remain completely faithful to the leader and his or her vision. Whether they simply turn a blind eye to the leader's character flaw or rationalize it away, they refuse to accept that a leader's character flaw has an impact on their organization. Often, the easiest way for the followers to deal with the issue is to rationalize it away. They may say to himself or herself "no one is perfect" or "their personal life is their business and it has no bearing on their effectiveness as the leader of our organization." That position is tenuous at best.

There is an old adage that says, "If you want to know how someone will behave in business, play a round of golf with him or her." Everyone who plays golf knows that most casual, non-professional golfers probably underestimate their scores by upwards of ten strokes. How do they do this? One way is called a "Mulligan" (that's when the golfer hits a poor shot and begs shamelessly of his playing partners to have a "Mulligan," otherwise known as a "free" shot. They dismiss the previous bad shot as though it never happened and do not count it for their score). Another is called a "gimmy." That's when a player "gives" the putt to another player. Usually, if a putt is within a very short distance from the hole, a player may just assume that they could not possibly miss the putt, so they simply assume it to be in the hole and pick up the ball.

Furthermore, players routinely pick up or move the ball off the fairway to clean the ball. Of course, this may casually improve their lie and so they hope to get a better next shot. Each of these actions is against golf rules and dictate stroke penalties on the golfer's score. So, next time someone tells you they shot 89, you can probably safely assume that their true score was closer to 100.

What's the point? Simple: if someone is willing to stretch the truth for something as insignificant as a golf score—which for people not earning a living playing the game should be meaningless—imagine what they may be willing to do when real gains or losses are involved as in the business world. The bottom line is this: our character is our character whether we are dealing in our personal life or our professional life. If a person is willing to lie in their personal life, they will have no trouble doing it in their professional life. Therefore, as it relates to a leader, it is naïve to believe that they can separate their personal and professional life and some how have two different set of values that drive their behavior.

Finally, what is the impact of the future of the organization? That depends on a few very important things. First, it has everything to do with what the leader does immediately following the revelation of the problem. Second, it has to do with the caliber of the other leaders in the organization. Third, it has to do with the level of commitment and loyalty the leader had achieved with the followers to this point. That is, the number of deposits that the leader had made in the emotional bank of the organization.

In doing the research for this portion of the text, I was at a loss to find a single example of a high profile case in which a leader, having been discovered to have committed some egregious act which uncovered a major character flaw, came forth quickly and with complete candor in honesty to his or her followers. What I did find, on the other hand, are example after example of cases where the leader did everything from deny the truth, distort the facts, evade the issues, and made every attempt to have it all just go away. Nixon, Clinton, Jackson, Condit, and Kennedy are names that most Americans would recognize as individuals who worked very hard to make their "issue" go away. Something they all have in common: the legacy as a person who was less than honest. It has long been a belief of mine that if a leader would just simply come out quickly and say: "I screwed-up. I'm sorry. I was wrong. I learned my lesson," that most of his or her followers would be willing to give them a second chance and move on quickly.

What role should other leaders play in times when the head of the organization is struggling with his or her credibility? And why are the other leaders in the organization important? Because, when the top person in the organization is down, that's who the followers will look to first. If there is a vacuum in leadership at that level, then the organization can quickly disintegrate or fall further into disrepair. So, leaders in the organization have to quickly step in to fill the gap left by the stumbling leader, albeit temporarily, to ensure continuity.

Finally, how quickly the leader can recover, if indeed they can, is intrinsically linked to their past behaviors and the level of credibility they have established for themselves over time. A pattern of strong moral and ethical behavior and H.E.A.R.T. would go a long way towards buying the leader an opportunity to recover. This presumes of course that the leader is not pre-disposed to some pattern of deceitful or otherwise negative behavior, which impacts their character. If that is the case, then it will only be a matter of time for the leader to fall again.

The undeniable conclusion is this: when an organization's leader is hurt, the organization suffers. The pain has a special stinging quality to it when the leader's injury is self-inflicted and the result of a character flaw. Why would it seem that this is a more severe blow to the organization? For a few reasons: first, it was completely avoidable. Second, it was the leader's poor judgment that pulled the trigger of the gun pointed at the organization's head. Third, the organization will have to spend time recovering. That time is, for all practical purposes, wasted resources and energy. Sometimes this could mean bad publicity for the leader and the organization, loss of customers and revenues, loss of employees who decide they can no longer stay in the organization. And the list can go on and on. Nothing good can come out of a leader having a flawed character and low credibility. The Legacy Leader must ensure that he has both of these critically important traits intact.

Establishing credibility requires a daily routine

In early 2001, I attended a leadership meeting hosted by Mr. Bob Salerno. He was the Vice President for Sales and Marketing for ETHICON, Johnson & Johnson. Mr. Salerno is a person who many, myself included, consider to be a leader of integrity and character. At that meeting, he presented his ideas of what leaders needed to do to gain credibility:

1. Be demanding but be able to satisfy

2. Be accessible, but not to familiar

3. Be decisive, but judicious

4. Be focused, but flexible

5. Be active without causing commotion

6. Be willing to make the tough calls, but act humane

Bob's message to his staff and extended staff was clear. First, he sent a clear signal that having credibility was of paramount importance if we were to lead effectively. Second, he left little room for misunderstanding that building that credibility takes daily actions. Actions that are decisive yet well thought out, determined yet negotiable, aggressive yet controlled, and tough but fair.

In his message, Bob directed his leaders and managers to be demanding, but be able to deliver themselves. No leader should demand without having the ability to deliver what the followers need to satisfy the request. Finally, he called leaders in his organization to be accessible, while not too familiar. In essence, he called leaders to be where the action is, but not in the way. To be close to those they lead, but removed enough to remain impartial. The wisdom of his six points is in their simplicity!

In their book, *The Leadership Challenge*, James Kouzes and Barry Posner devote a chapter to the leader's credibility. In fact, they title the chapter "Credibility Is The Foundation Of Leadership." In the chapter they write:

> "Honest, forward-looking, competent, and inspiring: these are the characteristics that have remained constant during two decades of growth and recession, the surge in new technology enterprises, the birth of the World Wide Web, the further globalization of the economy, the ever-changing political environment, and the expansion and bursting of the Internet bubble. The relative importance of the most desired qualities (of leaders) has varied over time, but there has been no change in the fact that these are the four qualities people want most in their leaders. Whether we believe our leaders are true to these values is another matter, but what we would like from them has remained constant.
>
> "This list of four consistent findings is useful in and of itself–and there's a more profound implication revealed by our research. These key characteristics make up what communications experts refer to as a source of credibility."

It is clear that these two leadership gurus understand the importance of credibility for the leader's success. It is also clear that they give it the correct level of importance by placing it right up-front in their book and labeling it as a key foundation of leadership. They are absolutely correct.

FIVE

THE LEGACY LEADER BUILDS ACHIEVING ORGANIZATIONS

Having established the importance of credibility as a key to being an effective leader, there are two related concepts that should also be understood. The first is the compounding nature of building credibility, and the second is the idea of building an "achieving organization."

The Credibility Building Model

To build credibility, a person must act consistently and correctly more than just a few times; they must do so over and over again. Moreover, there is a cumulative effect that one behavior adds to the previous one in terms of building credibility over time. Additionally, there is an order to the sequence of activities that leads to building credibility. This sequence of behaviors is illustrated in figure 1.

Credibility is earned. For a leader, every action, every word, every memo, every voice mail, every speech, every move is analyzed, scrutinized, and interpreted by the followers. Whether the leader intends to or not, every move they make communicates volumes of who they are. Their commitment to the vision, their ability to motivate others, how much they care or do not care about the followers, and whether they are willing to be where the action is.

The Legacy Leader understands the dynamics between each of these actions and they understand that they each are mutually inclusive. One builds on the other. Likewise, one can tear down the other. The leader's credibility will be a direct function of how well they do these things. Moreover, once the leader has demonstrated each of these behaviors, they must do so again and again. Each time, the slope of the credibility curve becomes steeper and the leader's credibility is increased exponentially. To be an effective Legacy Leader, you want to build your credibility as quickly as possible. Therefore, leaders must remain aware of the variables that drive credibility. These will be crucial to any success the leader will enjoy.

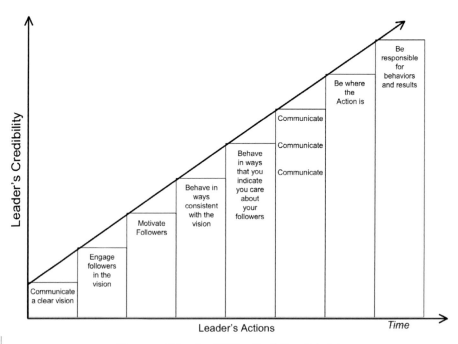

Figure 1: The Credibility Building Model

Anthony Lopez

The Achieving Organization Model

Ultimately, the purpose of leadership is to achieve a vision; to get results. The Achieving Organization Model, which will be presented next, highlights the direct correlation of the leader's credibility and the organization's level of achievement. There are many ways to characterize organizations. In this text, we will describe four types of organizations (see figure 2):

1. The Closed Organization

2. The Hard-Working Organization

3. The Performing Organization

4. The Achieving Organization

The Closed Organization

The bottom left hand quadrant of the model depicted in figure 2 describes the Closed Organization. This is an organization that is not performing or achieving results. Organizations in this quadrant can usually be characterized as suffering from at least one, and usually several, of the following problems:

1. Low morale

2. High employee turn over

3. A fair amount of organizational fear

4. Low trust among the employees

5. Little or no team work

6. Low empowerment

7. Change management issues

8. No clear understanding of the organizational vision

9. Poor communication among leaders and followers

10. Staffing problems

Often organizations that find themselves in this category replace their leader in hopes and with the expectation that the new leader can turn the situation around. But whether a new leader comes in, or the current leader remains, their main task will be to gain credibility. Only a leader with a high level of credibility can successfully affect the kind of change that will move the organization from being a Closed Organization to an Achieving Organization.

This process is usually slow and painful. The leader must follow the Credibility Model while working on all of the strategic and tactical issues usually associated with an organizational turn-around. However, as the Achieving Organization Model indicates, before the closed organization can move to the upper right hand quadrant, it has to move through the Hard-Working Organization stage. Moreover, before a leader can move an organization from this quadrant, they have to effectively deal with each of the ten problems outlined above. Thus, in addition to having to work to gain their credibility as leaders, they have huge cultural and organizational issues to deal with.

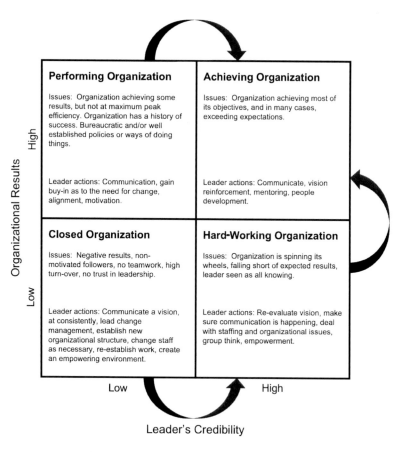

Figure 2: *The Achieving Organization Model*

The Hard-Working Organization

The Hard-Working Organization has the following characteristics:

1. It is not achieving all of the stated objectives, but it is meeting some goals

2. The leader has credibility

3. The organization may have inadequate staffing

4. There is good team work, but not a clear understanding of the vision and objectives

5. The organization may suffer from one or possibly more of the ten problems identified for the closed organization

The Hard-Working Organization is one that already has a leader with high credibility. Either the leader has earned it while at his or current post, or as is the case from time to time, they are coming in to team with a high level of credibility. How can a leader come into an organization with a high level of credibility? In some cases, a person reputation precedes them. They may have been the leader of another organization where they earned a reputation for being a leader of character, trustworthy, and effective; a leader who understands the concept of Leadership with H.EA.R.T. So, they come into the new organization with somewhat of a halo effect. That is, people assume that this person is credible and unless the leader gives them cause to change their mind, they will quickly yield their loyalty, albeit it, for a probation period while they "size-up" the new leader.

Coming in with a high level of credibility represents a tremendous opportunity for the Legacy Leader. They don't have to start from scratch! They can focus on issues of vision, alignment, and motivation—which have a profound impact on results - rather than having to put the patches on what's broken first (such as the issues the leader of the Closed Organization has to deal with).

This is a significant point and deserves elaboration. The leader who has and maintains credibility can impact organizational results much more quickly than the leader who does not have credibility. Time is the most precious commodity a leader has. The quicker they can impact the organization, the quicker the results can be achieved.

Each time that I have taken over a new organization, one of the very first things I have done is called a meeting with my direct staff to talk about trust and credibility. I tell them in no uncertain terms that as of that very moment, they each have one hundred percent of my trust and confidence. Regardless of their history with their previous boss, they start at one hundred percent. That means that they don't have to earn my trust. But, they have to work to keep it! If they violate my trust, I loose confidence with them and our relationship changes immediately. I then ask them to do the same for me. I ask for their trust and confidence and pledge to work hard to keep it. Each time I have done this, the reaction has been the same: first, people are surprised at my candor and wonder for a moment "what's the catch?" Moments later, they realize they have nothing to lose and agree to give it a go.

Invariably, over time, there will be someone who indeed violates the trust given to them, and when that happens, you deal with the immediate consequences of whatever their actions caused, and you redefine your relationship with that person. But, I can say with great pride and confidence that most people have never let me down. In fact, they have worked harder than ever to keep my trust and confidence. What did I gain by doing this? Time!

In most relationships, professional or otherwise, trust and confidence are usually earned over a long period of time. In some cases, that is the only way that it would be wise to give our trust to someone. Cases where catastrophic and life-threatening consequences can take place if trust is misplaced would be examples of occasions where you would not just simply start with one hundred percent trust. However, in the vast majority of cases in the professional setting, even if some take advantage of the trust you freely gave, the consequences of whatever action they took which violated your trust, can be reversed. The benefits of having 95% of your staff committed and loyal from the start, far outweighs the risk of the 5% who will violate your trust.

Moving an organization from the Hard-Working quadrant to the Achieving Organization quadrant requires significantly less effort and time that it does to go from a Closed Organization to

Achieving. That's the power of credibility. The leader who has it can use it to effect change quickly to achieve the desired results.

In the Hard-Working Organization, the leader must first focus on re-evaluating, and as necessary redefining the vision for the organization. It is imperative that this vision be clear in the mind of the leader so that they can go about communicating it effectively. The organization that is stuck in this quadrant can just as easily slip up to the Achieving Organization Quadrant as they can slip backwards into the Closed Organization quadrant; and the most important determining factor as to which direction this will go depends on the leader's ability to align the team behind a clearly defined vision.

The second thing that a leader needs to focus on if they are to move the organization to the Achieving Quadrant is to create an environment where people are empowered and can make decisions. This is important because another characteristic of the Hard-Working Organization is one in which the leader is looked to for very detailed direction at every step of the way.

This problem often plagues smaller companies where the leader is usually also the person who founded the company and hired all or most of the employees. Everyone looks to the leader for approval before taking significant action. That may not be because the leader is overbearing and a non-empowering kind of person, but rather because people may not clearly understand the vision that the leader has about where to go next.

People cannot know how their decisions will support or be in contradiction with the leader's vision if they don't fully understand what that vision is. So, they are reluctant to make major decisions without seeking the leader's input first. Therefore, while results may indeed be achieved, they will be slower in coming. Furthermore, as the decisions will almost always be funneled through the leader, they will more than likely always reflect the same style. Eventually, this will be the style that others will emulate, and this can lead to the phenomena we refer to as "group think;" everyone thinks alike.

I had a boss once who told the six of us on his staff that if we all thought like him, there were five of us who needed to go. He was right. A leader needs to have people around them who understand the vision, but who are independent thinkers and can make decisions that move the organization in the direction of the vision. But it is up to the leader to resist the temptation of making all the decisions. Moreover, they must reject completely the temptation to tell followers to make decisions only to later undo those decisions simply because it would not have been the way we choose to do it. The leader must be clear on what the goal is, and not be too restrictive as to how it is achieved. Only then will he start to develop people who are creative, risk taking, and goal driven, rather than followers who do what they are told.

The third task for a leader in moving up from the Hard-Working Organization Quadrant is to deal quickly with whatever organizational issues may exist within the group. Whether it is staffing issues, or any of the other nine problems described for the Closed Organization, the leader must tackle them head-on and forcefully. Members of the hardworking organization are getting results, and they know they are getting results. They also can tell that they have to work much harder than they should to do it. Thus, they welcome swift action by a leader that they perceive as attacking barriers that stand in their way of being an Achieving Organization. Therefore, the leader should feel confident in aggressively moving the group forward.

The Performing Organization

A few years ago, I received a call from a colleague who had just become the new plant manager for an auto parts manufacturer in Ohio. He had just taken over the plant a month earlier when the previous plant manager had retired after having been in the position for over fifteen years. It did not take him long to realize that the plant was a Performing Organization.

His organization had consistently delivered their customers with the parts ordered and had a better than ninety-five percent order fulfillment rate, which was good when measured against industry standard at the time. It also did not take him long to realize that while they were delivering results, their operating costs were much higher than he would have expected. The organization's overall profitability was significantly lower than expected by the corporate headquarters. In fact, when he was offered the position, the Vice President of Operations (also relatively new to the organization) had indicated to him that his first focus should be to increase the plant's profitability. He asked me to help him analyze the organization and make some recommendations of what he should do to get some costs out of the operation.

The first thing we did was map all the processes for the plant. Much to our surprise, many of the systems being used where still manual. Inventory tracking, expense reports, purchase orders, accounts payables, and other basic fundamental business functions had redundant systems in place. That is, while a computer system had been put in place to do these functions, the adoption rate by the employees had been dismal, and so the paperwork kept flowing. We drew flow charts for existing processes that literally ended in dead ends. A piece of paper or some other documentation was filled out and ended up in a file with no real purpose.

We tracked the flow of work-in-process through the facility and discovered that in some cases the flow was circular! The same part stopped in some stations more than once. This was usually a quality check of some sort. Even the way meetings were conducted was inefficient. It seems the plant was successful despite itself! Many of us have worked in organizations were we hear someone say, "We make money despite ourselves." That is a very telling comment. It indicates that the organization is perceived as financially successful, but very inefficient. The opportunity lies in discovering the inefficiencies and redundancies and eliminating them. And so was born the term *re-engineering* in the early 1990s, which came on the heels of several quality improvement initiatives adopted by companies throughout the world.

What W. Edwards Deming (father of the Quality Movement)

had preached for years before was finally becoming a reality throughout every industry and every company. Companies discovered that they were performing, but falling short of what they thought they could really achieve.

The Performing Organization is characterized by the following:

1. Organization is delivering some results

2. Moral and employee satisfaction are at fairly good levels

3. There are many bureaucratic and, in some cases, redundant control systems in place

4. There is usually longevity in employees with the organization. They know their jobs and have done them this way a long time

5. Organizational culture is strong

6. Informal networks are strong

7. Turn over is usually low or very controlled

My friend's auto parts manufacturing organization was the model Performing Organization! It exhibited all seven traits of such an organization. It soon became obvious to him that his biggest challenge was going to be changing the long-standing culture and breaking down the bureaucracy that was firmly in place. It was these two elements that caused people to do things the same old way they had become accustomed to. We both realized quickly that for him to succeed at effecting change in these two critical areas, he would need to earn the credibility with many key staffers first. Without that there was no way that anyone was going to follow his lead. After all, this was an organization that was indeed achieving fairly good results, so change was not seen as a necessity by most.

Through this experience, we learned that there are three key things that a leader must do to gain credibility:

1. The leader must demonstrate that they understand the company, its mission, and its customers

2. The leader should quickly establish the organizational culture, through consistent behavior that supports that new culture

3. The leader must communicate their vision of the organization, specifically outlining the result that will be expected and the need for change

These worked well for him. He quickly gained the team's credibility and he was able to put in place many of the processes we developed to drive improvements. Within nine months, the organization's profitability had risen more than 18%.

Unfortunately, not all stories have a happy ending. Nevertheless, leaders can significantly improve their success rate if they work hard on their credibility. As was the case for my friend in the auto part manufacturing plant example, leading change in a performing organization can be terribly difficult. For those of us who have worked in organizations that are delivering results or have significant market share leadership, we know how difficult making change can be.

Why change when you are successful? What motivation is there for rocking the boat when the boat is floating on calm waters and there is a gentle trade wind keeping the corporate sails taut? That's the leader's greatest challenge in a performing organization. They must offer compelling reasons as to the reason for the changes. They must get the buy-in from the organization that getting out of the comfort zone, and doing things differently than they have in some cases for many years, will be worth the pain. They must find ways to convince the follower that the rewards for changing far outweigh the risk of change.

The leader that has credibility will have a much easier time of accomplishing this than the one that does not! Therefore, the very first thing that the leader must do in this situation is make sure that they have the credibility with the organization to make things happen.

As previously stated, there are three key behaviors that leaders—particularly if they are relatively new to the organization—must demonstrate in order to gain credibility. These important ideas deserve further exploration.

The leader must demonstrate that they understand the company, its mission, and its customers.

The leader should roll-up their sleeves and get down into the details of the organization to understand what they do, how they do it and why they do it. I'm reminded of when I first took over as the Business Unit Manager of one of the business units in the ETHICON, Puerto Rico plant. I "lived" at the plant for two months. My family was still living in New Jersey because we were waiting for the school year to end for my daughter, before moving the family to Puerto Rico. This gave me the opportunity to really focus on my new assignment, and since I had nothing but an empty hotel room to go back to in the evenings, I stayed at the plant many hours each day.

Often, I would pack a change of clothing and, after sleeping two or three hours at the infirmary, I would shower and change, and get back to work. It did not take my employees long to realize that I was spending long hours getting to know our business. No doubt, this level of hands-on work and commitment demonstrated to them that I was genuinely interested in understanding the organization.

It also afforded me the opportunity to have a very steep learning curve. That meant less time wasted later in trying to fix problems I may have potentially created by my lack of understanding of the systems and processes that made our organization tick.

The leader should quickly establish the organizational culture, through consistent behavior that supports that new culture.

During those first two months as the leader of the manufacturing organization, I made few process changes. I did, however, make significant cultural changes. It did not take long for my supervisory staff as well as the employees to realize what I expected in terms of personal and professional behaviors, both of which have impact on organizational results. We established clear lines of communications between all shifts, I moved certain people from one area to another, and even to different shifts as necessary. But, for those first two months, I did not change much of how the organization went about doing its work. I first wanted to demonstrate that I understood how it was being done and why it was being done a particular way.

It was then that we began to actually change the way in which we did things. A leader who starts making changes without first gaining credibility with their followers may be perceived as arrogant and only interested in their way of doing things. That perception of the leader will be counter productive to the organization in the long run.

The leader must communicate their vision of the organization, specifically outlining the result that will be expected and the need for change.

Once I understood my organization, its mission, and its customers, and once I had demonstrated my genuine interest in the organization and its success, I set about the task of communicating my new vision for the organization. No doubt this was a performing organization. We were shipping product out the door each week. Sixty thousand dozens of suture products left our back doors each week. But our production efficiencies were low, we had too much product in quarantine awaiting a quality inspection before being released, we spend too much on overtime, and our absenteeism was too high.

With the help of my direct staff, we developed a new vision and mission for our organization. We involved several employees to represent the production staff, as well as some of our professional support staff from Engineering, Quality Assurance, Human Resources, and Finance. Together we decided that we would maintain production levels and we would dramatically improve our costs of goods sold by dealing with our in-efficiencies, overtime, and absenteeism rates.

We set about "preaching" to all the employees the reasons why we needed to do this, and making sure that every action I took, and that my supervisory staff took, was consistent with this message. At every meeting with the employees, we delivered the same message about the importance of our quality and efficiency. I explained time and time again, that these two important factors would drive our competitiveness in the marketplace. They understood this very well and began accepting many of the changes we were making. We made these changes relatively slowly at first, and with increasing speed as time went on.

Two years after we started this movement, we had made significant progress, although not everything was perfect. We still had room to improve in our efficiencies and our shipment levels. But the change was evident. The organization was becoming more productive. Perhaps more importantly, the organization had learned to change, adapt, and move on. We had become an Achieving Organization.

The Achieving Organization

To be an Achieving Organization does not mean that everything is perfect. It does not mean that every single corporate objective is being met. If they are, then I would suggest that perhaps the objectives were not aggressive enough for the organization. If all objectives are being met, it may be an indication that they are not set to stretch the group to reach a higher level of achievement. An Achieving Organization has the following characteristics:

1. The organization is meeting or exceeding many of its objectives

2. Motivation levels are high, turnover is low

3. The leaders are trusted and respected

4. There is a culture of empowerment, and followers accept this empowerment

5. Organizational systems are effective

6. Bureaucracy is minimized

7. The vision is well understood by all

The leader's role in this kind of organization is probably the simplest, not to mention the most rewarding, of all four types of organizations. The leader's job now is to continue to communicate the vision, ensure that the organizational processes are in place to support the vision, and to mentor and develop people around them. One other very important job for the leader of an Achieving Organization is to look from the outside in. That is, to look at the organization from a different perspective, to be sure that the current organizational design and its culture are ideally suited for the environment in which they exist. The leader must consider the economic, political, and social trends that may affect his or her organization.

In their book *Transforming the Organization*, Francis Gouillart and James Kelly write:

> "As we learn that the process of organizational evolution is at least as important as the organizational structure that overlays it, organizational design may not seem as important as it used to be. But make no mistake: organizational design still matters, and picking the right one remains one of the most important tasks of the leader...Organizational design is an area in which leaders most directly exert their influence, re-

defining and reassigning roles and responsibilities among the employees of the firm."

They are right on the mark. The leader's legacy will be forever linked to the organizational design and culture that they leave behind.

While it is certain that all leaders must be able to deal with all of the issues associated with all four types of organization, it is clear that the leader of the Achieving Organization will have more time to focus on the important issues of mentorship and organizational design. The leaders of the other three types of organizations will be spending a great deal of their time dealing with the problems facing the organization. The link between all of these is credibility. The leader with integrity and credibility—that is the leader with good character—will be more effective in moving the organization where it needs to go.

SIX

THE LEGACY LEADER
AS MOTIVATOR

The power that can be unleashed when people are motivated is impressive. A motivated person does not quit. A motivated person remains positive. A motivated person perseveres. Achieving the desired results is the only expected outcome that a motivated person will accept. Failure has no place in a motivated person's thinking. If a motivated person exhibits these characteristics, a motivated team multiplies these by several orders of magnitude. A team of motivated people is competitive, energetic, focused, results driven, aggressive, and always hard to beat. A motivated team has a "you go, we go" attitude. "One for all and all for one" is their understood motto.

Motivation is contagious. Motivation is obvious to those who witness it. It's desired by those who don't have it, and missed by those who lost it. Motivation is allusive. It can be short lived and difficult to maintain. Motivation need not be expensive, yet the absence of it can be extremely costly.

The Legacy Leader understands the power of a motivated person. They realize that the key to their success as leaders rest on their ability to motivate their followers. They also understand the basic principles of motivation we will discuss in this chapter.

Care first about your followers

In the fast-paced world of business, it is easy to overlook the needs of those around us, particularly when we are pre-occupied with our own affairs, both personal and professional. Yet for the Legacy Leader, putting the concerns and the needs of their followers before their own is of paramount importance.

In his book *The West Point Way of Leadership*, Colonel Larry Donnithorne writes:

> "There are many, varied styles that leaders use to influence their followers. Some are soft spoken while others shout; some are dramatic, or understated, or funny. But with any of these styles of interaction, it is still possible for leaders to show that they care—or that they don't. The greatest challenge leader's face is to show that they care deeply about both accomplishing the mission and the people who accomplish it. The leader's true effectiveness arises from a sincere regard for each member of the team."

Caring first about your followers does not mean to pamper them. It simply means that a leader should never place his best interest before that of his followers. That kind of behavior is transparent and obvious. It leads to resentment among the followers and it reduces the leader's credibility and trust levels with his team.

Some years back, I had a very talented young woman working for me. Angie was a Process Supervisor and was responsible for about half of the supervisors who reported in my business unit. When we first started working together, each morning I would say to her, "How are you doing?" She would immediately, almost instinctively, go right into describing what had happened the day and night before on the product floor. She would focus on what our production levels were, what problems we may have had, and what was on hand for today. She was good! She always had the latest information and was completely aware of what needed to be done. She would go on for a few minutes and when she was done, I would say something like, "Thanks for the update. We can talk more about that in a bit. How are you doing?" She would crack a smile and tell me about how she was doing. She realized that I was interested in her well-being. The job environment we worked in was very stressful and extremely demanding in terms of the number of hours worked each week. This could clearly take a toll on a person's family and personal life, and I needed to make sure that all was well with her.

One morning, I got into the office quite early after having received a call from my Process Supervisor letting me know that we had experienced some major equipment malfunctions the night before and production levels had been seriously affected for the week. She had been in the plant since 3:30 a.m. that morning. I also knew that she had not left the plant until 7:30 p.m. the night before. I knew this because that's when I went home as well.

As soon as I arrived, I found her busy on the shop floor and I asked her, "How are you doing?" She was about to start giving me the download of information, when she stopped herself halfway though the first word coming from her mouth and she said to me, "You mean, how am *I* doing, right?" That was exactly what I meant. We talked for a moment about her being very tired, having missed the day off she planned on taking that day, and her husband not being very happy with her work hours. I told her that as soon as she briefed me, she could go home, sleep, take the rest of the day off and invite her husband to dinner and bring me the bill. She smiled and proceeded to tell me about the night's events. We always got to the business issues. There's always time for the business issues. But the leader must care about the person, and the person is not just about work.

By the way, it was 2:00 p.m. before she finally left for the day. I had asked her three times to go home. Finally on my third request she said, "I have to make sure we looked good for your boss before I leave." That's the magic of caring for your followers first; it motivates them to care about the leader and his or her best interest.

General Omar Bradley wrote, "A leader's true effectiveness arises largely from a sincere regard for each member of the team. People are not robots and should not be treated as such. I do not by any means suggest coddling. But people are intelligent, complicated beings who will respond favorably to human understanding and consideration. By these means their leader will get maximum effort from each of them. He will also get loyalty."

Be a cheerleader

Some years ago, I had the opportunity (thanks to my wife volunteering me) to coach my seven-year-old daughter's soccer team. There is no more rewarding or challenging job than that of coaching soccer for a team of six and seven year old girls! I knew nothing about soccer, other than that the objective is to kick the ball between the two poles. The team that does that most often wins. That was the extent of my knowledge of the game of soccer. What I did know is that these little girls needed encouragement, a few basic skills on the game, and they needed to have fun!

Our team was lousy. We lost every game that first season that I coached them. Each time we played, however, the girls got a little better. More importantly, each time we scored a goal—which sadly was not that often—we celebrated by playing "ring around the Rosie" right in the middle of the playing field. I will admit that the most amusing part of this was how frustrated the opposing team's coach would get with us every time we did that. It seemed to me those other coaches, and the parents, sometimes took the game a bit too seriously and behaved in was that were always counterproductive to motivation for their players. I find that yelling and insulting six and seven year olds never yield the intended result. The same is true for adults!

The part of the coaching job I enjoyed most was watching the girls play a game and just have a great time at it. They played their hearts out for no other reason than to please their moms and dads who were cheering from the sidelines. They also reveled in the light of having their coach cheer them on and give them a high five when they gave it their all.

Do adults react any differently to cheering? No, they don't. There are few things more powerful in the Legacy Leader's arsenal than an arm wrapped around a follower's shoulder followed by some encouraging words.

"I know you can do this." "I have every confidence in you." "I trust you," or, "You're the right person for this job," are simple statements that cause a follower to stand a bit taller, walk more proudly, and try harder to make things happen.

I remember one example of a leader who managed to motivate an entire organization with inexpensive Matchbox toy formula racecars. Mr. Jesse Penn was trying to get the entire Operations organization within ETHICON, Johnson & Johnson, to think and act more like a team. Jesse must have been impressed by the teamwork demonstrated by pit crews in car races. He once told me how fascinated he was when he saw the speed and accuracy with which these teams of people could service a car, fill-it up with gas, replace all four tires, and get it back into the race in a matter of seconds. In fact, the driver with the fastest, most effective pit crew always has a tremendous advantage in the race. Jesse wanted to capture that spirit and motivate his people to strive for those high levels of teamwork. He purchased many toy Matchbox racecars, and had a small label affixed to the side of the car with the name "ETHICON."

Each time Jesse saw or heard of someone in the organization doing a great job or exhibiting the behaviors that he felt were in agreement with his vision of teamwork, he made sure they got one of the toy cars.

I recall the first time I saw one of the cars on a colleague's desk. I was immediately curious about it and questioned him on where he had gotten it. There was a big smile across his face as he told me he had received a visit from the Vice President of Operations. The VP had dropped off the car as a thank you to him. I wanted one!

Soon, everyone wanted one of Jesse's cars. Before long, these little toy cars became trophies that people proudly displayed on their desk. I still have mine, and I am sure so do many other people. It wasn't the size of the prize that motivated people to want one. After all, we are talking about a 2-inch toy car that probably cost less than $2.00. Yet, people worked hard to get one, and they worked even harder after they had it. Jesse understood that he needed to be a cheerleader, pumping his people up and encouraging them to go, go, go!

Be available, but not imposing

There is a fine balance that a leader must keep between being close to the action, but not in the way of the action. For the leader who finds themselves closing their door to read through hundreds of e mail and answer dozens of voice mails, or moving through an airport to catch yet another airplane, or running to one "behind closed door" meeting after another, there's only one thing that can be said: cut it out and stop making excuses!

Nothing is more important than being visible and available to your followers. Everything that keeps you from doing this is reducing your ability to generate energy and motivation around your vision. We all have suffered from the tyrannical hold of the "schedule." Most of the time spent in these trips and meetings is wasted, and we all know it! So, why do we keep doing it? A leader who is a slave to their schedule is not a master of their destiny.

Leaders must focus on being available. As a leader, you must make time for it. Put that on your schedule and keep the appointments made with your folks. Go down to the cafeteria at lunch, and sit with people who did not expect you. Insist that other leaders do the same. You want to motivate your followers and establish a good legacy as a leader? Be visible. Be available.

Reward often

Over the past years I have had the opportunity to work with, and be exposed to, many different companies each with its unique culture. The leaders in these organizations always reflected that organizational environment. Of course they did; after all they determined it with their behaviors, attitudes and styles. The opinions about how to reward followers or how often rewards should be handed out are as varied as the styles of each leader. In one company that I have worked with, their idea of rewarding is not punishing someone. They reason that the absence of being punished is, in and of itself, a "reward." The old joke that goes "the floggings will continue until morale improves," has more truth to it than many of us care to acknowledge.

Rewarding people comes easy to some leaders while others would rather have root canal than reward a follower. Is there a correct answer as to when and how often to reward? The answer is yes. Reward as often as appropriate and make sure the reward is appropriate. The size and physical form of the reward is often not the motivator to the recipient. The leader must never forget the purpose of rewarding:

1. Rewards are intended to motivate

2. Rewards are intended to recognize and encourage a behavior. The behavior must be in complete agreement with the vision and with the organizational cultural norms that the leader has established

3. Rewards can have a positive or a negative effect on both the individual and the organization at large

Keeping these simple principles in mind, the leader can use everything from a cash bonus to a sincere "I'm proud of you" to achieve the desired effect. Only the leader's imagination restricts how he or she can reward the followers. But if they reward the wrong behavior or the wrong person, or if their rewards are inconsistent and poorly communicated, the negative effects will be swift and will permeate through the organization like a foul smell running though the ventilation system of a building. It will reach every person in every corner of the organization, and they will question the validity of the reward, the person receiving it, and no doubt, the person handing it out.

It is probably for fear of risking this negative outcome that many leaders shy away from rewarding people. Worst yet, they choose to reward in private and even instruct the recipient "not to tell anyone else." That is the cardinal sin when rewarding someone. A leader should never fall into that trap. Instead, the leader should work harder at finding ways to reward individuals and organizations that fits with their personal style. They must ensure that they are consistent and that only the right behaviors are rewarded.

In more than twenty years of managing and leading people, going back to my days as an Air Force cadet, I have never found a more powerful form of reward than the right words, spoken at the right time, and to the right people. Nothing can be further than the truth than the saying "words are cheap."

Words such as "nicely done," "you really impress me," "thank you for a job well done," and "keep up the good work," are far from cheap. They can become meaningless, however, if they are poorly delivered or not sincere; they can become transparent and a complete waste of energy to even say them. What people will remember most about being rewarded are the words said by the person presenting the award.

I was honored to receive a number of military commendations while I served in the Air Force. I proudly display the medals and accompanying certificates in my home. But recently, when I had a friend visit, he was looking at some of the framed awards and asked me, "What was this one for?" I had to think about it for a bit. I wasn't sure I remembered what I had gotten it for. Luckily, most military awards come with a certificate in which the actions being recognized are described in a short paragraph or two. So I was reminded and was able to tell my friend about the award.

But there is something I do remember about every single military commendation I ever received, and of those I witnessed being presented to others; and that is the statement that ended each of the presentations. Usually, military commendations end with a statement such as: "The singularly distinctive accomplishments of (fill in the person's name) while serving his country reflect great credit upon himself and the United States Air Force." Having those words read out loud before my peers and family meant as much to me personally as the medal itself. So much so, that I recall that, but frankly struggle to remember the reasons for having received it in the first place.

Many organizations today use financial rewards as their main form of recognition. What sales representative would not like to take an all expense trip to Hawaii for two because they achieve outstanding results for the year? What executive is not happy to receive an obscene amount of stock options as a reward for exceeding corporate profitability objectives? Is there an employee who would file a grievance for getting too large an end-of-year bonus for outstanding performance? I think not. Yet every one of these individuals will only be motivated for a relatively short period of time in the vacuum of a more continuous form of recognition that can really only be done with verbal communications from their leaders. Cash is good. Twenty-four percent lead crystal salad bowls and Movado watches are nice. An upgrade to a company car is very nice. But these, and other forms of recognition, have a relatively short half-life. The leader's words on the other hand, can and often have an enduring quality about them.

Most normal human beings enjoy being rewarded. However, they don't all enjoy being rewarded in similar ways. Some prefer it with big fan fare, others would rather it be done in a more subtle way. So the leader must adapt to this, and must do everything possible to ensure that the effects of the reward are what was intended; that is to reward the recipient for past performance and to motivate them to continue to perform at a high level of achievement.

In the book *Management Skills*, Chapter 19 is titled "Motivating and Satisfying Excellent Individuals." In it, Edward E. Lawler III writes:

> "Motivation and satisfaction are at the same time complicated and simple topic areas—complicated because of the enormous individual differences that exist and the complexity of human beings; they are simple in that there are some key truths that can be used to guide the design of effective rewards systems. These are worth repeated here because they are so fundamental:
>
> - Rewards must be important to be motivators
> - Individuals differ in the importance they attach to rewards
> - Individuals are motivated to perform when they believe they can obtain rewards they value by performing well
> - Individuals are attracted to jobs and organizations that offer the rewards they value
> - Satisfied employees are unlikely to quit and be absent"

Leaders must never underestimate the value and power of recognizing properly!

Discipline swiftly and fairly

Shortly after I took over a large organization of more than three hundred people, I found it necessary to fire one of the employees. That same day, while I was standing in the cafeteria line getting lunch, one of the more senior (both in age and in years with the company) employees in my business unit approached me and she extended me a handshake. She said, seriously and loud enough so that people around us could hear her comment, "It's about time somebody did something about that guy. He was getting away with his antics for a long time. Thank you for finally doing something about it." Within seconds there were echoes of supports coming from many people who heard her comment to me. People know when discipline should and must be handed out. They expect the leaders to do it swiftly but fairly. Taking this kind of action can have very motivating effects on the rest of the team.

One of the biggest demotivators in organizations is when people perceive that there is unequal or unfair treatment. In some cases that can mean that people receive more than they deserve, and in others it can mean that people are perceived with "getting away with pulling less than their weight" towards achieving the goals. Both have equally devastating effects and both are a reflection of the leader's credibility, their judgment, and ability to take action. Both are a test of the leader's character. People will watch intently to see how the leader will deal with these circumstances and will decide how much they can trust the leader to be dedicated to the vision, the good of the followers, and the overall health of the organization. When discipline is required, the Legacy Leader does not shy away or delegate their responsibility. Done correctly and fairly, discipline can be a great motivator. Conversely, the effects of poorly administered discipline will have a demoralizing effect on the organization.

Use a personal touch: Notes, voice mails, and drop-in visits

Most people have a scrapbook or some other place where they keep pictures, letters, or other memory joggers such as ribbons, medals, and certificates. For many of us, that usually includes personal notes we have received from people who are important to us. Some of my most precious keepsakes are a few hand-written notes that I have gotten over the years either from people I worked for or from people who worked for me. I keep these in a very special place and once in a while, I look though them and remember. I remember how I felt when I received them. I remember what I did to receive them. I remember wanting to please that person again.

Sadly, these days it seems most leaders are content with sending an electronic mail message to give a word of thanks or encouragement. Perhaps they reason that they can copy more people on the email and give the person being addressed wide recognition. There is nothing wrong with that, but it can not, and does not, replace the personal touch of taking the time to write a note with your own pen, affix your name to it, lick an envelope and send it to the person. The effort that this takes to do is what motivates and excites the recipient. It makes the leader a real person, someone who is in touch with the needs of his followers. It makes the leader a person rather than just the person who holds an office.

While an electronic mail message can have a cold and removed feeling to it, a voice mail message can very effectively get a message across and can be very motivating. When the recipient can hear the excitement, sincerity, or other emotion in the leader's voice, it motivates and excites them. They feel good to receive the message. People who receive these messages usually are anxious and happy to share with their colleagues and co-workers the news of having received the message. The leader's credibility is increased and the followers are endeared to the leader.

Another very powerful motivator is the casual drop in visit by the leader. Just popping in and saying a quick hello can have very long lasting positive and motivating results. There does not have to be a special reason to do it. The very fact that the leader would take the time to simply stop-in and check to see how a person is doing is reason enough. This, like the personal notes and voice mail messages, makes the leader approachable, open and available. It increases the channels of communications and affords the leader a chance to get the pulse of the organization and to promote their vision. All of this from a simple drop-in visit. Of course, the leader must be careful not to use these drop in visits only when there is something that they need, or when they are searching for information. They must certainly want to avoid dropping in only when there is something going wrong. That can turn these casual drop-in visits into dreaded and feared occasions. It would be much like being sent to the principal's office only in reverse; the principal comes to you!

Clearly, we should never abuse this method of motivation. Doing so can in fact have the opposite effect on both the individual and on the organization or other team members. They can be demoralizers and contributors to organizational fear. The wrong words in an electronic or voice message can have devastating effects on the moral of an organization. Legacy Leaders never underestimate the power that their words, whether written or spoken, private or public, can have on their followers. Evidence of how important these words are can be found in many museums that have preserved the notes written by leaders, and in the countless scrapbooks carefully protected by their owners.

"Watch" the jokes

Jokes are often a reflection of a deeply held belief of the person telling the joke. Therefore, if you want to get a good idea of what a person believes or the nature of their character, pay close attention to the jokes they make. Humor is as important to life as breathing. I am a firm believer that it needs to be an every day part of the job. But, an ill-worded or poorly delivered joke by a leader can undermine days, months and even years of trying to build a legacy and motivating people towards a vision. Indeed, it can mean the immediate loss of credibility and trust, and a re-evaluation of the leader's character by his or her followers.

If, as a leader, you have gone to one of your constituents after having made a remark or a quick joke at their expense and said something like, "You know I was only kidding right?" you were too late! The damage was done, not just with that person, but also, perhaps, with many more. Of course, they may tell you it was okay, but you are naïve as a leader if you believe they are being completely honest with you. You see, while you may have said the comment in jest, others who heard it, may not understand your relationship with the person. They may not know that you indeed trust them and think highly of them. They only know what they heard and they can't be sure of what the intent truly was. The best advice here is: don't do it. If you want to make jokes, poke fun at yourself—you might as well, after all your followers are! The wise leader understands what is worth making fun about themselves, and finds ways to use this humor to make themselves more personable and approachable to their followers.

Results motivate

Drive results, and it will drive motivation. Of course, nothing happens in a vacuum; therefore, how we drive to achieve results can also determine whether these results will indeed motivate a group of people. The leader who drives organizational results at the expense of his followers will have only very short-term results. Nevertheless, people associated with winning teams are easier to motivate. So, focusing on building a winning team to drive results will lead to motivated followers.

One of the problems that plagued the manufacturing organization I led was our backorder. In certain industries, such as the one we were in, having some backorder was acceptable, as we sold through distributors who kept weeks, and at times, a few months worth of inventory. So while, we may have a manufacturing backorder, our end customer was not always significantly affected. Nevertheless, we had a goal to eliminate out backorder. Realistically, my goal was to reduce it as much as possible. At one of the quarterly meetings, I challenged my entire business unit to reduce the backorder to $50,000. That would be an impressive feat given the complexity of our business and given that the current backorder was in excess of $900,000. I promised them that if they accomplished the goal, I would dust off my saxophone and play "En Mi Viejo San Juan" for them. This is a very old, meaningful, nostalgic, and favorite song for people in Puerto Rico.

The time for the next quarterly meeting came very quickly. We always held the meetings in the largest conference room in the facility. When I walked in to the meeting, I was amazed at what I saw. The room had been transformed to look like a street in old San Juan. The walls were fully decorated, and even a small stage had been prepared to look like one of the forts in San Juan.

We went on with the business of the meeting, and at the end I did what I always did, opened it up for questions. They all screamed in unison "play us our song." I teased them for a bit, and reminded them that they had not really hit the goal. They had missed it by $5000. The lowest our backorder had gotten was $55,000. They screamed louder, demanding their song, fully expecting that I would recognize the tremendous effort and accomplishment, which they knew, was impressive. More importantly, they knew that I knew it was impressive. I had hidden my saxophone in a closet in the conference room the day before the meeting. I pulled it out, donned a hat, and played my very poor rendition of "En Mi Viejo San Juan." The applause when I was done was deafening. Surely they were not applauding how well I played—they were probably happy to have me stop. But to them, my playing the saxophone was a public recognition of their tremendous teamwork, effort, and accomplishment. This worked so well, I threatened to play again if they let the backorder go back up!

Listening motivates

Listening has to be one of most underestimated motivational tools used by leaders. It may be because it is so difficult to learn to do it well. Leaders are by nature assertive and take-charge kind of people. It seems counterintuitive to think that you can take charge when you are listening; after all, it appears to be such a passive activity. Nothing could be further from the truth. A leader must train herself or himself to listen well. They must turn off their natural inclination towards being heard, and tune in to what is being said. Not to just hear what is said, but to process it, think about it, and consider it, before even thinking about what, if any, the response or reaction should be.

Regrettably, most people spend the time that others are talking formulating what they will say next. This is clearly evidenced by the number of times someone is interrupted in the middle of a sentence during a meeting. When a leader does this, they manage to shut down the conversation. If the leader interrupts a follower, the follower yields to the leader and then carefully considers whether they should try speaking out again.

If a leader wants to gain immediate credibility, they should learn to listen actively. There is no greater form of respect that a leader can afford a follower, than taking the time to listen to them. People understand the urgency of a leader's schedule. They realize how very busy most leaders are. So, when a leader takes the time to listen well, internalize what is being said, and respond appropriately to the statements they've just heard, the followers feel respected, valued, and acknowledged. It is almost impossible to motivate someone who does not feel respected, valued and acknowledged, thus logic would point us to the inevitable conclusion that to be a great motivator, among the other traits a leader must exhibit, they must be great listeners.

On August 1, 1997, I was sitting in my office, when I heard a faint knock on the door. It was one of production workers in my organization. The day before, she and I had spent more than an hour talking about several important personal and work related issues. She had been having some performance problems, which prompted the discussion in my office. Rather than discuss her performance problem first, I had given her a chance to speak about what was happening in her personal life that she felt was affecting her ability to do her job. These non-work-related issues were distracting her.

Frankly, I did nothing to solve her personal problems. All I did was listened to her and give her a chance to talk through her problems. After she spoke for a while, I told her I understood her dilemma, and that I understood how these issues could indeed have an impact on her performance. I encouraged her to use the services of our employee assistance program, which is staffed with professionals capable of helping people with personal problems. I also made it clear that while I understood her situation, I did expect her performance to improve immediately or we would have to take other action.

She had come back to see me the next day with a small box that she handed to me and said thanks, smiled and walked out. Inside the box was a small car, sculpted in tin, with a musical box that plays "Happy Days Are Here Again." There was also a small note that read: "Por entender y escuchar, simplemente gracias, Ada." Translated it means, "For understanding and listening, simply thank you," and her name, Ada.

A few months later, her performance had improved significantly, and although she had not used the services of the employee assistance program, she had resolved her personal problems. Legacy Leaders need to take the time to listen!

Situational Leadership Motivates

Followers want to have a leader they can look up to. They want a leader who they can count on to make the right decisions at the right time. People don't expect leaders to always be right. What they do expect is for them to always act appropriately in light of the circumstances for that particular moment.

In 1984, Dr. Paul Hersey wrote a great book entitled *The Situational Leader*. In it, he outlines four fundamental styles of leadership and accompanying follower readiness level. Hersey suggests that a leader can do one of four things: delegate a task to a follower, participate with the followers in getting the task done, sell the followers on the reasons for doing a task, or tell followers what to do. According to Hersey, the style that the leader adopts depends on the situation being dealt with and with the level of readiness that a follower has. For example, if a follower is an expert in his or her field and the leader has confidence in their ability to get a particular job done, the leader should choose to delegate the task to the follower giving them as much autonomy and flexibility as possible to get it done without interference from the leader. By doing this, the leader motivates the follower because he has indicated their trust in them.

On the other hand, if the follower is a novice or inexperienced, the leader may choose to be specific and tell the follower exactly what they need to do. If they don't take that approach, they risk a few outcomes: first, the task may not be completed correctly or on schedule. Second, they may succeed in frustrating the follower, who despite their best attempts, because of inexperience, may not be able to deliver that which is being demanded of them. The end result may be a poor result and a de-motivated follower.

Hersey puts it like this:

> "Research has shown that a leader's success is affected by the environment … Leader effectiveness depends upon the interaction among the leader, follower, boss, associates, organization, job demands, and time constraints. These are factors that tend to be present in the environment at any particular time. A change in one may create a change in the others."

He goes on to write:

> "Followers also bring attitudes and behaviors to the situation, both individually and collectively."

Clearly, the effectiveness of the leader and his or her ability to motivate his or her followers will be determined by the interaction between the leaders behaviors, attitudes, and styles, and those of their followers.

Imagine for a moment that you're standing in front of your house and that it has caught on fire. You hear the fire engine siren screaming down the road and soon the big red truck comes to a stop and fire fighters jump off the truck ready for action. You notice one fire fighter that has a big "C" on the front of her helmet, so you assume that she's the chief. What style of leadership would you like for her to exhibit at this very moment? What if she gathered everyone around and said something like, "So folks, any suggestions on what we should do here?" and started patiently listening to each suggestion made by each of her team members, being careful not to interrupt them and then trying to reach consensus on a decision? All the while, your house is being reduced to ashes.

Clearly, that participative style of leadership would not be the right style to adopt at the moment by the chief. What you would want and expect is for the chief to bark out the necessary commands to make sure that the team works effectively and efficiently to get the fire out. You want her to tell people what to do if necessary; whatever it takes, just get it done! That would be the appropriate style to adopt at that time.

Later, after the fire has been extinguished, and the firefighters are back at the station, that same leader may call her team together to discuss the team's performance. She may start by praising them for a job well done, and then ask for input as to how everyone thinks the team performed and how they can do an even better job next time. Using a different approach, appropriate to the moment, the leader can successfully get the team to switch gears with her and follow her lead, whether in a moment of crisis, or during the calm evaluation of the team's performance. The leader, who demonstrates that ability and flexibility, gains the followers trust and in doing so motivates them to new levels of performance.

Whether you subscribe to the four leadership styles proposed by Hersey, or some other variation of them, the point is clear: the right leadership style for the right conditions exercised consistently and with H.E.A.R.T., is very motivational to followers. Followers understand that different circumstances require different leader behaviors. As long as the leader's character, integrity, and credibility remain constant, they (the followers) are willing to support the leader as they adopt varying styles to match the situation.

SEVEN

THE LEGACY LEADER
AS COMMUNICATOR

Picture this: you arrive just in time for an important meeting called by the president of the company. You are anxious to hear what he has to say. Finally, the room is called to order, the president takes the podium, and after a few introductory remarks and greetings proceeds to say:

"We have been considering the internal ramifications of all potential scenarios as we realize that in this corporate environment we must have an energized and globally aligned company, where people sense that there are no boundaries or challenges for all vertical as well as horizontal communications to help us overcome the obstacles we face. Moreover, realizing that our pipeline is indeed our lifeline, we must ensure that we balance all critical base business activities and expenditures to have a vibrant and meaningful, value added, research development strategy, staffed with highly creative and aggressive product developers, to drive product innovations for our company. We must have the finest and most motivated leaders in the industry. Charismatic leaders who will provide clear direction, and create an empowered qualified group of followers, driving them and the organization to the highest levels of synergy and performance. Finally, I would expect that each of you talented people would focus on results. Not working harder, but smarter. Re-engineering your daily tasks and eliminating all non-valued added activities from our processes and systems; utilizing all the Six-Sigma Process Improvements tools that we have equipped you with, and working in a true spirit of cooperation and global alignment with your European and Asian Counterparts to increase our world wide reach and penetrate into yet uncharted and unexploited markets in other parts of the world. Now, I will take any questions you may have...."

Here's a question: what in the world does all this mean? Does this sound familiar? Would it surprise you to learn that this is almost a direct quote from the CEO of a major Fortune 100 company addressing a group of his followers? Run-on sentence after run-on sentence, this leader managed to say nothing of substance.

The jargon that many leaders use today to address their followers often leaves them wondering what was said. They are left pondering what the actual meaning of what was said is. Many of us have heard speeches made by leaders or read letters written by them, addressing seemingly important issues, that have left us wanting more, or worst yet have left us with more questions than answers.

Politicians have taken this type of communication skill to an art form. In fact, you hear the term "spinning" as it refers to how a message should be delivered to focus on a point, or to avoid making one. Leaders often are so rehearsed that they come across as robotic in their communications to followers, using rhetoric and corporate lingo that sound sophisticated and educated, but has no real substance.

We all would agree that communication is the lifeline of a leader. Without effective communication to their followers, leadership is meaningless. In the vacuum of information, uncertainty reigns supreme. Uncertainty leads to assumptions; assumptions lead to erroneous actions; erroneous actions often lead to failure in execution; and failure in execution leads to the execution of the leader.

What is it about a leader that makes them good or poor at communications? Why do some leaders engage their followers while others struggle to get their message across? Can it be just a matter of style? Can we teach a leader how to be an effective communicator? Understanding the answer to these questions begins with clarifying our definition of communication.

What is communication? What are the essential elements embodied in the concept of communications that are critical to the leader's success as a communicator? It seems some people think that if a person is a good speaker or a good writer, they are therefore good communicators. It's more than this.

Good communication is successfully getting someone else to understand your message. That implies a two-way information exchange. The person communicating the message must have confirmation that the message was received and understood. This is where most leaders fall flat on their face as it relates to communication. They may do a terrific job of expressing their message, but they have no clue whether the message was received and understood.

Ironically, as it relates to leadership, that is the most significant part of communication. If a general in the army gives an order, and never verifies that the order was received and understood by the intended subordinate or unit, they should not scratch their head in wonderment when the order is not carried out. Worse yet, they need to consider themselves completely responsible if their order, having been misunderstood, is executed and results in the wrong objective being accomplished.

Whether the leader uses verbal, written, hand signals, body language, actions, or smoke signals is not the point. The method of communication is never as important as whether the message is received and understood. Therefore, for a leader to simply communicate is useless. They must communicate effectively. The definition of effective communications stretches the definition of communication to include knowing that you were successful in getting someone else to understand your message and having them act according to your expectations.

Does this mean that the communication style of the leader is irrelevant? No it does not. Few would argue that it was Mr. Obama's impressive orator skills that help him win the White House. Clearly there are some individuals who are more charismatic than others in their communication styles. There are those who can speak well in front of audiences and those who cannot. There are people who write well, and people who do not. Could someone with less passion and inflection in their voice have delivered Dr. King's "I have a dream speech" and have the impact that he did? Probably not. But Dr. King's speech was not uniquely impressive because of the words used or even because of his classic abilities as an eloquent orator. His words had special significance because of who he was as a leader. It is because of his credibility as a leader that his words are so moving and compelled people to action.

People will look at the leader's character first, and listen to his or her words second. People will consider the leader's actions long before and long after they trust their words. Style is important. We can teach the mechanics of becoming a better communicator in the traditional sense of the word. That is, people can learn to become better public speakers, learn to manage their body language, or improve their writing skills. But, no well polished and delivered speech or well-written letter can possibly replace or make-up for the leader's character and credibility with their followers. These are the elements that will ultimately determine the level of effectiveness that the leader will enjoy as a communicator.

Legacy Leaders should always strive to improve their effectiveness as communicators and to do so they must keep a few simple rules in mind:

1. Communicate to inform, not to impress

2. Communicate to clarify, not to confuse

3. Communicate directly, not with double talk

4. Communicate honestly and transparently

Informing vs. Impressing

Some time ago, when I was heading the manufacturing Business Unit in ETHICON's San Lorenzo Plant in Puerto Rico, I held quarterly meetings with all the employees. We usually brought them together by shifts. These meetings were intended to give all employees a sense of our performance for that past quarter, highlight accomplishments and recognize top performers, as well as to layout plans for the next quarter. It was also a time for employees to ask their questions.

I invited our General Manager to join us from time to time, and sometimes, he would make some remarks at the meeting. I remember one of these meetings when one of the employees asked a very direct question about the future of the manufacturing facility. The employee wanted to know if the plant was at risk of closing, and operations moving out of the island of Puerto Rico to someplace else such as Mexico. This was a question I got at almost every meeting with the employees. This time, I thought I'd pass it to the boss to answer. So I asked the General Manager if he would field the question.

The General Manager stood up, and without missing a beat, began by telling a short story. He spoke in Spanish so this is not a direct quote, but the story went like this:

> "When you go to the local neighborhood bakery to buy fresh bread, you go there with the expectation that you will find bread, freshly baked. You expect that the bread will taste just as good or better today as it did yesterday, and you expect to pay a fair price for it. If you go to the bakery and discover that the bread is only available some of the time, and when it is, it does not always taste good, and after a while the price goes up, what would you do?"

The audience all in unison answered, "I'd go to another bakery to get my bread."

"Right!" the GM continued. "So let's make sure we make great bread!" Once he said that he sat down.

His point was clear. Just as in the case of the bakery, so it was true in our business. As long as we maintained high fill rates, no backorder, provide superior quality product, and control our cost so that our profitability remains high, our business here in the island would be secure. When we stop making the best, freshest bread consistently, we will have to start worrying about it.

The answer was clear and so was the message. He had delivered the message using simple and very relevant language. You see, in Puerto Rico, the local bakery is an icon. Getting fresh "pan de manteca" or "pan de agua" is a part of daily life for many Puertorricans. He had used an example that made the point clearly and used words that they could all understand. He could have chosen to use more eloquent and sophisticated business terms and lingo to address the question. That may have impressed a few, but no doubt would have minimized the impact of his words. Instead he spoke in simple terms they could all relate to. From that moment, every time I was asked the question about moving the facility and the jobs to Mexico, I reminded the team about the bakery example. For the next two years, I heard employees using the bakery analogy within my Business Unit to help keep us focused on the important aspects of our business.

Leaders should aim first to get their point across in their communications and second on how impressive they sound in doing so.

Communicate to clarify, not to confuse

In his book, *Competitive Leadership: Twelve Principles for Success*, Super-Bowl-winning coach Brian Billick describes his use of "blue language." It's not something that he is proud of, but he writes:

"Sometimes, 'locker room language' seems to be the only verbiage that fits the situation. I would love to have the time and demeanor to approach a player and coolly and calmly comment, 'Gee, because you are playing in a manner that would indicate that you are not fully focused on the task at hand, I would like for you to endeavor to regain some sense of focus on your duties.' All factors considered, it is just more telling (and expedient) to say, 'Hey get your g _ _ d _ _ _ head out of you're a _ _.' The former may be civilized, but the latter seems to be a lot more to the point and more effective."

I agree with him. Coach Billick obviously understands that the leader's communication needs to be clear and concise. Moreover, follower confusion as to the message and what the expected behavior is should never be the outcome of the leader's communication. I don't think the player in this case had any problem understanding the coach and what he was expected to do.

Communicate directly, not with double talk

We will all remember watching President Clinton give testimony under oath regarding the Monica Lewinsky affair. He was asked a question by the attorney leading the investigation, and answered the question this way: "It depends on what the meaning of the word *is* is." Really? It depends on the meaning of the word *is*? What followed was one of the most circular reasoning answers ever given by any leader to a rather direct question.

People often use this technique to avoid answering a question or more specifically, to seem as if though they have answered when in fact they have not. Few things can be more frustrating to a follower than to listen to one of their leaders speak in circles, using hundreds of words to say nothing of substance. This leads to an immediate mistrust of the leader. It also leads to more questions as people's appetite to discover what the leader is so unwilling to share, grows.

A leader should choose words carefully, making every attempt to be direct, honest, and completely forthright, never giving the impression that there is something that is being hidden. If indeed the leader is unwilling or unable to share some information with the followers, they should say so plainly and explain their reasons why. I have never been disappointed with my teams when I choose to be one hundred percent transparent in my communications with them. Leaders who always speak the truth, honestly and transparently, earn the right to also say, "I can't speak about that right now. But when I can share more information I will." People understand the need for confidentiality at times, and they understand that leaders are exposed to information that needs to be "managed." However, we must never withhold information as a general rule. The opposite in fact should be the case! Leaders must share information freely and completely whenever possible.

Leaders need not make apologies for withholding some information from their followers when they deem that it is appropriate and necessary. If they have earned the trust and credibility with their followers, they will have significant leeway to do so. But as soon as the followers sense that there is some hidden agenda or begin to believe that the leader is being dishonest with them, the leader will loose his effectiveness.

There are several other dimensions of communication skills that are clearly important for effective leaders. They are: nonverbal communications, listening skills, and, to a lesser degree, writing skills. Let's look at each of these.

Nonverbal Communications

No one would argue that our body language sends deafening screams that can be heard by all who see them. Body language is not a part of communication, it is most of it. Ralph Waldo Emerson once said, "When the eyes say one thing, and the tongue another, a practical man relies on the language of the first."

We all know that actions speak louder than words, so the leader that pays little mind to the language of their actions, their eyes, hands, posture, and even their appearance, must willingly accept the certain outcome that the followers actions will be directly related to the message sent by these non-verbal cues. A military officer whose uniform is not immaculately pressed and boots shinned to a high gloss would be foolish to expect that his or her troops would look any better than they do. The leader whose eyes have no sparkle when they speak about their vision tells his followers that he is not excited or truly committed to the vision. If a leader looks bored, they probably are. The impact of the body cannot be overstated.

While the leader's body language and other non-verbal cues are very important to the organization and to the followers, what most leaders failed to realize and capitalize on is what they can get from paying close attention to the followers non-verbal cues. Followers say more to their leaders with actions than with words. So, while the effective leader certainly concerns themselves with managing and using their body to convey the proper messages, they are constantly in-tune and reading the non-verbal language being "spoken" by those around them.

Sitting plainly on the surface of the follower's body language, leaders can gain volumes of information regarding the follower's motivational levels, their level of understanding, and, more importantly, buy into the vision. They can also gauge the followers' level of trust in them, and whether or not they are saying everything that they would like to have said. The effective leader is always interpreting the body language of their followers and turning that non-verbal exchange into actual communications by asking probing, non-intimidating, questions, and making encouraging statements. In essence, the leader wants to make sure that they are creating an environment where communications can indeed take place.

Listening

I have come to believe that listening is the most important communication skill a leader can possess. I have also come to the conclusion that listening is one of the most difficult skills for a leader to develop. Contrary to popular belief, listening is not a passive activity. It is an active sport requiring extreme concentration, focus, and a Herculean amount of effort. For leaders, who are accustomed to being heard, listening is a debilitating weakness that minimizes their effectiveness as communicators, reduces their ability to influence followers, and diminishes their impact as motivators.

Some time ago, I was asked by a client to facilitate a contract negotiations meeting between the company's management and the worker's union. We sat for several hours of talks, most of the talking being done by the representatives of both sides. The union president, who was by now somewhat frustrated, turn to me and said, "You're not saying too much here. All that you've been doing is sitting there listening." I responded by saying, "It is infinitely more important for me to know what you are thinking than for me to have you know what I am thinking." My point was this: I already knew what I was thinking. I needed to know what others thought. If I had engaged in speaking, I would have failed to focus on listening to what was being said.

Listening to what they were saying as well as to what they were not saying was very important. I could not do that and talk simultaneously. I was either going to focus on what I was saying, or I was going to focus on what they were saying. To effectively lead the discussions and bring resolution to the negotiations, listening, rather than talking became my most important tool.

Too often people don't listen well because they are too busy formulating their next thought. They plan their comments and look for the next possible opportunity to jump in and be heard. Leaders who do this jeopardize several things: first, they risk shutting down conversations. Followers will not interrupt when leaders are speaking.

Second, they risk being perceived as poor listeners and people who think they know it all. Third, they risk not getting all the pertinent facts and information that would have been available to them if they would speak less and listen more.

Listening must be practiced. It is a skill that takes time to learn. Some of the basic principles of good listening are:

- Don't create or tolerate distractions
- Keep some notes as you are listening
- Give positive non-verbal feedback as you are listening
- Ask only important clarification questions
- Avoid going off on tangent or off subject
- Avoid getting concerned over the delivery style of speaker
- Be patient
- Visualize as you listen
- Avoid giving too much thought to what you want to say next. Listen first and pause as necessary to formulate a question or a response

If for no other reason, effective leaders should become good listeners because of the motivating effect that listening can have on people. When a follower feels that the leader has heard them and considered their words, it causes them to gain confidence in the leader, and gives them a feeling of importance. Leaders listen up!

Writing Skills

If there is a skill that leaders often neglect to develop it is their writing skill. E-mails and voice mails have all but replaced the need for formal letters and other forms of writing. This trend must be reversed. Leaders must never underestimate the impact, importance, and value that their followers place on words written by their leaders. The bottom line on writing is that there is no excuse for a leader not having well-developed writing skills. There is a boundless supply of educational materials available for all levels of skill development in writing and I would not presume in this text to try to teach composition and other writing skills. Clearly, that subject can easily fill a book of its own. Suffice it to say that the importance of good writing cannot be overstated. It is the leader's writing that often survives them and contributes to their legacy. Leaders must therefore make it a priority to become good writers.

There are two other communication issues that leaders must deal with in their organizations: perceptions and rumors. Left unchecked, these two can have negative ramifications including organizational fear, mistrust by followers, inefficiencies, turnover, low moral, and ultimately lack luster results achievement.

Dealing with Perceptions

Many people say, "Perception is reality." I do not agree. Reality is reality. Perception is someone or some group's idea of what the reality is. That perception can, and usually is, based on some portion of reality, but it is often (and almost by definition) distorted or incomplete in some way. People fill in the blank with information that they have gathered through the organizational grapevine or, worst yet, from stereotypical thoughts and attitudes that they have had engraved in their minds from early childhood.

Thus, based on perceptions, people believe in almost anything; and while perception is not reality, it is a major driver of attitudes and behaviors that in a very real way can turn this "virtual reality" into actual reality. Expressed in a different way, this means that actions of those who allow their perceptions to drive what they do, can in essence change the environment around them and therefore create a new reality.

We all have perceptions about most things. Whether it's individuals, organizations, groups, products, cultures, or anything else that we may not have complete information about, people form opinions based on what they know regardless of how much or little they know. Although these perceptions can sometimes be positive, sadly, in many cases, they are quite negative. It is negative perceptions based on stereotypes that lead some people to group all motorcycle riders into gangs, or causes discrimination of other kinds against people of color or of a particular religious belief.

There is one example that I often use when leading a group discussion on the subject of diversity to get people to understand the power—and the danger—of perceptions. I describe the following scenario: suppose the phone rings and you pick it up, say hello, and the voice you hear on the other end is that of a person with an English accent. You don't know the person, but they engage you in a short discussion. What thoughts come to mind about the person? After giving folks a few moments to consider this, I ask them, suppose the accent was German instead, what would you think then? A few more moments go by, and I ask, suppose it was a Spanish or Latino accent?

I've done this exercise with at least ten groups over the past few years, and there are clear themes evident from one group to the next. Words used to describe what people thought when they considered the English accent are: sophisticated, educated, well mannered, intelligent, and even trustworthy. For the German accent the themes are: cold, calculating, specific, intelligent, and arrogant. The Spanish or Latino accent elicited the following reactions: unsophisticated, uneducated, not very intelligent, and hard to understand.

All of this from a short telephone conversation with someone they have never met before? Obviously, most people can see immediately the profound stupidity of these themes. We have absolutely no way of knowing whether the English person is indeed sophisticated or well educated. They may be neither of these.

There's no way to know if the German speaker is arrogant or intelligent; they may be both, but we just don't know. Surely, we can't assume that because we have a hard time understanding the person with the Latino accent, it means that they are not intelligent. Indeed, they may have a PhD, and speak five other languages. Yet can anyone deny that we all have these kinds of perceptions about someone? Moreover, can anyone deny that, whether consciously or subconsciously, some people act on these perceptions? No doubt, the answer to both of these questions is no. It is precisely because people do act on perceptions that leaders must deal with them in their organizations as part of an active communication strategy

What should a leader do about these perceptions? There are a number of alternatives. First, leaders can ignore people's perceptions. Second, they can try to convince people that their perception is not correct. Third, they can accept and deal with the new reality created as a result of actions taken based on perceptions. I believe that a leader must deal with the perceptions. They can be strong feedback to the leader as to the organization's culture and its beliefs. As with any feedback, the leader can ignore it, rationalize it away, or we can act on it. Leaders, who ignore the feedback, do so at their own peril. Those who rationalize it away are foolish and again, do so at their own peril. Finally, the leader who acts on the feedback looks to change something in their own behaviors and in their verbal and written communications, to proactively deal with and dispel the perceptions.

Dealing with the Rumor Mill

If there is one constant from organization to organization, group to group or even industry to industry, is that rumors abound in all. Where two or more come together, the potential for rumors spreading is almost certain. In more than twenty years of holding leadership positions, from the time I was an Air Force cadet while in undergraduate school, right up to the present, dealing with rumors and their impact on organizational effectiveness and moral, has been a part of the daily routine. In his article "Rumors: Pruning the Office Grapevine," Bill Hunter writes:

> "Rumor has it that U.S. Industry is confronted with no fewer than thirty-three million fresh bits of grist for the grapevine mill every working day. That's enough to cause constant concern for management, most of whom see the grapevine as a form of office crabgrass—a weed that roots too easily, propagates too quickly and bears the wrong kind of fruit. However, historians, sociologist, psychologist, business consultants, and others who have studied the grapevine and its messages see it as a legitimate form of communication that's not all bad if it's properly understood and controlled."

Mr. Hunter makes some excellent points here. Rumors do spread like wildfire, and management does need to be concerned about them. But more importantly, leaders need to be concerned about them because they can do something to minimize their impact on the organization.

Rumors have many characteristics. They usually are composed of bits and pieces of true information typically surrounded by assumptions, guesses, and exaggerations. Each time a rumor is spread from one person to the next, the story changes, usually to be made into a more fantastic story to tell. Typically, we can categorize rumors in four main types: divisive rumors, fictional rumors, bogeys, and "scenario-stretchers" rumors.

Divisive rumors are intended to drive wedges between individuals or groups. Fictional rumors are complete fabrications that someone created for reasons that, frankly, boggle the mind. Bogeys are rumors that are intended to feed people's fears and concerns. Finally, "scenario-stretchers" are rumors that make predictions on possible outcomes given a certain number of inputs. Whatever the types or the source, these all can and usually do have destructive effects on productivity and organizational effectiveness.

It seems apparent that in many corporations, rumors are an integral part of the culture. In fact, many conversations between colleagues begin with, "So what's the latest rumor?" That's not just a new way to say "good morning," it's a serious request for information. People really do want to know what the latest is. We have all heard someone say, "you know what they say about rumors: they are usually right." And amazingly, they are!

It is spooky how accurate the rumor mill can be. I remember some years back, I received an e-mail from a person who I had met only once at a training session. In the e-mail the person said they had heard I had accepted a certain position and that they would be reporting to me. He welcomed me into the organization and said he looked forward to working with and for me. Interestingly, while I had been offered the position and was seriously considering it, I had not yet made a decision, to accept the position. Yet apparently, the "fact" that I was coming was already common knowledge at the facility!

My first concern at that point was for my current staff. I knew immediately that if people at the facility already knew that there was a chance that I would be moving into the new role, that people who currently reported to me must have heard about it as well. I immediately called my staff together for a meeting. We found those who were away on business trips and patched them in via telephone conference. I told them directly that while I had been offered the position, I had not yet accepted. I also told them that as soon as I made the decision, they would hear it directly and first from me and not via the rumor mill.

Why did I feel compelled to act so quickly and address the rumor? The answer is simple: rumors can only have negative effects on an organization's effectiveness. It leads to confusion. It can lead to resentment by followers who feel that there isn't sufficient communications between them and their leaders. It adds to the feeling of mistrust that can naturally exist between employees and managers. It is a complete waste of time for people to talk about rumors.

When they are talking about rumors, new ones get generated. New possible scenarios of the potential outcomes are created. People start to guess what it might mean to them, or to the organization.

As a leader, I have learned that the best approach is to have complete and open communications to address the issue and dispel the rumor quickly. However, if a leader is not careful and takes this approach with all rumors, they would be doing nothing but addressing them each day. There are just too many of them in an organization. It seems they have a life of their own and they reproduce faster than they can be killed. They also move faster than fire through dry leaves on the forest ground, burning everything in site. In the final analysis, rumors are: insidious, fast moving, usually destructive to organizational cohesiveness and effectiveness, perpetuated until addressed, difficult to dispel, primary contributors to perceptions, time consuming, and a leader's worst enemy.

Anyone who has been a part of an organization for any period of time has been exposed to the rumor mill. We have all sat in small groups in offices, cafeterias, at airports waiting for the next flight, or on a golf course, when someone lowers their voice and start by saying, "Guess what I heard." When those magic words are spoken, all ears perk up and the person receives our undivided attention. Sadly, we've all been a part of it. It is almost unavoidable. Yet, as a leader, depending on how we act, we can make something positive come from just having heard the rumor.

What should a leader do about rumors? First and foremost, they cannot be ignored. But, the leader who tries to keep up with them is foolish and will find themselves frustrated and feeling completely inept in dealing with them. The solution to dealing with the problem of rumors is:

1. Demonstrate to your followers that you are a person of character and high integrity. That you are trust worthy and credible

2. Communicate often with your followers

3. Communicate openly, honestly and completely with your followers

4. Anticipate rumors and communicate facts that would prevent them from taking root in the first place

5. Do not condone followers who actively engage in spreading rumors. Call them on their behavior and deal with it for what it is—a performance issue

Having led large organizations with thousands of people, it is quite clear to me that trying to keep up with rumors is pointless. Each day there are one or two new ones that are added to the ones of the day before. Even if I tried day in and day out to be available, whether by walking around the shop floor, or being in the cafeteria at lunchtime, or even catching someone in the hallway, to address rumors one-on-one, there is no way that I could keep up with them. I always thought that if I just could have people hear the facts, the rumors would be reduced. But again, the volume was too great and it was evident that we needed to do something else to deal with it.

One approach that was effective in dealing with rumors in the organization I led in manufacturing began when I called a staff meeting with the line supervisors and middle managers to discuss communications and specifically rumors. We had a discussion about the way we should communicate with each other and how they should in turn communicate with their employees. We agreed that each day during our morning production-planning meeting we would address all rumors that anyone had heard. We would agree on what the answer to it was, and what the accurate facts were that people needed to have. We also agreed that we would be completely consistent, honest and forthright with the information at all times. Next, we called a meeting of all associates; all three hundred and fifty of them. We met with each shift, about one third of the group at a time. I told them how I wanted to handle dealing with the rumor mill from that point forth, and laid out a few rules:

Rule #1: If you have a question about something or you have heard something you want to confirm, ask your supervisor or me directly.

Rule #2: Spreading rumors is not an acceptable behavior

I also made them several promises:

Promise #1: We will tell you the truth every time.

Promise #2: If we don't know or cannot tell you yet, we will tell you that.

Promise #3: We will keep you informed

Promise #4: We will try to anticipate your questions and provide you information in some cases before the questions even come up.

I was very gratified that it did not take as long as I thought it would to have people accept this new way of dealing with the rumor mill. We did not eliminate them completely, but no doubt the number and impact was significantly reduced. More importantly, each of the supervisors and I gained a significant amount of credibility with our followers as we were perceived as honest and open communicators. At each of the quarterly meetings thereafter, there was always one slide that I used at the end of the business meeting. It was titled: "The Rumor Mill: Anticipating your Questions." In that slide we listed every question and concern that we felt our employees may be having at the time, and we addressed each one of them completely.

Left unchecked, rumors can choke an organization. To defeat them, the most effective weapon in the leader's arsenal is pro-active and preemptive communications with their followers.

In his book, *Leadership Lessons of The White House Fellows*, Charlie Garcia wrote:

> "In his job as chief strategy office and executive vice president for Univision Communication, America's premiere Spanish-Language media company, Cesar Conde (WHF 02–03) has worked with some of the biggest stars in the Spanish-speaking world. Thus, the day he watched his White House Fellows principal, Secretary of State Colin Power, deliver a speech in person, he knew he'd just seen something extraordinary. While riding in a limousine after the speech, Conde complimented Powell on his speaking abilities, and Powell revealed something that Conde would have never guessed: Communicating well with others had not come naturally for Powell. Perfecting his communication skills had taken years of study and hard work."

He goes on to write this:

> "He (Powell) felt that the strongest public speakers were those who used their notes in a smooth, non-distracting way. Some of the best communicators have the ability to look down at their notes and digest the whole page with only a glance, whereas most people would have to look at a page three to five times. Everyone has his or her own style, but the best speakers work hard to fully develop their personal styles and make it seamless."

The bottom line on communications is this: leaders have to be good at it if they hope to be successful. They have to work hard to develop their personal styles and make their communications seam effortless and more conversational in tone. This will go a long way in helping them be more genuine and transparent when delivering their messages.

There is one more thing on communication that all leaders must always keep in mind: effective communication leads to empowered teams. Albert Einstein is probably best known for his famous theory of relativity and the equation $e = mc^2$, where e = energy, m = mass, and c = the speed of light. For a leader, there is an equally powerful equation. That equation is $e = fc^3$, where e = empowerment or energy, f = frequency, and c = clear, concise, consistent communications (hence the c^3). Put simply, the level of energy and empowerment that an organization will enjoy is directly correlated to the frequency with which leaders in the organization share concise, consistent, and clear communications with their followers.

EIGHT

THE LEGACY LEADER
AS MENTOR

There are few things that have brought me more joy over the years than to see individuals who I have had the privilege of mentoring grow personally and professionally. Nothing is more rewarding that to watch as someone you've helped becomes wildly successful. Frankly, it is humbling and heart-warming when a person that you have had the opportunity to mentor says, "Thank you for all you have done for me." It is the greatest feeling a leader can experience.

Leaders are duty bound, completely responsible for, and should be held accountable for mentoring those around him or her. The time that a leader spends mentoring others is time very well spent. The dividends that the leader will receive from this activity can hardly be measured.

It seems absurd and totally contrary to what a leader should desire, to not expend a significant amount of energy on mentoring the growth of those from whom the leader will, and should, expect so much. Of what lasting value is it if the leader, focusing constantly on the path that lies ahead, forgets to look back to ensure that those whom she leads are indeed on the same road. Even more so, that they are prepared to effectively navigate the road themselves. In fact, the leader would want them to be ready to anticipate turns and obstacles.

Ultimately, the leader would want to create a group of followers who can create the opportunity for new paths, and who would themselves learn the fine art of mentoring the next generation behind them.

In his book, *Developing The Leader Within You*, John Maxwell has this to say about mentoring: "The more people you develop, the greater the extent of your dreams."

Investing in mentoring people is the highest return-on-investment activity that a leader can engage in. However, it is unlikely that a leader can be a good mentor if they have not had good mentorship themselves. Or at a minimum, they have observed with envy as others were mentored and nurtured by leaders they admired, and were proud to serve and follow.

Mentoring is somewhat akin to the leading wagon of a caravan traveling on a dusty road. On a dusty trail (as in a road never before traveled, or one traveled infrequently), the leading wagon must ensure that it does not create sufficient dust behind it as to negligently limit the visibility of those wagons following behind. The leading wagon stays just far ahead enough and moves at a speed that pushes those behind to drive at the pace set by the leader without jeopardizing the integrity of the caravan. Eventually, the lead wagon can cede way to another wagon that has clearly demonstrated that it has learned from the pace set by the first. Leaders should treat people they mentor in a similar fashion, pushing them by driving ahead, not leaving them so far behind that their visibility is clouded or they end-up derailing off the road.

Stephen Ambrose captures one of the finest examples of mentorship in the book *Undaunted Courage*. Mr. Ambrose tells the story of how Thomas Jefferson helped develop and prepare Meriwether

Lewis for his adventure across the yet uncharted western portions of the country. In his book, Ambrose writes:

"In 1792, Thomas Jefferson proposed to the Philosophical Society of Philadelphia that a subscription be taken to engage a daring traveler to undertake an expedition to the Pacific. George Washington subscribed, as did Robert Morris and Alexander Hamilton. In hearing of the project, Lewis approached Jefferson and, in Jefferson's opinion, "warmly solicited me to obtain for him the execution of that project..." Jefferson's high opinion of Lewis apparently did not extend that high. In any event, he passed over the teen-age Lewis and chose instead a French Botanist Andre Michaux, who got started in June 1793."

The story, of course, does not end there. As a leader, Thomas Jefferson had already seen and written about the raw talent he saw in Meriwether Lewis. But he felt that Lewis was not ready. Lewis continued to toil as a farmer and landowner on Locust Hill (his home), but worked each day to prepare himself for what he really wanted: exploration. Jefferson realized what his role was as well: to help this young man realize his potential. Jefferson needed to mentor him. To help unleash (and simultaneously tame) the raw talent that lie within. And so he took a very active and personal interest and concern over Lewis.

In 1801, then-president Jefferson made Lewis his secretary. He had Lewis live in the president's house. In fact, his quarters were in what became the East Room. Jefferson made sure that Lewis was involved with him in almost every activity of significance, to include the evening events and socials. So much so was Jefferson's development of Lewis that Lewis even delivered Jefferson's first State of the Union Address to Congress.

"Beyond vicious partisanship and vile journalism, what else had Meriwether Lewis learned from his first two years of his life in Washington? A great deal about practical politics. Further, he advanced his scientific education. He was introduced to new instruments of navigation; he listen to discussions of the geography of North America and the World, and of Indians of the United States; he heard experts on the birds and animals and plant life of the eastern United States, and speculation on what lay beyond the Mississippi River. In addition to the school of the practical and the scientific, he greatly expanded his understanding of philosophy, literature and history. He read extensively from Jefferson's library. And somehow, from someone–who else could it have been but Jefferson?–He learned to write…Moreover, the journal he (Lewis) wrote are among the greatest achievements and constitute a priceless gift to the American people all thanks apparently, to the lessons learned from Mr. Jefferson during his two years of intimate contact with the President in his home."

—*Undaunted Courage*

What a powerful and remarkable example of mentorship taken to the heights of excellence! The results were unquestionably of tremendous historical and long lasting value. What better legacy for Thomas Jefferson than this? Because of his mentoring of Meriwether Lewis, the successful exploration of the yet untamed western part of the United States was achieved and preserved in a magnificent way for all time.

There are simple analogies that can be drawn between the lessons that Lewis learned while under the mentorship of Jefferson to the kinds of lessons that all leaders must teach those who follow them today. Lewis learned about politics, and in today's competitive world and global market economy, the skill of knowing about politics is a key for any successful businessperson to have.

Lewis was introduced to new instruments of navigation. This would be akin to learning new business tools such as decision-making. He expanded his understanding to other areas such as philosophy and geography. Today, gaining cross-functional understanding of business segments is of significant value. Importantly, Lewis learned to write! Writing is a very powerful form of communication and arguably one of the most significant traits of a leader. It comes naturally to a blessed few, but for the rest of us, we have to learn it the old fashion way: from someone who teaches us how by example if nothing else. Jefferson took mentoring as a duty, a responsibility, indeed as an honor. What a shame that so little of that idealism and of mentoring attitude survives today. Leaders must make this of utmost concern and of the highest priority. Leaders must see this as a duty.

There is much we can we learn from the Jefferson-Lewis mentorship relationship and a Legacy Leader must do to be a great mentor. Maxwell puts it like this:

> "From my own experience and through observation of other leaders who excel in this vital area, I have discovered that there are three areas in which successful people developers are different from those who are not successful in developing others. Successful people developers:
>
> 1. Make the right assumptions about people;
>
> 2. Ask the right questions about people; and
>
> 3. Give the right assistance to people."

I think Maxwell's points are excellent and very insightful. It speaks to the leader's need to be personally engaged and committed to the process of mentoring people. In the remainder of this chapter, we will outline in greater detail the specific responsibilities that a leader must tackle to be great people mentors.

The Legacy Leader recognizes their responsibility to nurture and develop talent

No one told Thomas Jefferson that he had to "look after" Meriwether. He saw the talent and accepted his role in developing it. A leader should never be so focused on their day-to-day activities that they forget to proactively look for opportunities to develop others. Having highly talented and constantly growing people around the leader will only enhance the leader's ability to be effective within the organization and to have people prepared who can continue the work created by the leader's vision.

More importantly, the leader must create an environment where people can be developed. In fact, you want to have an environment where people want to be because they realize that people are being developed. There are clear pockets of excellence within any large organization where the differences between leaders who make it a priority to develop their people and those leaders who don't, are very evident. What is also clear is that people who are fortunate to be in the organizations where there are opportunities for development are more motivated, focused, energetic, and productive, than those who are not.

Also implied in the responsibility of the leader to nurture and develop talent, is the need for the leader to identify the areas that need development in those individuals selected. This means the leader must be close enough to know the strengths and weaknesses of the person to be developed. They must first be clear as to what their potential is and what type of activities, whether assigned projects, readings, educational courses, or some other special assignments would be the most appropriate to help develop the hidden talent.

Finally, while it may seem trivial and obvious, it is important to select the right individuals to develop. Leaders ought to look for people of high character and integrity, intelligent, trust worthy, positive thinkers, self-starters, good followers, and willing. All other qualities that a leader should have can be learned.

The Legacy Leader stays close to those he or she mentors

Jefferson had Lewis move into the White House with him so that he could do his tutoring and developing up close. This is an extreme case of course and in today's world probably not very practical. But what should not be lost here is simply this: the Legacy Leader makes time to be with their mentee in professional and social settings as each of these provide unique opportunities for development.

Furthermore, leaders need to encourage people they are developing. They must be close enough to gauge how well the person is doing and what course corrections may need to be made. Rewarding the person with a well deserved "nicely done" is powerful and motivational. Staying close also means proactively seeking feedback from other key members in the organization who can give insight and feedback as to the performance and development of the person. This feedback represents a gold mine of information, which helps people grow.

The Legacy Leader takes mentoring personally

Mentorship can and should extend to multiple facets of a person's life. Developing someone's technical expertise while allowing him or her to remain an incompetent communicator, does little to help the individual reach his or her maximum potential. Jefferson extended his mentoring of Lewis to personal and social events during which Lewis could be exposed many different types of personalities, subjects, and points of view. There is no better school than the real world. But Jefferson allowed Lewis to gain the wisdom of this real world without being eaten by it first. And so it goes in today's world; a mentor should expose the person they are mentoring but pay close attention and help prevent major derailments or catastrophic falls and failures.

There is a nurturing aspect to mentoring. It's hard to imagine that a leader can be nurturing towards a person they are developing, if they don't take their role as the mentor personally. The leader must recognize that they have the ability to transform the life of the person they are working with. That is a serious responsibility and it's one that should not be taken lightly. The impact of the leader's development can and will have long lasting implications to both the person's professional and personal life. That awesome responsibility must be tackled with purpose and good intentions. More importantly, it must be followed through to a logical conclusion.

Mentorship relationships are not necessarily life-long. Surely the friendships that will more than likely result can be. But the teaching and coaching relationship may evolve to more of a peer or colleague type of relationship. Nevertheless, when the time does come for the nature of the relationship to either change or end, it is the leader's responsibility to make that clearly understood by the follower. At some point, the leader must "cut the cord" and commission the person to go forward and lead, and to assume their responsibility for developing others.

One final point on this: if a leader can't accept their duty as mentors personally, it would be best for them not do it at all.

The Legacy Leader creates and helps find opportunities for his or her mentee to grow and learn

Jefferson watched Lewis and actively sought opportunities to have him around and involved in as many activities as practical. Again, translating this into today's world, it may mean that the Legacy Leader proactively seeks to involve his or her mentee on projects and assignments that exposes them to as many aspects of the business as possible.

The Legacy Leader stretches his or her mentee's abilities

Jefferson had Lewis deliver his first State of the Union Address to Congress! If Lewis had a fear of speaking in public before this, he most surely overcame that problem after completing this incredible assignment. No doubt there are times when leaders want to step aside and let those they are mentoring shine in the limelight. By doing so, the Legacy Leader shines the brightest of spotlights on themselves!

Also important in the development process is to place people in circumstances that take them out of their comfort zone. To give them assignments that forces them to think from a different perspective than that to which they are accustomed. Moving a person with a technical engineering background into a marketing position will cause them to learn to think in a different way. Giving a person with a marketing background an opportunity to run a manufacturing organization will definitely cause them to learn to think differently.

Many organizations, Johnson & Johnson included, work hard at developing people across organizational boundaries. In some cases even helping people cross sector lines; that is, a person who has traditionally worked in the medical device industry, may move into the pharmaceutical segment, or the consumer product sector. The cross-functional experience gained by these individuals will no doubt make them more valuable as leaders.

Finally, it is critically important that leaders not shelter those they are developing. The opportunities presented must be significant and have a certain amount of risk level to them. I have always believed that people learn just as much, if not more, from failure than they do from success. Providing people only with opportunities in which they have a very limited risk of failure, is meaningless development. It is of much greater importance to be ready to provide help when needed by the person being developed, than to limit their growth with a false sense of accomplishment.

The Legacy Leader finds people to mentor

In today's corporate environment, the pace is fast and furious. Often times, people development takes a back seat to getting things done. In this kind of environment, too often talented people who are either too humble or shy to seek out a mentor are left under-developed. In some other cases, people who are assertive, seek out a mentor, and demand development, are often labeled as egotistical, self-centered, and too career-minded; and so they too are left underdeveloped because of a perception of the person being overly concerned with their careers. We all know people who may fall into one of these two groups of people. Yet, finding these, and other talented people, and mentoring them to bring out the best in them, can be one of the most rewarding experiences for a leader.

Over the years, particularly in the "post-empowerment era," managers and leaders have become fond of telling their followers that they must take charge of their careers. Leaders and managers insist that people must be responsible for their own development. They tell their followers that they should be accountable for their careers, setting their goals, and demanding support from their managers to be developed.

For a long time, this philosophy made sense to me. I still agree with the basic tenet that people need to be responsible for their own careers and seek out development. I certainly preached that to my followers every chance I had. However, I have also come to the conclusion that too many leaders are using this as a cop-out. They are using this as an excuse to escape their responsibility to seek out people to mentor, and to make sure that other leaders in the organization do the same. It has become an excuse for not making it a higher priority in the "to-do" list. It is far too easy for a leader to reason that it is not their responsibility to spend the necessary time actually mentoring people.

How realistic is it for a leader to tell her followers that they need to go to their managers and demand that they be developed? Leaders must remember how things really were when they were lower in the pecking order. That is one of the main reasons I wrote the book *The Leader's Lobotomy*. It seems to me that leaders forget some of the basic tenets of leadership and the importance of mentoring is certainly one of those things they often forget. Leaders need to think back to a time when they reported to someone who wasn't a good people developer; or perhaps to a time when they worked for someone who played favorites with people, and they weren't one of the favorites.

Leaders should think about feedback they may have received in the past that wasn't very favorable, and what they had to do to overcome it. They need to recall a time when they saw other people getting opportunities that they felt they themselves deserved or where more qualified for just because the other person was "well-liked," came from the "right school," or, worse, had the right network of friends. They need to think back to a time when they saw behaviors in their managers and leaders that made them believe that there was favoritism being used in determining who got the next promotion or choice assignments. They need to think back to friends and colleagues, who they can remember, were labeled a particular way, when in fact it was professional jealousy or personal bias at work. That's reality! It happens day in and day out.

Thus, telling a follower to just go and demand to be developed can lead to some frustrated followers who realize that they will get nowhere doing that. Moreover, leaders who behave this way, make it very clear to their followers that they are disconnected with the world in which the follower lives.

What the leader needs to do is demand that the leaders and managers that work for them make it a point to develop people. Not just to say they do it, but they must actually make it happen. They should not wait until someone asks to be developed. It should be the leaders and managers who are aggressively seeking out people to work with and mentor.

If a follower needs to go ask a manager or leader to be developed, then either the person is not really someone who should be developed, or the leader is not doing his or her job. It's that simple. If the person is not going to be developed, or there is no reconciling their personal and professional goals with what their manager or leader sees them as capable of doing, then they should be told clearly and directly. This gives them a chance to make an informed decision of what they want to do next; they can either leave the organization or be productive in an area and at a level that both, they and the manager, can agree to.

Leaders must not assume that just because there is a formal process of development included as part of the performance appraisal system of their organization, that people are indeed being developed. Some are, and some are not. It's up to the leader to make sure that talented people are not neglected.

Furthermore, leaders must be on a constant watch for people who were once considered high-potential, talented people and suddenly are "off the list." Is it possible for that to happen? Of course it is. There are times when a person who was thought to have promise, provides evidence to the contrary and demonstrates that they are really not prepared for higher level of responsibilities. However, the leader should look with a suspicious eye on the circumstances under which this "fall from grace" took place. He or she must be convinced that personal biases, professional jealousies, erroneous feedback, or simply the dislike of one manager or leader towards the person, are not the causes for this. Many talented people are victims of this phenomenon. Most of us know someone who has fallen prey to this black hole.

What evidence do leaders have of this occurring in their organizations? They simply need to look around and ask themselves and others who have been around for a long time: who were the superstars five years ago? How about ten years ago? Surely, you will find that some have moved up the corporate ladder as expected. Others left and developed their careers elsewhere. Finally, others are still in the same position or perhaps have even been demoted. One leader I know refers to these people as "Heroes to Zeros." What happened? Some would argue that this is exactly what should happen. They reason that the law of "survival of the fittest" ruled the outcome. That may be true in some cases, but in many other cases, the people who did not fair well, were passed over for the wrong reasons. They were overlooked for the reasons that were listed above.

One leader in a major Fortune 100 company once said to me, "I tell good people that if they don't like how their career is going, just hang in there until the new management comes in and then they'll get another chance at reviving their career." I'm sure this leader meant well in giving people that advice, but analyzing what he said makes it very clear that it was not a performance issue holding back the people he was telling this to, but rather a personal bias or personality issue. There's no room for that kind of nonsense in the Legacy Leader's organization.

One way that a leader can make sure that people are being sought out and aggressively developed, is simply to ask the question of all other leaders and managers: "Who are you developing?" Demand to know the name of the person and what the plan for this individual is. Then take the next very important step of asking the person whom this leader is developing: "Do you think you are being mentored and developed?" If there is a disconnect between these two answers, go no further in trying to find the problem with mentorship in your organization. The conclusion is obvious.

Leaders should be held accountable for seeking out and assertively mentoring and developing people. The best people to judge whether or not they are doing that are the people who are supposed to be the benefactors of these mentors. When it comes to mentoring, Legacy Leaders take off the blinders, remember what they went through in their early years, and hold themselves and others accountable to mentoring talented people.

In the book *Servant-Leadership*, in one of the essays, Jeffrey N. McCollum writes:

"With growing recognition of the importance of character to successful leadership, mentoring, in the sense of helping someone learn how to *be* rather than what to *do*, is coming back into vogue. In the height of the Industrial Age, mentoring had a machine and parental quality to it. Mentors were frequently described as 'pulling strings,' 'greasing skids,' or 'putting wheels into motion' on behalf of others. In fact, most organizational mentoring programs involve pairing a senior manager, chosen for his or her power position in the organization, with a junior manager. What is emerging now has a decidedly more spiritual quality to it. Mentoring is what Robert Bly describes as a 'vertical' process—one in which young members of a society learn how to 'be' in that society. Bly's thesis is that the breakdown of these vertical relationships has created a sibling society—one in which the members live out a perpetual adolescence. His observation explains why it's sometimes so difficult to get employees to accept more responsibility for the organization and for themselves."

He goes on to write:

> "Clearly, mentoring is about the use of personal example and not about the use of organizational power."

Being a mentor is not about "taking care" of someone or being a person's "godfather." It is entirely about imparting to another person the wisdom of your experience. To afford them the benefit of lessons learned before them. To aid in creating an environment in which the person can smooth out rough edges, learn from mistakes, gain insights from experts, and become the best that they can. Leaders should understand that those they mentor will overwhelmingly define their legacy.

Sponsorship vs. Mentorship

Some years back, in 2002, I had the opportunity to attend the Johnson & Johnson Diversity Leadership Conference. During the conference, we heard from several of J&J's Executive Committee

Members during a discussion on the subject of mentorship and sponsorship. We heard Ms. Coleen Goggins discuss the role that mentors and sponsors had played in her career. She explained that while she had not had many mentors in her career, she did have leaders she thought had been her sponsors.

When asked to describe the difference between sponsorship and mentorship, Ms. Goggins said: "A mentor shows the way. A sponsor clears the way." She went on to explain how she had benefited from individuals who had been willing to give her a chance. These leaders cleared the way for her to be given opportunities to lead organizations within Johnson & Johnson. They were willing to take a risk on her.

Wow! Think about that! That is precisely what people need most: a chance. Given that chance, most people will drive results that may surprise even themselves. Sponsors clear the way! That's taking mentorship to a whole new level; a proactive, hands-on, fully committed level. Ms. Goggins was very fortunate to have leaders like that around her. Legacy Leaders must be mentors, sponsors, and opportunity makers.

I love the quote from John Maxwell that says, "You teach what you know but you reproduce who you are." As a leader and mentor, we can and must share our knowledge. Imparting wisdom to those who will come after us is important. Helping them avoid the same trappings and mistakes that we made along our leadership journey is also important. But we must always keep in mind that as leaders we will create other leaders who will be very much like we are. So we must not only talk about it, we must do it! We must demand of ourselves the very best, modeling the behaviors that we know are the right ones. People will do what we do, not what we say!

To mentor someone is a privilege and a supreme responsibility, and the Legacy Leader makes it a priority.

NINE

THE LEGACY LEADER
AS CHANGE AGENT

Not too many years ago, an apple was a fruit we ate to keep the doctor away. Today it's a personal computer or an iPhone that can hold not only our entire directory but plays our favorite tunes. A short ten years ago, a blackberry was something you added to your cereal in the morning. Today we use it as a powerful communication tool including emails and text messages. When I was a kid, hip-hop was what we did in the schoolyard with a jump rope rather than in a dance club with eardrum busting music. Not long ago, googling was what babies did as they dribbled. Today, Googling is the way we search for information online. Things change. In today's technologically driven global economy, they change quickly. In some cases, the half-life of a product line is measured in days, weeks or maybe months.

Perhaps the greatest evidence that things have changed dramatically is illustrated by this trivia question: what is the one question you never had to ask someone when you called them on the telephone? The answer is, "Where are you?" Before cell phones, when you called someone, you knew you knew exactly where they were.

Today, I can be anywhere in the world and receive a call from anyone at any time. Today the very first question we ask when they answer the phone is, "Where are you?" Things change!

Many times, when I speak to a group on subjects such as leadership, team building, diversity, coaching, time management, or change management, I begin with a short exercise to break the ice. I start by asking each person to take a blank piece of paper and a pen. I give them each fifteen seconds to sign their name as many times as possible in that period of time using a signature similar to the one they would use when they are signing a check or some other legal document.

At the end of the fifteen seconds, I poll the group to see what the average numbers of signatures were. Usually the range is from two to fifteen signatures in fifteen seconds. Then I ask them to do the exercise one more time. This time, however, they are to use the opposite hand to do the writing. If they usually write with their right hand, they use the left, and vice versa. After the laughter subsides—and there is always laughter and a few comments made by the group—they get set and I give them twenty seconds to do the same task again.

This time the range drops from five to fifteen to one to ten signatures. It's a fun exercise and a good icebreaker, but more importantly, it helps to illustrate a very important point. Once we finish the exercise, I ask the group a simple question: "What one word describes what happened between the first time we did the exercise and the second?" The answer, of course, is change. We changed something. We changed the conditions under which the task was being done.

I then ask the group to tell me how they felt the first time they did the exercise. Words such as comfortable, no problem, at ease, confident, relaxed, and competent are common themes with each group when describing the feelings during the first exercise. Uncomfortable, stress, stupid, incapable, silly, and reluctant are among the words used to describe their emotions the second time through. That's the nature of change. It makes people feel uncomfortable, stressed, incapable, reluctant to do it, and at times even silly or stupid. We are, by nature, creatures of habit.

Most people have daily routines that govern their lives, and to deviate from these can cause them a great deal of anguish. Consider as an example the daily commute to work for many people. Most of us do it on automatic pilot. Even when we are driving, without giving it much thought, we make the car turn left or right at the correct intersections, and eventually get to our destination often without being able to recall details of our trip. We are in "our zone;" and our zone is comfortable. We understand it. We like it. We don't want to change it.

Yet, while nature tends to make many people resistant to change, the world and our environment are in a state of constant change. The evidence is clear; those who refuse to change are doomed to be left behind. In the not so distant past, many people in the workplace refused to accept the computer as a daily part of their job. These were the people who insisted this trend was a passing fad. Those people were left behind. As a father of a teenage girl, I resisted as long as I could to allow her to get her own Facebook account. There's just something about the cyber world that is scary for fathers of teenage daughters. But that change was inevitable because every teenage kid has a Facebook account. So I did the only thing that I could, I allowed her to have the account, only after I created one of my own and befriended her so that I could view the same things she was seeing! We can either resist the change, or figure out a way to adapt to it. The latter is the better choice.

Change is inevitable and despite what some would say change is not always good. Change can be painful and unpleasant. On the other hand, under different circumstances, change can be a breath of fresh air. Change can be positive for an organization. It can lead to increased follower productivity and motivation. Regardless of the nature of the change, whether large or small, or whether wildly popular or not, all change has a few critical similarities:

- All changes have an owner and sponsor who wants the change to take place
- All change must be managed
- All change must be monitored and evaluated
- All change must be fine tuned

Effective leaders must understand their role in the change process. They must embrace change and breathe life into the change. They must want it, define it, drive it, expect it, and live it. There are countless of great books focused on change management. The number of techniques and models used for defining business and process improvement by companies is as varied as the styles of those who adopt them. There is probably not one model that works well for all kinds of industries or organizations. The change management model that would be used by a financial services company may be quite different from that used by an automobile manufacturing company.

The purpose of this chapter is not to put forth yet another change management model, but rather to focus simply on the leader's role in making change happen. What the leader does and how they do it is independent of industry, because change ultimately affects people. And people, while they may have different technical backgrounds or work in different economic environments, most share common feelings and thought processes about change that affects them personally.

If a leader is to be successful in driving change in his or her organization, they must concern themselves, first and foremost, with how their followers will accept the change. Moreover, they must work to ensure that people not only accept the change, but come to think of the change as necessary, positive, achievable, reasonable, and ultimately good for them and for the organization.

Without this support, the change will fail to reach its objectives. The leader's ability to accomplish this will not rely on the change methodology chosen. Followers can quickly be trained on the mechanics of the change model, assuming that it makes sense for an organization. In fact, there are usually process facilitators who assume the role of managing teams that go about developing the strategies and tactics that will be implemented to make change happen. Moreover, while the leader does have responsibility to ensure that these teams are formed and get to work, his or her primary concern is not about models, mechanics, or tactics, but rather about the people's attitudes.

The leader's ability to be an effective change agent will be determined by their ability to influence their follower's thinking. Essentially, the change will come about as a direct function of how well the leader can make people believe in the need for change, how well they can communicate their passion for the change, and how well they motivate the followers to want to change.

The leader must become a force for change. To do so effectively, they must be perceived as honest, ethical, and credible; and so it seams we are back to the basic fundamentals of legacy leaders. The leader that has demonstrated character and has therefore earned the respect of her followers will be more effective at driving change than the leader who has not.

For the leader to be a successful change agent, they must do the four fundamental things:

- Clearly communicate the "why" for the change
- Secure leadership and management support for the change
- Remain connected to the organization
- Start acting in ways consistent with the end goal of the change

Communicating "the why"

Most people will want to know in very specific terms why a leader believes a change is necessary before they will support and adopt it.

The basic question of why is enormous in its consequences. Properly addressed by the leader, it can form a coalition of followers who will themselves become change agents moving the change forward at light speed. If on the other hand, the leader poorly communicates the reasons for the change, the result can be a lethargic organization that will move at the speed of mud.

Instead of having an organization that is adopting change and moving forward, what the leader will be contending with will be an organization where rumors will begin to fly, scenarios of all sorts will be formulated by people, fear will be generated—as it usually is when there is uncertainty about people's future—and resistance to the change will be strong. This resistance, while it may not be overt—because some people behave in politically correct ways not to appear as negative towards the change—will have a crippling effect on the leader's ability to be effective.

People are motivated when they understand why a change needs to happen. They feel more a part of the decision making process, and more involved with their own destiny. They will need to have a clear understanding of the nature of the change. Will this change fundamentally alter the leader's vision? If so, how? If a follower has bought into the leader's vision, and the change seems to be inconsistent with this vision, they need to understand how the leader reconciles this. Clear, concise, honest, and transparent communications by the leader is the only option if there is to be the hope of effective, swift, and long lasting change in an organization. That is the leader's number one priority. All else in the change management process is dwarfed by the importance of answering the very simple question of why.

I can think of one exception when the leader can move an organization to change–whether is to adopt a new way of doing business altogether, or just doing one task or mission which is out of the ordinary–without explaining the why and still be successful. In this case the leader would have had to already earn the credibility of his followers. He has already demonstrated through consistent and sustained behaviors that he or she is a person of character and high integrity. They have demonstrated time and time again that they care first about the well being of their organization and their followers before their own interest. A leader who enjoys this kind of reputation can ask the organization to trust him and follow her on a particular change and the followers will abide.

Sometimes, the environment or business conditions require that a change be made immediately whether to take advantage of a new opportunity, or protect the organization's interest from some external or internal problem. This gives the leader little or no time to clearly formulate a vision statement and communicate the need for the change. In these circumstances, the leader can make withdrawals from their credibility bank account and effectively lead the organization through the crisis, leaving the detailed communications as to the "why" until a bit later.

Two things are important to point out: a bit later means just that, a bit later. It does not mean indefinitely or for an extended period of time. It means communicate the why as soon as possible. Secondly, the leader should be careful to reserve this kind of unilateral change action for opportunities or threats that are real and pressing, leaving little doubt later that the sense of urgency was indeed warranted.

The importance of communicating "the why" for a change cannot be overstated. It is mind boggling that this very simple idea is the Achilles heel of so many leaders who wonder why they have difficulty making change happen effectively within their organizations. They lock themselves behind closed doors in change planning meetings that go on in perpetuity, and are shrouded in secrecy. Leaders often think that they know best, and that followers will just blindly align themselves behind their vision for change. There is only one form of leadership that I know of where this works; it's called a dictatorship. This form of approach will not yield positive results in the long term in an organization.

The leader who wants to be effective as a change agent will

slam open the door of communications, and will as much as possible execute the change planning process in plain view for followers to understand what is happening. This does not mean that some information and some planning should not be kept confidential. Followers understand and appreciate the need for confidentiality when it comes to planning. They know that some things are best kept under control for competitive reasons or even to protect personnel privacy. They are fully aware and accepting of this. But they also fully expect to be informed of all else. Moreover, the leader who simply addresses the issue of confidentiality by saying something like, "There are some other items that I can not discuss right now that will be communicated as soon as possible," can help to dispel the cloud of secrecy that surrounds most change.

Secure leadership and management support for the change

There are many ways to get somebody to do something. Any parent knows the different methods to get a child to clean their room. You can ask the child politely, you can force them to do it by threats, you can pay them to do it, or you can try to make them feel guilty about not doing it. Most of us with kids end up resorting to "because I said so" as the most compelling reason why they need to do it.

In an ideal world, we would be able to reason with our children, and using our well-developed parental influential skills along with the concepts we've learned about being legacy leaders, get them to accept our vision of a clean room. We would help them understand why it's important for them to keep a clean room. We would want them to understand that they would learn discipline and develop organizational skills as a result of keeping their rooms in order; not to mention the value of living in a dust and pollution free environment. Once the child buys into these reasons, they are happy to clean their rooms. I would imagine that this would work in a small fraction of homes, but the rest of us rely on "because I said so" as still the most compelling reason for our kids to clean-up their rooms.

Humor aside, essentially leaders in organizations have similar options in terms of influencing those around them to take some action. But one fact is certain, if they enlist the support and gain the buy-in of key members of the management and leadership staff, as well as the support of influential followers, their task will be dramatically reduced in complexity. The greater the base of support that the leader can gain from his key staff members the quicker a change can become a part of the organizational culture.

Gaining this support can mean that the leader has to spend some time on person-to-person discussions. Few people can resist when a credible leader they trust, sits down with them and takes the time to personally explain the need for a change and ask for their direct support. When the President of the United States wants to influence Congress and the Senate to take some action or support some policy, the most effective tool available to them is the one-on-one meeting with an individual or small group of Senators or Congressmen or Congresswomen, in the oval office. The President, using the home court advantage and the virtual power of the oval office, invites individuals to join him in moving his agenda forward. This personal touch is much more effective than sending memos or e-mails or relying on other senior executives or middle manager to deliver the message.

Some may read this and shake their heads in disagreement and think of this as a time consuming task and a waste of their effort. They would be tempted to spend the time in meetings just making things happen. But experience tells us that they would be wrong. Time spent building a base of support is not wasted; it is invested in the change process. It will ultimately save time in the adoption and execution of the change, and it will build the credibility of the leader as one who builds consensus, listens well, and respects followers enough to make them an integral part of the change.

There is one more thing that a leader must take into account when securing the support of management and other leaders in the organization, and that is dealing with those who oppose the change. There will almost always be one or more individuals who are in opposition to a particular change. Often they will have sound and seemingly reasonable objections to the change. The actions a leader takes to deal with this resistance to the change are critical, and send loud echoes throughout the organization as to its culture and ability to deal with conflict. The leader should:

- Listen carefully to the objections
- Consider the person's opinions and reasons for their objections
- Try to incorporate the suggestions made by these individuals into the proposed change
- Directly ask for their complete unwavering support
- Agree on a reasonable time frame for meeting again to check for progress and commitment
- If agreement can't be reached, replace the individual

This simple process, if managed well by the leader, can be very empowering and can demonstrate to the organization that the leader can deal effectively with differences of opinions. It also demonstrates the leader's fairness, yet firm commitment to the change. Objections are fine and must be welcomed. They can have a strengthening effect on the ultimate change that is made. But left unchecked, dissension among the management and leadership of and organization will surely lead to its dismal failure.

Remain connected to the organization

There is a saying for those who are in the market to purchase real estate. It goes like this: "When buying real estate, there are three things that matter most: location, location, location." Similarly, when it comes to driving change, there are three very important things that matter most and a leader must do: communicate, communicate, communicate.

The leader must seek out opportunities to be available to communicate directly to followers about the changes being made. Sometimes we spend too much time planning to communicate. Organizations prepare elaborate and colorful presentations with graphs and tables and roll out communications in large group settings. There is nothing wrong with that approach. But there is a certain amount of informal and impromptu communications that the leaders must do in order to bring the changes to the people on the shop floor directly. Making the time to visit the manufacturing floor, or the cubicles where people work on a daily basis and taking the message directly to them has a power that can not be harness in a cold conference room with large screens, pretty charts, and a microphone.

Moreover, by remaining connected to the roots of the organization, the leader will be exposed to the true feelings of the followers. She will hear things that her middle managers and executive leaders did not know or were unwilling to share with her. The leader will get direct and unfiltered feedback about the changes coming, and will even pick-up excellent suggestions on how to proceed. But the most important win for the leader who remains connected to the lower levels of the organization will be the increase in credibility that he or she will gain. This alone will ultimately help them achieve their intended change more easily.

Start acting in ways consistent with the end goal of the change

Motivational speakers are fond of telling their audiences that they should believe in themselves, set goals for themselves, and start acting in ways that are consistent with those goals. They say that one should visualize the goal as having already being achieved thereby creating a positive energy within themselves that motivates them to move in the direction of the goal. Who could argue with that logic?

Is there an Olympic gold medalist that during the months and years of training and in the moments just before the starter's pistol is fired indicating the beginning of a race that thought, "I will not win the race?" We teach our children about the "little engine that could." "I think I can, I think I can, I think I can ... " What if the message was, "Maybe I can't, maybe I can't, maybe I can't?" Would the little engine make it over the top?

The leader who wants change to happen in their organization must live and breathe it each and every moment. Their behavior must be completely consistent with the end result of the change both in public, but more importantly in private. If the leader sends a mixed message and behaves one way when in public, but a different way when they are in a small group setting behind closed doors, the impact is clear and definitive. Those who see it will understand that the change is meaningless and will, whether consciously or subconsciously, behave in ways that betray that fact.

A colleague of mine once related to me a story that illustrates this last point. He recalled a time when he worked in a manufacturing facility as one of the leadership staff members, and they were incorporating the process of diversity into their plant. They had established training sessions that each of the leaders and managers were required to attend. They held some of these meetings off-site at a hotel and one of the meetings in which they were discussing gender bias issues ran into the evening hours.

Immediately after the meeting was over, a few of the staff members got together for some refreshments. Among them, was the general manager and the corporate headquarters human resources director. After a drink or two, everyone was relaxed and they started discussing the day's events. A few of them where amazed, not to mention disappointed, at some of the remarks made by the GM and HR leader. They joked about some of the women in the group (those not present of course), and even about some remarks made by other men in the group. It was immediately obvious to the subordinates present that the diversity process was not really going to take root in their organization at that time. The lesson here is simple: the leader must act consistent with the change if the change will have any chance of taking hold.

There are many things that a leader will be remembered for. The leader's legacy will be enhanced or diminished by their ability to effectively lead change. It is inevitable that those who will come behind you will change what you've worked so hard to put in place. The question remains as to whether they will choose to build upon what you've left behind because it created a solid foundation for growth and a legacy worth keeping, or whether they will look to tear down your foundation and replace it anew.

TEN

THE LEGACY LEADER
AND DIVERSITY

When used in a business setting, the term "diversity" immediately connotes certain ideas in most people's minds. Usually people think of race and gender differences when they hear the word. Other dimensions of diversity may also come to mind such as language and cultural differences, sexual orientation, and others. Diversity as a concept presents a very interesting and no-doubt-complicated challenge for a leader. But one thing is for certain: there is evidence to suggest that diverse organizations yield better results than non-diverse organizations. This alone provides leaders and business managers a compelling reason to ensure that they are creating a diverse and inclusive culture in their organizations. The question this begs is how to do that?

Fortunately, the path to creating a diversity aware and inclusive organizational culture is not as much of a black art today as it was just twenty years ago. There has been great progress made by companies such as Verizon Communications, Coca-Cola Co., Procter & Gamble, Johnson & Johnson, IBM, and American Express, to name just a few. These, along with many other fine companies made it to the 2008 Top 50 best companies for diversity in America according to Diversity, Inc. They have blazed a trail for cultural change, and in the process, created a road map for others to follow.

Every organization is different, and they all have their own unique set of values and culture; thus there is no one recipe for success. The basic steps that we will outline in the Diversity Engagement Model presented next, can serve as a guide to help organizations and leaders chart the appropriate course that will help create an effective culture.

When I first joined Johnson & Johnson (J&J) in 1991, the concept of Diversity was in its infancy, not just in J&J, but throughout corporate America. While social issues had already been center stage since the 1960's in our country, many corporations operated business by long reigning principles of non-inclusion. In these companies the roles of men and women were firmly established, and largely determined, by their race, ethnicity, and other not so obvious dimensions of differences.

The winds of change were just beginning to blow in the late 1980s and early 1990s, and diversity was taking center stage as a business issue. We were all about to be introduced to a new way of thinking that would challenge our contemporary view of the world. A few pioneering and forward thinking leaders were taking the risks of tackling organizational cultural issues, and championing adoption of the concept of "diversity" in their companies. In the case of ETHICON Inc, Johnson & Johnson, the company I had just joined, that leader was a man by the name of Robert Crocee. As the president of ETHICON, Mr. Crocee was about to make diversity a business imperative in our company. I don't know if he really understood what he was unleashing at the time. Twenty years later, there can be little doubt that ETHICON, and the rest of J&J, is a stronger and more competitive global corporation because of the course that he, and other strong leaders like him, set us on.

There were many questions that needed to be answered before a fundamental change in our company's culture could really take root. After all, to deal with the various elements of diversity, one must first expose the raw nerve endings of each of our beliefs and pre-programmed biases. Whether we are talking about race and gender, socio-economic and family status, sexual orientation, language, religion, age, or the many other dimensions of diversity, getting people to confront these is not an easy task. However, there are two important and overriding questions when it comes to diversity and the work place. Those questions are: *Why should companies care? And why should a company do anything about it?*

The answer to these two questions can be illustrated by the following example. I had just left the Air Force when I joined J&J. The term "diversity" was not a part of our vocabulary in those days. However, the military was in the middle of driving awareness around sexual harassment issues given the exposure that the Department of Defense (DoD) and the Navy were under because of the "Tailhook" incident. In September 1991, during the 35th Annual Tailhook Symposium held at the Las Vegas Hilton Hotel, 83 women and 7 men were assaulted during the three-day aviators' convention, according to a report by the Inspector General of the DoD.

While none of the 140 cases that resulted from Tailhook ever went to trial, one thing was certain: this incident represented a turning point for the U.S. military in dealing with sexual harassment. It was a pivotal movement that brought attention to the broader dimensions of diversity.

From 1991 to 1996, I served as a Human Resources and Social Actions Officer in the Air Force Reserves. I was responsible for training troops on the changing rules of how the military was going to deal with "diversity." The end goal was to "ensure unit mission readiness." No doubt some of the solutions implemented by the military were far from perfect—as evidenced by the now infamous "don't ask, don't tell" failed policy on how to deal with sexual orientation.

What the DoD and the military did correctly surmise was the reason "why" units and their commanders should care about diversity. They should care because of its potential impact on mission readiness and unit effectiveness. To put it in business terms, commanders should care because it can help improve the "bottom line."

There is growing evidence that representational diversity is one of the factors that can make a difference in driving organizational results. In 2006, Diversity Inc. surveyed the top fifty companies for diversity. Forty-three of these fifty companies were publicly traded. They used the criteria of human capital investment, CEO commitment, communications, and supplier diversity. The results were quite compelling. Over a ten-year period, these companies had 23.5% better returns than the S&P 500.

In another study conducted by Catalyst, looking for a connection between gender and financial performance, they examined Fortune 500 companies with the highest and the lowest number of women in top management ranks from 1996 to 2000. The companies with the highest number of women in top management spots had a return on equity that was 35% higher, and a total return to shareholders that was 34% higher than the companies where women were underrepresented in the highest levels.

While these results may surprise some, the data does seem to support the notion that greater diversity within a team or company makes for higher performing organizations. Thus, it may also be reasonable to conclude that the organization may benefit from the accompanying diversity of thought that comes from a diverse group of people.

If more diverse teams yield better results, therein lays the real and sole reason for caring about diversity in business. Some individuals, primarily people of color and women, myself included, may be inclined to want to establish the more righteous and philosophical reasons for tackling the issues of diversity. However, we can all agree on this: in the end, the reasons of 'why' an organization cares about diversity are of some relevance. Yet, the fact that they do something about it is of much greater value and significance.

This leaves leaders and business managers with the daunting task of bringing about organizational and cultural change to ensure that their teams embrace diversity and all of its dimensions. As with any change, there is a process that organizations will go through. There is certainly no recipe or step by step "do-it-yourself" diversity awareness program that can be blindly applied to all companies. The Diversity Engagement Model, explained next, lays out a foundation from which a plan of action can be developed and implemented in individual companies or organizations to create a more inclusive mind set among all members of the teams.

The Diversity Engagement Model (DEM) (figure 3) outlines the steps needed in order move a team to action around the subject of diversity. Starting from a point of presumed ignorance, lack of awareness, or denial about an issue, there are steps that someone (or group of people) must take in order to reach a point where that person (or group) is compelled to take action. In the DEM, the building block steps, or stages, are: Ignorance or denial, Awareness, Education, Action, and Measuring Results. We will examine each of these stages, and discuss the drivers necessary for the leader to move the organization from one stage to the next.

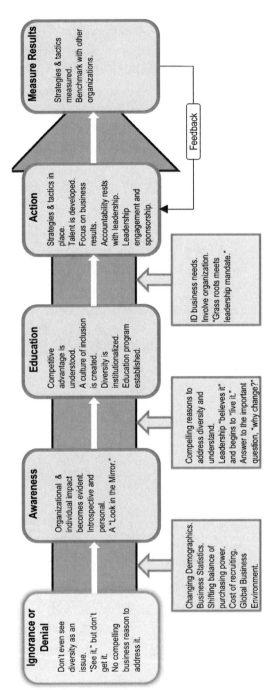

Figure 3: The Diversity Engagement Model

Ignorance or denial

As the saying goes, "The first step in recovery is admitting you have a problem." The same can be said about diversity. Before a company can move towards a culture of inclusion where diversity is acknowledged, and potentially leveraged as a competitive advantage, it must recognize that diversity is an issue that must be dealt with. Ignoring the issue in hopes that it will go away, or that it does not have an impact on the business, is foolish. More foolish, however, is denying that the issue exists and indeed plays out in every aspect of a company's daily life. Statements such as, "In our company everyone is treated fairly and equally," "We all get along and we don't have any diversity issues," or "Our plant is composed of all Hispanics, so how could there be diversity issues?" are indicative of denial or ignorance.

In this stage, leaders and managers in an organization either do not see diversity as an issue, they "see it" but don't get it or they have no compelling business reason to address it. As a result, these leaders have no attachment to the concept of diversity, and are therefore not compelled to act. Thus the question becomes, what would have to happen to compel leaders to act? The answer begins with a set of compelling data. In the case of diversity it requires gaining an understanding of the following:

- The changing world demographics
- The relevant business statistics and indicators
- An understanding of the shifting balance of purchasing power
- The cost of employee turn-over and recruiting
- The evolving global business environment

There is a mountain of empirical evidence and data regarding the change in world demographics, and the resulting global market economics that have emerged as a result. According to a report from the Henry J. Kaiser Family Foundation entitled, "Key Facts, Race, Ethnicity and Medical care" (1997):

> "The United States is racially and ethnically diverse, and the nation's diversity is growing over time. As of 2005 nearly one third of the U.S. population identified themselves as a member of a racial or ethnic minority group; by 2050, this share is expected to increase to nearly half."

Business indicators are clear regarding the increasing purchasing power of the diverse consumers. For instance, the U.S. Hispanic purchasing power has surged to nearly $700 billion and is projected to reach as much as $1 trillion by 2010 (HispanTelligence). The rate of growth is nearly three times the overall national rate. Leaders who ignore this growing and important trend in market demographics, do so at the peril of their company's profits.

Only the nimble and quick to respond organizations will implement the right strategies to ensure that their products and services remain relevant to the changing customer base. It seems reasonable to suggest that companies that are most diverse in their make-up will be able to leverage the diversity of thought that comes naturally with a diverse team. This could give them an edge in ensuring that their strategies are more in-tune with the complexities and the needs of the new/diverse market place.

Another compelling set of data that leaders will be faced with is the increased cost of recruiting and retaining the highest caliber talent. There is ample evidence to suggest that the need for qualified workers will outpace the available talent. Therefore, the race to recruit, and more importantly retain employees, is on! In his article "Cost of Employee Turnover," William G. Bliss (2006) estimated the cost of replacing a $50,000 per year salary person would likely reach $75,000. He estimates that the cost would be significantly higher (200% to 250% of annual compensation) for managerial and sales positions. Taking the cost of turnover at 150% of salary, for the mid-sized company of 1,000 employees who has a 10% annual rate of turnover, the annual cost of turnover is $7.5 million. These are real dollars, and the costs of time and lost productivity are no less important than the costs associated with paying cash to vendors for services such as advertising or temporary staff.

Bliss uses the cost of recruiting, training, productivity loss, and lost sales as factors in estimating the cost of turnover. He concludes: "The costs and impact associated with an employee who leaves the company can be quite significant. This is not to say that all turnover should be eliminated. However, given the high cost and impact on running a business, a well thought-out program designed to retain employees may easily pay for itself in a very short period of time."

Why is this important and relevant to a discussion on diversity? For one simple reason: when polled about why they left a company, people of color and women often cite that they did not feel valued and respected, and they did not feel they had equal opportunity for advancement as their non-diverse colleagues. There is also evidence that people of color and women generally have higher turnover rates than their counterparts. If companies reduced their turnover, they would save significant dollars that could be invested in other parts of the business. Therefore, addressing the reason why people leave the organization can become an important strategy for any organization.

A study published in the Journal of Business Ethics entitled "Leveling the Playing Field for Women of Color in Corporate Management; Is the Business Case Enough?" (Giscombe & Mattis, 2004) was conducted in order to examine the unique experiences of African-American, Hispanic, and Asian-American women in business careers. This multi-phase research design included: a survey of professional and managerial women of color in thirty companies with 1735 survey responses, and analysis of national census data. It looked at qualitative analyses from almost sixty focus groups and more than eighty individual interviews. It also included a diversity policy analyses at fifteen companies. The study found that retention of women of color was positively correlated with supportive behaviors of supervisors. The authors of the paper argued "that the financial business case for diversity, e.g., the cost of turnover, is necessary but not sufficient for developing and sustaining supportive relationships between supervisors and their women of color direct reports."

It seems the old adage is true: people leave managers, not companies. People of color and women seem to leave them more often. The smart business leaders understand that these are costs that must be avoided and that valuing and nurturing a culture of inclusion is one way of doing this.

Thus, through the process of considering the data, leaders can move their organizations from ignorance to awareness.

Awareness

Even the most rigid of business minds succumbs to data and its implications. In the case of diversity, when data becomes overwhelming, it leads to a moment of enlightenment. Simply stated, data lead to awareness.

When the organizational and individual impact of diversity become evident, people generally begin to take an introspective and personal look at their actions and behaviors. We "look in the mirror," if you will. We begin to observe our own and other's behaviors in a different way. Our perspective begins to evolve in how we look at advertisements and television broadcasts. Some comments and jokes that were funny to us before are no longer something we want to laugh at. We become emotionally invested in the issue of diversity.

Three things begin to happen at this stage:

- Compelling reasons to address diversity start to become evident

- Leaders become believers in the process of diversity and inclusion, and they begin to lead by example in their own rhetoric and behaviors

- The answer to the important question "why care?" evolves and begins to take shape

Many organizations never even get to the awareness phase. Many more probably get stuck there, and never move past it. They have "Diversity Awareness Sessions" for employees, and they create Employee Resource Groups (ERGs) or Affinity Groups (AGs) without giving too much thought as to "why" host these diversity sessions or why sponsor ERGs.

I am a firm believer in the effectiveness of ERGs and AGs in helping companies drive business results, affording employees developmental opportunities, and having a positive impact on recruitment and retention. However, ERGs or AGs are not the sole solution to a company's diversity issues. Well-organized and executive sponsored groups will serve a company well and be a part of the solution.

The awareness phase is entirely about driving emotional engagement with the issues of diversity. It is this emotional engagement combined with a clearly understood and compelling reason for why we should care, that will allow an organization to transition to the next phase: education.

Education

With any change-management process that an organization embarks on, education is always key to its success. Whether implementing a product development or quality control process, introducing a new employee recognition system, or driving significant cultural change around diversity, educating all members of the company will in large part determine the effectiveness of the change.

In the early 1990s, ETHICON implemented a diversity-training program for all associates in the company. From the members of the Board to the employee on the manufacturing shop floor, all were engaged in a formal training around diversity. In some cases, that training took the form of three day facilitated workshops. Some of us even had a chance to be trained as "trainers" in the process of diversity. The goal was to make sure that all employees in the company had a basic and fundamental understanding of diversity, including why it was important for the corporation to learn how to manage it. These training sessions were tough at times, as people came in close contact with their emotions and feelings about the different dimensions of diversity. Many of us were humbled by the experience as we discovered that we had some biases to deal with. The process was effective and it put the company on the road to learn to leverage diversity as a competitive advantage.

In those early days of diversity awareness and education initiatives in Corporate America, companies created positions at the manager, director and even the executive level. These dedicated resources were designed to help manage and implement diversity policies in their corporations. Today many major companies have a Chief Diversity Officer, and provide formal diversity education to keep employees engaged in the process. Additionally, over the past twenty years, Employee Resource Groups (ERGs) have flourished in these companies. They too play an important role driving employee education.

In the DEM's education phase, the end in mind is to ensure that the competitive advantage that the company can enjoy by embracing diversity is understood. Furthermore, with the help of dedicated diversity managers, and ERGs, diversity is institutionalized and woven into the DNA fabric of the company.

Having achieved emotional engagement in the previous phase of the DEM, people in the organization now begin to make a more logical assessment of diversity. The more we know about an issue, the better we are able to reason, draw conclusions, and develop action plans. Maybe the organization realizes that they simply do not have enough diverse talent in their company, so proactive recruiting plans are put in place to improve the number of people of color and women hired. Perhaps the company realizes that their marketing initiatives are not targeting the changing demographics and implement programs to address this gap. Or maybe they simply realize that they don't have a fair representation of women in their senior ranks, and they put mechanisms in place to make sure that women are developed and promoted at the same rate as their men counterparts.

We can make a long list of scenarios, and provide numerous examples of initiatives that different companies have put in place as they embarked in their diversity journey. What the actions are is never as important as the fact that leaders allow the process to take place. It is far more important that leaders embrace the process, live it, and model the appropriate behaviors that will create a culture of inclusion. The diversity process will succeed only after the leaders have clearly articulated their diversity vision, explained *why* diversity is important to the organization, and detailed their expectations of cultural change.

Action & Measuring Results

At least two things need to happen for a company to enjoy the benefits of having a diverse organization and a culture of inclusion. First, leaders must create an environment where awareness and education around the issues can take place. Second, leaders have to insist that there be an action plan developed and implemented to get after the strategies that will take advantage of the new culture.

Managing the process of organizational culture change, diversity and inclusion is no different than managing any other business process. It requires dedicated resources and strategies focused on delivering business results. It also requires accountability, specifically with the leaders of the organization. Leaders should not only be accountable for the results and for driving the change, but they should be personally engaged and champions of the diversity process.

Finally, as with any other business process, diversity must be measured if it is going to become a permanent part of the company culture, rather than just a passing fad. There are many measurement tools that can be employed by companies to understand how they are doing relative to diversity. An employee engagement survey is an excellent tool that can be used to measure progress in organizational culture. There are also some basic data that can be benchmarked against other companies and used as a measure of progress. As it relates to women and people of color, companies can track their recruiting and promotion rates, percent of turnover, number of people in development programs, and the number of people mentored. Other measures can include the number of ERG members, how active these groups are, and their business contributions.

As we stated at the beginning of this chapter, there is growing evidence to suggest that diverse organizations yield better results than non-diverse organizations. Companies who did a better job managing human capital investment, who had CEO commitment to diversity, better communications, and a focus on supplier diversity delivered better results. As demonstrated, data are also compelling that the cost of recruiting new hires can be quite significant. Trends suggest that the need for qualified workers will outpace the available talent. It would seem reasonable that developing and retaining the best diverse talent is an important business consideration. These data provide leaders and business managers compelling reasons to create a diverse and inclusive culture in their organizations.

Following the example and the path already charted by other great organizations that are tackling the issue of diversity as a very real business differentiator and value generator, is one way to for leaders to help create a diversity aware and inclusive organizational culture in their organizations. The basic steps outlined in the Diversity Engagement Model can serve as a guide to help organizations and leaders chart the appropriate course that will lead to an effective culture; a culture where diversity is appreciated, fostered, and appropriately managed.

ELEVEN

THE LEGACY LEADER AS FARMER

Years ago, it was very common for a person to spend an entire career with one company. When someone was referred to as a "company man," it was a compliment. It meant that the person was loyal to the company, and the company was loyal to the individual. The relationship between the person and the company was life long. Those days are long gone. In today's economy, statistics indicate that a person can expect to move to four or five companies within their career. The reasons for moving range everything from simply seeking more money, changing career paths, looking for upward mobility, or wanting to do something new. More often than not these days, individuals at all levels are being displaced from their positions as a result of organizational downsizing.

There are many good reasons why people move from one organization to another. Some of that movement is healthy for an organization. Bringing in new talent with a different background can often infuse new ideas and new ways of doing things that can be very helpful to the gaining group.

What is often overlooked however is the harm of losing talent for the wrong reasons, such as poor development, lousy leadership, or not enough pay. Why are they wrong? Because there is no excuse for them! People should be developed, lousy leaders should be fired, and people should be paid well so that money is not a concern to them. Companies always underestimate the cost of replacing a talented individual. The cost goes well beyond that of recruiting and training a replacement.

When a company loses a talented individual, they lose, among many other things, that person's experience, his or her network, not to mention his or her future contributions. Moreover, if the person leaves for the "wrong reasons," it can affect those who remain behind. When good people start leaving, it causes those left behind to wonder why they should stay. Therefore, a Legacy Leader must be concerned with understanding why people leave and prevent good people from leaving.

While conducting some of the research for this book, an interesting pattern emerged as I looked at the careers of some very successful leaders in a variety of industries and organizations. It seemed that in a number of cases, high potential individuals left organizations midway through their careers (between the ages of thirty-five and forty-five). They moved to other organizations where their careers quickly exploded and they moved to the very highest levels of management within their new organizations. Whereas, perhaps they had been held back or overlooked in their pervious organization, in their new home, they were quickly recognized as talented, highly valuable, and very promotable.

A possible explanation of why this happens could be that in some of these cases the person leaving felt frustrated with their progress, or seem to be frozen at a particular level in the organization. Yet when they transition to another organization, it appears their full potential is not only recognized, but it is exploited by the gaining organization. They (the gaining organization) move quickly to take full advantage of their leadership capabilities. Why does this happen? What does the gaining organization see in this individual that the losing group did not? I believe that it is as simple as, and can be explained by, the old saying, "familiarity breeds contempt." Said another way, "We take those closest to us for granted." When an individual with great skills is around an organization for a significant period of time, it is possible that his or her positive characteristics and performance results become overshadowed, or in some way tainted, by an emphasis in flaws or what has been identified as "areas for development."

Clearly, these "areas for development" are important. Everyone has something they need to improve. However, some organizations and some managers focus so much on the "gaps" an individual has, that they miss the significant talent and contributions the person has made, not to mention the potential they demonstrate. In fact, most development plans focus on "fixing the gaps." They identify activities, projects, and educational courses that the person can do or take in order to correct some flaw. Whether it's writing or verbal communications, or strategic planning, or even some technical skill, the development plan is created to fix what is wrong.

What is almost never included in development plans are activities, projects and courses geared towards increasing the skill of a person around areas they already happen to be fairly proficient at. Why not continue to develop the positive traits in a person to help them achieve even higher levels of success in those areas? That is because we tend to focus on the negative rather than the positive. Thus, leaders need to be alert to these dynamics. They need to ensure that people are not pigeonholed or labeled because of data which often is quite outdated.

Consider the case of an individual who has been with the company for twenty years. Perhaps they arrived at the company as a recent MBA graduate, and joined the company when they were just twenty-five years old. Maybe they earned a bit of a reputation for being overly aggressive and self focused, although always were given high marks for great performance and for talent potential. Yet as the person matured over the years, it is entirely possible that they were unable to shake the "baggage" they collected as a young professional. While it is entirely possible that they still have the same tendencies they had as a young person, it is more likely that they have matured and learned from their twenty years of experience. Yet the organization continues to view them with those same biases they had years ago. Does it happen? All the time! What is this person to do? Often times, they do the only thing they can to overcome these erroneous or outdated perceptions; they leave the organization and go elsewhere.

Perhaps the most telling example that I can use to illustrate how pervasive and damaging this can be to an organization is the in how one leader dealt with it in their team. The President of a major company had in mind to promote a woman in his organization to a key leadership role as a director of an important area of the business. He was convinced that she had all the skills, experience and talent necessary to do a great job in the position. She was a seasoned employee who had been with the company a very long time. As part of the interviewing process, he had her meet with several members of his staff, most of whom were Vice Presidents. After the interview process was complete, he reviewed her candidacy with his team during one of the staff meetings. It came as a big surprise to him that the feedback on the woman was not very positive.

Alarmed by the feedback he was receiving about the woman, he decided to do an experiment. He took her resume, and changed a few data points. He changed her name of course, and altered the names of companies she had worked for and the descriptions of her positions slightly. He made sure to keep the integrity of the resume intact. That is, the mock resume was in essence the same as the original with one exception, the name of the person was different and there was no way that anyone would immediately know that it was essentially the same resume as they have previously reviewed.

He forwarded the resume to his staff members and asked them to consider this "new" candidate.

At this next staff meeting, the President asked for feedback on the resume and the candidate he was proposing, and he got rave reviews from all involved. "This is precisely the kind of person we need in this important position," one VP said emphatically. Imagine their surprise with the president divulged the details of his experiment! First, he appropriately lectured them on the bias they had demonstrated towards the woman that they had turned down for the job. Next, he gave the woman the job.

How could this happen? I believe it's quite simple. Too often we become enamored with a candidate who has a very strong candidate and who interviews well. We are quick to consider them a strong candidate and only see the positive traits of this individual. What else would we see during an interview process? Certainly no one is foolish enough to have a resume full of their "areas of development" or their "baggage." Surely, no one would provide references who would do anything other than give glowing reports on the person's skills.

Too often, we are willing to give that virtually unknown candidate the opportunity over an internal candidate simply because we know the internal candidates "dirty laundry." The reality is that all of us have "baggage." So why do we take a chance on the new person, but not on someone we already know? That's a question that the leader must make sure is being asked and answered. There are times when the outside candidate is better and deserves the job. But if talented people are leaving the organization, it may be worth a look to see if this dynamic is playing out, and do something about it before more talented people go impress some other company during their interview with them. If this sounds like the voice of experience, that's because it is!

The evidence is clear that organizations tend to focus on the negative aspects of a person's abilities. This can be easily seen during the talent audit process most companies have. This is a process where managers get together once or twice a year to discuss succession planning. This is a critically important activity for companies to undergo. However, most companies probably fail in how they go about it. They are intended to review each person in the organization, understand their strengths and weakness, determine what feedback to give the individual, and to make some decisions around what the person's next steps or positions could be. This process is very important to an organization.

Having participated in several of these kinds of audit meetings as one of the managers involved, it became clear very quickly that there can be a tremendous amount of personal bias and personalities involved in how a person is presented and rated by the group. Sadly, I have seen several people misjudged and improperly labeled. They don't usually last long with the organization after that. Interestingly, several of the ones who have left after such a process, usually became wildly successful elsewhere. So who was wrong? Was it them or was it us? No doubt in my mind, it was us who missed out on keeping the resource within our organization.

As a result of these kinds of audits or personnel reviews, almost by default, we focus on the weaknesses. So much so that individuals with this strong leadership potential can at times end up frustrated and even pigeonholed within the bowels of the organization; their skill begging to be used and their desire stifled by company politics and in some cases jealousy.

Why is it that these individuals can move to a new organization and succeed? It is because when people such as these leave, they move into a new environment, as most people do, with a clean slate. They are able to start anew with only a two page resume, a few interviews, credentials such as licenses and diplomas, and perhaps a few solid references which highlight all of the positive and impressive skills sets the individual possesses—the same ones that the losing organization had ignored or taken for granted.

In the new surroundings, the person shines because they have an opportunity to perform unencumbered by previous perceptions of weaknesses. Does that mean that this person really had no weaknesses? No, it may not mean that at all. It simply means that the new organization is able to focus on the good the person has to offer rather than on whatever the weakness may be. Chances are that those weaknesses, whatever they may be, are not significant enough to prevent the person from making significant contributions. And even if they are significant, they will be uncovered quickly in their new organization anyway. But that does not bear out to be the case most times. Most times, the person does very well in their new role and quickly moves up in the new company.

So what must the Legacy Leader do in order to avoid losing good people for the wrong reasons? They must focus on the positive traits of the people around them and build on these characteristics. They must optimize the use of these skills, and exploit the best in people. Furthermore, the Legacy Leader must ensure that:

- Managers and other leaders in the organization focus on the positive traits first and foremost

- People are evaluated for their strengths first and then their areas for development

- Plans are put in place to ensure that both the strengths and weaknesses are worked on

- People are not unduly held back. No one is perfect. If you wait for someone not to have gaps before you promote them, they'll go some place else

- Make sure that there is a fair and well-executed audit process in place and that professional jealousy or unsubstantiated perceptions are not perpetuated

- Ensure that the process of developing and moving talented people rest on merit, performance results, and level of preparedness and not on personal relationships

In bureaucratic organizations, we sometimes hide behind "development" as a reason for not moving people along. We want to develop the individual until "they are ready." When we do this, we fail to realize that it is much more effective, and dramatically more motivating, to challenge the individual with a position that perhaps is just beyond their current reach, and mentor and coach them as they complete their development and grow into the position.

The military successfully uses this model, stretching people at times to their breaking point. What can be the problem with this approach? The answer is that there might be some casualties. Some people may fail. However, if the leader has done a good job of selecting the person in the first place, the chances of this are minimized. The up side to this approach is that there will be some superstar leaders created as a result. It has been my experience that, given the opportunity and a challenge, more often than not, people will rise to the occasion to pleasantly surprise those who took the risk and provided them the opportunity.

This approach can lead to a wonderful cycle of success. When an individual, stretched at first, succeeds, they gain a confidence that propels them to repeat that success at much higher levels. More importantly, they become leaders who themselves will realize the value of developing others and affording them opportunities to be stretched.

Law of the Harvest

The Legacy Leader's role in the process of nurturing, developing, and maturing future leaders is crucial. They must engage in the process themselves and make sure that others around them do the same. In addition to this, the Legacy Leader must understand the "Law of the Harvest."

Some time ago, the senior pastor at the church I attend preached a powerful sermon on the Law of the Harvest. The principles of the law are very basic, yet fundamentally profound. They are:

1. It is impossible to reap, until you have sown

2. It is impossible to reap something other than what you have sown

3. You not only reap what you sow, you get more of it!

4. It is impossible to reap if you quit

It is impossible to reap until you have sown

Where do leaders come from? The eternal argument of whether a leader is born or made has no answer. You could find individuals who would make sound and logical arguments on both side of that coin. As for this author, he believes that a leader is made, but it sure helps to be born with a few traits that truly make a great leader.

If we believe that a leader is born, we would dismiss the impact that education, environment, opportunity, coaching, mentoring, successes and failures can have on developing a leader. Would Ike Eisenhower been the leader he was had he not gone to West Point? Would Kennedy ever have a chance to become President had he not been exposed to the education and environment that he was raised in? Was Martin Luther King, Jr., born a civil rights leader, or did his upbringing by a Christian mother and father instill in him the beliefs, ideals, and desire to do what he did?

On the other hand, had these same individuals not been born with the qualities that they possessed, whether their physical abilities or personalities, would they have been great leaders anyway? If Eisenhower had not been educated at West Point, or Kennedy raised in the right environment, or King have Christian parents, would they have become the leaders they became? And so the debate goes on. Is a leader born or is a leader made? Ultimately, what's the difference? We can't do anything about how someone is born, but we can indeed do something about how a person is educated, trained, coached and mentored. That, in the final analysis, is the most important job of the leader. For where do leaders come from? They come from other leaders!

All great leaders can point to one or more other leaders that inspired them to achieve. Whether directly, or indirectly, there is always someone that the leader has looked to in order to model their behavior and emulate them. So a Legacy Leader must sow some seed. Plant in individuals the desire to be leaders. Help them see what they must do to succeed as leaders. Get personally involved at times to make sure that others behind them are learning to lead with H.E.A.R.T. and that they understand the fundamentals of good leadership. That will not happen by accident. The Legacy Leader must not only plant the seeds, but they must water it, nurture the growth, and prune the parts that need pruning. Only then will they see fruits.

Leaders who look around them and don't see several individuals who could in a matter of moments step-in to fill their shoes are failures as leaders and will never be a great Legacy Leader. How could they be? If they were to die that moment or leave the organization, there would be no one who could take over and continue the work. What kind of legacy is that? Sadly, it is the kind of legacy that most leaders will have.

When I was a Business Unit manager in a manufacturing facility in Puerto Rico, the general manager called two employee audit meetings per year. At each of these meetings, each manager was responsible for presenting his or her people: their strengths, weaknesses, and a list of possible future assignments with timing for these. We also discussed the development plan for each of these individuals to a certain degree. It was also an opportunity for other managers to offer feedback about the individual. No doubt this system had its flaws, and from time to time, it became painfully obvious that there were biases and personalities involved in the process. Nevertheless, we managed through them, and did a fair job of evaluating people and providing for their development and future opportunities.

As part of the process, each manager was also required to indicate who from their respective staffs was being developed to take over the Business Unit manager's spot. We would draw an organizational chart, and fill each box (including the top spot—that is, our own position) with the name of an individual whom we were developing to fill those spots. I recall one such meeting when one of the managers presented his staff and he put up his organization chart with the top box empty. He said that at the moment he had no one who could back fill his position.

When the Plant General Manager saw the empty box, he quickly stopped the manager from making his presentation and stated, "That is unacceptable! You're trying to tell me that out of a plant of more than 1200 people, there is not one person who can replace you?" There was silence. It became very clear that our leader expected each of us to make developing leaders a first priority and that empty boxes would be a reflection of us, and not those we led. That is leadership. I learned more about leadership that afternoon from Mr. Jorge Rivera, than I have in reading several leadership books. He understands the first principle of the "law of the harvest": it is impossible to reap, until you have sown. Jorge was going to make sure that we did not ignore what is possibly the most important aspect of leadership–developing the next generation of leaders.

It is impossible to reap something other than what you have sown

Every gardener knows that if you plant a tomato seed, you get a tomato plant and ultimately you get tomatoes. If you plant corn seeds, lo and behold, you get corn stalks. No one would expect anything else to happen. It is impossible to reap something other that what you have sown. If you want to know why an organization has the culture that it does, you have only to look at the seeds that the leader planted. If you want to know what kind of leaders are being developed in an organization, you need look no further than the behaviors exhibited by the current leaders. It is as simple as that.

A funny thing happens to us when we grow up and have children of our own. One day, in our everyday dealings with our kids, we stop and, in a moment of sheer panic, we ask ourselves, "Oh my God, when did I become my father?" All of a sudden, we realize that we are in many ways (much more that we would care to admit) very much like our parents. The way we talk, the way we think, and in large part, the way we act. That's not surprising is it? We become a product of our environment. We learn from those around us. Leadership is exactly like this. How will leaders act? The way they are taught to, that's how. Legacy Leaders understand that they must instill in those they are developing the right behaviors. They must plant the right seeds. They are responsible for not just their behaviors, but also the behaviors of leaders below them. The leader's legacy will be judged by the seeds they planted.

You not only reap what you sow; you get more of it!

Whatever behaviors the leader plants will be magnified many times over and echoed right back to them. This is the third principle of the "law of the harvest." You will not only get what you sow, but you will get much more of it in return. If you don't like pumpkins, don't plant a pumpkin seed because that one seed will spring up a plant that will give you many pumpkins and will stretch out and spread to cover the entire garden if left unchecked. If you don't want an organization full of people running scared and timid of taking risk, don't plant fear. If you want people who will tell the truth, plant the value of honesty.

You want to motivate many? Start motivating one. It will spread. You want loyal followers? Start being loyal to them. It will spread. You want to have leaders who will listen? Listen to them. It will spread. You want followers who will trust you? Start trusting them. It will spread. You want followers who will communicate? Start communicating with them. It will spread. You want to align your followers? Start getting a few on the right track. It will spread.

You want followers who will take some risk? Reward the risk takers. It will spread. You want followers who are willing to ask for help? Ask for help yourself. It will spread. You want leaders that develop people? Start developing them. It will spread. You want leaders that empower people? Empower them. It will spread. You want an organization that manages change well? Embrace change. It will spread. You want followers who will make decisions? Start making decisions. It will spread. You want followers who will be responsible for results. Start making yourself accountable. It will spread.

And the list can go on and on. Whatever behavior you want to see in your followers, plant the right seed for it and you will have what you planted many times over. The opposite is, most certainly, also true!

Legacy Leaders cannot afford to underestimate the power that they possess in an organization. They set the mood of the organization. They establish the culture of the organization; and they do so, on a daily basis.

While I was in the Business Unit manager position, I enjoyed getting to the facility before the third shift let out in the morning, and as the first shift was arriving. This gave me an opportunity to see two thirds of my team at one time. I would gown up (we worked in a clean room environment) and just walk the shop floor; checking out the production records for the night before, talking to some of the employees and supervisors, and just getting an overall sense for what was happening. Most times, I did it just to talk to people. Pat them on the back and see how they were doing. The power of a handshake, a smile, and a sincere, "How are you doing today?" is amazing. I was usually done by 6:30 a.m. or so, and then went to my office to prepare for a 7 a.m. production meeting with the supervisors and planners.

One morning, one of my Process Supervisors (middle managers to whom the line supervisors reported to) came in just before the 7 a.m. meeting, she closed the door, sat down and very directly said to me, "What the heck is wrong? The entire shop floor is asking,

'What's wrong? Tony did not look very happy today.'" I looked at her with complete shock and surprise.

"Nothing's wrong. What do you mean?" I asked.

She explained that she had entered the shop floor after I had left that morning, and that several people, including the third shift supervisor had asked her what the problem was because I seemed completely removed, distant and upset. Wow! I searched my short-term memory bank as this had just happened less than twenty minutes earlier and quickly realized what the problem was. I did act differently that morning. I was so preoccupied with a very pressing machine breakdown issue that had surfaced the day before with one of the packaging machines that I went to the shop floor completely focused on the task of getting to the bottom of it. What was the status? That was all that I was interested in at that moment. I probably walked past several people and unknowingly, ignored them. Perhaps rather than a smile and a good morning, a few people got a nod of my head as acknowledgment.

I remember getting to the machine, talking to the operator and the engineer about the problem, got the answers I was looking for, asked the questions I needed to ask, and left the shop floor. I was not upset. I was not angry. There was nothing really wrong; after all it was not terribly unusual for a machine to break down. Nevertheless, the people noticed and reacted to my mood in a big way! One person, in that case me, set the mood for more than fifty people in an instant. That's the third law of the harvest. I sowed a bit of "bad mood," and got a bunch of people worried.

By the way, I immediately went back to the shop floor and made a public apology to my team. There was laughter and a sigh of relief from them. From then on, it became something we could joke about. I believe it made me more accessible to them and it increased my credibility. That leads to the final point about this third law of the harvest: you have to pull the weeds. Left unchecked the weeds can choke a garden in no time at all. It seems they grow in greater number and faster than the plants you really want. The Legacy Leader acts quickly to correct the mistakes he or she makes. The impact of this action is almost always positive and your credibility as a leader will sky rocket.

It is impossible to reap if you quit

"Never give in—never, never, never, never, in nothing great or small, large or petty, never give in except to convictions of honor and good sense. Never yield to force; never yield to the apparently overwhelming might of the enemy."
—Winston Churchill, October 29, 1941

"I have not failed. I've just found 10,000 ways that won't work."
—Thomas Edison

"We didn't lose the game; we just ran out of time."
—Vince Lombardi

"Obstacles are those frightful things you see when you take your eyes off your goal."
—Henry Ford

"He conquers who endures."
—Persius

Each of these individuals understood that you cannot get something if you quit. Legacy Leaders persevere, adapt, learn, change, and they don't quit.

TWELVE

THE LEGACY LEADER DEALS WITH CHARACTER FLAWS

George Washington once said, "I hope that I shall always possess firmness and virtue enough to maintain what I consider the most enviable of all titles, the character of an honest man." The character of a leader is on display for all to see all the time. Character matters! Perhaps now more than ever before in our history as a nation, we need leaders with unblemished values and of an ethical mindset. It should be considered a key qualification for leadership.

Dwight L. Moody believed, "If I take care of my character, my reputation will take care of itself." I agree with him. If we take care of our character, being mindful to behave according to the highest levels of ethical and moral behaviors, our reputations will indeed be taken care of. The reality is that we all have some character flaw. The only questions are whether we recognize them, and whether we take proactive steps to deal with them.

It requires a healthy level of emotional intelligence and courage to confront our character flaws and determine to take action to correct them. Taking the time to do a personal self-assessment and to seek out valuable feedback to help us as leaders is very important first step. One way that I have found useful in doing this assessment is using a process called SIPDE.

All good motorcycle riders understand the SIPDE concept. Each time I ride, I am reminded of these simple, yet very useful rules for safe riding. The acronym SIPDE stands for, Scan, Identify, Predict, Decide, and Execute. When riding a motorcycle, taking your eye off the road, or being distracted, even for a moment, can have devastating consequences. So you keep your mind occupied scanning for threats or problems that lie ahead. You identify the dangers, and predict how they may affect you. Whether it's an icy patch of road ahead, a dog that's about to charge the bike, or a car pulling into your lane, you identify the condition and predict what can happen next.

Also part of identifying the dangers is predicting what a driver may do next, or what possible scenarios can play out in the next few seconds. Armed with this information, you make a decision as to what action you should take to avoid getting in the situation you have identified as a possible safety threat. Finally, having decided what to do, you wait until just the right moment, and without hesitation, you execute your move. SIPDE can save your life. When you ride, you do it constantly. You are always in one stage of SIPDE or another It's a process, not a task you do once and forget about it.

Leaders need to apply the SIPDE process when doing self-evaluations of their character. If a leader believes and understands how important their character is to their ability to be an effective leader, then they should concern themselves with conducting personal audits of their behaviors and attitudes to ensure that they are in agreement with the character they want to be known for. To perform a valid self-assessment of character, the leader must be honest with themselves. They must accept that there is an excellent chance that they will identify some flaw in their character, be willing to accept input, and they must have a passionate desire to change their behaviors. This is the only way that a leader can expect to affect their character, and therefore, their legacy.

Self-assessment begins with scanning. Scanning for information about oneself means seeking feedback from family, friends, colleagues, superiors, subordinates, or anyone who you can trust, knows you well, and will tell you the truth. You want to know from them what they think of your character. Next, you want to identify the source of whatever flaws you may have. This requires that a person be willing to dig deep into their psyche to establish root cause for a belief that causes a particular behavior, which is interpreted by those around you as a character flaw. Without getting to this root cause, a person will struggle fruitlessly in a vain attempt to make a change.

I witnessed a prime example of how this can be manifested during a time in the early 1990s when the world of corporate America was dealing with the concept of diversity. Any person who was working in a major corporation in the United States in those days was affected in one way or another by the idea of managing diversity. Many books were written on the subject. A great number of consultants made vast sums of money helping organizations deal with diversity, training all of the employees, from the lowest to the highest-ranking member, on what it meant to manage diversity. In the company I was with at the time, we spent significant resources training everyone.

Each person attended a three-day workshop on the subject of diversity, and some of us even became diversity trainers. Often, people of color (a term that evolved and became en vogue as a result of diversity initiatives) attended three and four workshops a year. This was necessary primarily because there wasn't enough of "us" to go around ensuring that each session had sufficient minority representation.

The workshops were intense and often became volatile as people expressed their feelings about once taboo subjects such as race, color, sex, and gender biases, all in an attempt to get people to better understand others and themselves so that they could work together more effectively. That was indeed the motivation for making people aware of diversity issues: to make them be able to work together.

The ultimate goal was of these sessions was to create more effective teams. The end in mind was for all of us to perform better. It was also to change people's behaviors so that high performance teams would not be held back because of issues of prejudice, or stereotypes, or other biases. Companies understand that inefficient teams cost money. Thus, investing in changing behaviors that caused this inefficiency made sense then, and still does today.

As a supporter of the diversity process then, and still today, I strongly believe that having people understand and appreciate the differences between themselves and others, is a very good thing. But I have clearly observed that while going through a three-day workshop may have had a profound and life changing effect on some people-a change that affected their character—to most, it represented a superficial, albeit positive change. That is, most people, having gone through such training, learned ways that they should behave in the workplace. They learned what was politically correct to say and what was not. They checked their behaviors and became more aware of their surroundings. However, behind closed doors, or in less formal setting such as a company picnic (particularly after a beer or two) their true beliefs became evident in their jokes, comments, and personal behaviors.

This behavior was an indication that their character remained unaffected. If their true character was unchanged, then ultimately, their behaviors and actions, while masked behind the right words, would be no different than before. In fact, their actions may be even more dangerous to the organization now than before because they are hidden behind a veil of deceit. Our beliefs are so ingrained in our mind and they are so much a part of us, that even when we think we've conquered a bias or an attitude, we come to discover that in fact all that we have done is learned to manage it. This is not intended to be a condemning statement on anyone. It's a reality we must all deal with. But more than anyone else, the Legacy Leader must work to identify their biases, deal with them, and do their utmost best to delete these from their long-term memory banks.

Once the leader has scanned for and identified any of his flaws, they can predict how these flaws will affect the organization and those they lead. Understanding the outcomes that can result from character flaws will help the leader in taking the next step, which is deciding what to do about them. Finally, the leader has to make the necessary changes in their attitudes and behaviors.

The SIPDE process is no different than any other business decision process. It has a data gathering phase, an analysis phase, a decision phase, and an execution phase. And, as implied by the fact that it's a process, it repeats itself. Leaders use all kinds of different business models for making decisions that affect their businesses. Why would doing an analysis of the leader's character be any different? After all, the leader's character is by far the key to the organization's ultimate success or failure. A leader not spending time evaluating his or her character and making necessary changes is no different than driving a car on a winding country road, in the middle of the night with the lights out. The Legacy Leader is wise and strong enough to face his or her flaws, deal with them, and make necessary and permanent changes to ensure that he remains effective as a leader.

Character flaws in leaders are usually quite obvious. To illustrate this point when I teach a class on leadership or management, I always tell the audience about "the monkey climbing the flagpole." Here's what I say: "the higher a monkey goes up a flag pole, the more of his ass you can see," and after a few chuckles I explain what it means. As a person climbs the organizational ladder, there is more and more visibility of their actions. Everything the leader does and says is scrutinized, analyzed, and depending on whether they have credibility, it is either supported or criticized. Thus if the leader is unprepared, that will be evident. And so for leaders, character flaws are like flags waving high on a flagpole for everyone to see. A legacy leader is willing to face their flaws head on and change behaviors to improve their effectiveness as leaders.

Some years ago, a good friend of mine, Dr. Tom Divilio, a retired general surgeon, gave me this analogy between character flaws and hernias. Tom told me there are there are three rules for hernias: they don't get better, they don't get smaller, and they only get worse with age. There is currently only one true way of fixing a hernia and that is to have surgery. Having a hernia is almost never a fatal condition if treated properly. In fact, many millions of people ignore the symptoms and just live with the pain of the hernia, rather than dealing with it. The same is true for character flaws: they don't go away, they don't get smaller, and they can get worse with age, unless we do something about them.

Character flaws may not always be fatal to the leader's effectiveness, yet logic would seem to dictate that it certainly could hinder the leader's effectiveness. Repairing character flaws requires intervention to effect a change. It requires someone to diagnose the condition, make a determination of the best course of action to fix it, and then to execute the repair.

There are five character flaws that this I consider the "Cardinal Character Sins of Leaders." When the leader suffers from any of these, the effect on their effectiveness, and therefore their legacy, can be devastating. Ignoring them or rationalizing them away is pointless.

Arrogance

Overbearing pride, haughtiness, assurance, presumption, loftiness, imperviousness, vanity, conceit, self-importance, contempt, and scorn are just some of the words that can be found in a thesaurus when looking up the word arrogance. It is not very hard for a leader to suffer from this flaw. The old saying, "Total power corrupts totally" has, as do most sayings, roots in some truth. At times, leaders can become consumed in themselves. They can be surrounded by people who are so committed and so loyal that they provide the leader a complete sense of infallibility. This may cause the leader to believe that they can do no wrong. A leader who believes they can do no wrong can do no right!

Arrogance can be displayed in many ways. Some ways that a leader demonstrates their arrogance are:

- Not listening to others
- Interrupting while they are in the middle of a sentence
- Dismissing ideas because of the source, rather than considering the merit of the idea
- Being impolite or rude
- Not being sensitive to people's feelings
- Speaking only with people who are at certain levels of the organization
- Expecting special treatment

And the list can go on and on. What do all of these have in common? It's an overt behavior. One that people can see, feel, and hear. It does not have to be the words used; it can be how it is said. It can be body language, or even the way a person walks that expresses arrogance to others. True arrogance is founded in the person's deep-rooted belief that they are really better than those around them are. It may be by virtue of their education, the school they attended, their socioeconomic position, title, or some expertise that causes the arrogant person to consider themselves above the others. That belief, manifested in actual behaviors, is the embodiment of arrogance.

There is an interesting dynamic that seems to take place in organizations as it relates to arrogance. It is easy to label someone as arrogant when they exhibit some of the behaviors, such as the ones listed above, which can be interpreted as arrogant. Most times in fact, it is not arrogance at all. Some times a person who is assertive, intelligent, experienced, and has a progressive work ethic—a "get it done" attitude, if you will—is labeled as arrogant. I don't believe that is necessarily true. In fact, as a leader, I want people who are assertive, intelligent, experienced, and who have progressive work ethics and a "get it done" attitude.

The true test of arrogance needs to be how the person feels about their position relative to their peers, subordinates, and superiors. Do they indeed believe that they are better than the rest? It may be that they are in fact better than the others in the group. After all, in a group, someone has to be the best at whatever the group does. Thus, the fact that they may be the best does not make them automatically arrogant. How they behave given that fact, however, does. Again, arrogance is about a belief and a behavior that demonstrates that belief. It is about the intent of the individual to have things done their way, just because their way must be better and right. Arrogance is not about a belief that you are better than someone else; it's about behaving in ways that indicate that you think you are better than someone else! Legacy Leaders must not allow themselves to fall into this trap, and they must not allow others to be mistakenly characterized in this way.

In an article by Frank Koch of the Naval Institute, he writes the short story of a ship captain, and how his arrogance nearly cost him his ship. The story goes like this:

> Two battleships assigned to the training squadron had been at sea on maneuvers in heavy weather for several days. I was serving, on the lead battleship and was on watch on the bridge as night fell. The visibility was poor with patchy fog, so the captain remained on the bridge keeping an eye on all activities. Shortly after dark, the lookout on the wing of the bridge reported, "Light, bearing on the starboard bow."
>
> "Is it steady or moving astern?" the captain called out.
>
> Lookout replied, "Steady captain," which meant we were on a dangerous collision course with that ship. The captain

then called to the signalman, "Signal that ship: We are on a collision course, advice you change your course 20 degrees."

Back came a signal, "Advisable for you to change course 20 degrees."

The captain said, "Send, I'm a captain, change course 20 degrees."

"I'm a seaman second class," came the reply. "You had better change course 20 degrees."

By that time, the captain was furious. He spat out, "Send, I'm a battleship. Change course 20 degrees."

Back came the flashing light, "I'm a lighthouse."

We changed our course.

Sometimes, arrogance can blind a leader. Some get lucky and figure it out before they run their ship ashore. Most people are not arrogant. Yet for a leader, arrogance is the worst of all character flaws. It can make a person feel invincible and incapable of being wrong. No one is either of those. Legacy Leaders cannot be arrogant.

Dishonesty

Trust is the foundation of leadership. Without honesty, there can be no trust, and therefore no leader can be dishonest if they expect to be effective. It's that simple. No exceptions, no special circumstances, no rationalizing being anything less than honest in their communications and actions is acceptable for the Legacy Leader.

What the leader says she will do, she must do. When the leader speaks, his words must be the truth. Not truths hidden in rhetoric that can be interpreted in a number of ways—an art that politicians have perfected and mastered—but crystal clear truths in the form of simple, unambiguous talk.

The leader who is anything less than one hundred percent honest with his followers will have a legacy that will reflect one hundred percent of his flawed character.

Disloyalty

If trust is the foundation of leadership, loyalty is the cement that binds the leaders and followers together. The relationship that exists between leaders and followers at times has a unique quality that transcends logic and encompasses the emotional realms. A leader who has loyal followers commands a strong machine, which, when properly utilized, can achieve impressive results.

Loyalty means to be faithful, steadfast, true, constant, reliable, trustworthy, dependable, unwavering, firm, and dutiful. To the leader it means everything we've talked about in this book thus far—putting your follower's interests first and sincerely caring for them. It means never compromising your values and integrity at any cost, but most certainly not at the expense of your followers. It means never giving your follower any reason for wondering and questioning the intention of your actions.

Among the many words that describe the opposite of loyalty are the words false, treacherous, traitorous, and treasonous. We probably have all felt the sting of being betrayed at one point or another. Whether by a close friend or loved one, a colleague or a subordinate, the pain is always sharp, and the lesson is always harsh.

Being disloyal doesn't happen only in acts of great significance. Often, disloyalty is accumulated and grows as a result of many small actions that take place over an extended period. Sometimes, leaders give cause for their followers to eventually see them as disloyal only after a prolonged period of time. Nevertheless, the effect is the same. Whether the leader betrays the followers in one highly-visible and impactful way or they do it in daily actions, behaviors, and attitudes, the end result will not be dramatically different. The leader will not be trusted; they will lose all credibility, and will be seen as disloyal.

The Legacy Leader is loyal.

Self-centered

With a leader, adjectives that begin with "self" can be positive or negative traits for them to possess. Self-control, self-confidence, and self-assured are good traits for a leader to demonstrate. Selfish, self-reliant, and self-satisfied, on the other hand, are among the negative ones.

Probably the worst trait in this "self" category is self-centeredness. It implies conceit, someone who is swellheaded, vain and immodest. It refers to someone who practices self-love. Not the kind of healthy self-love that we should all have for ourselves, but rather an extreme passion with our own self-interest at the expense of others. It goes to the core of arrogance, which we already stated was the first of the cardinal character sins for a leader. When the leader is wrapped-up in himself or herself, how can they possibly be committed to the followers and the vision?

The Legacy Leader must work hard to replace self-centeredness with self-esteem which connotes someone concern with self-respect, independence, self-regard, confidence, and pardonable pride. The fine line between pardonable pride and arrogant pride is humility. Being proud, confident, self-assured and in control, while maintaining a humble spirit does not mean that the leader is meek or whimsical. It simply means they don't need to boast and push their chest out while thumping on it with clenched fist like King Kong to get attention.

The Legacy Leader has self-esteem, but is not self-centered.

Egotism

Like self-centeredness, egoism refers to selfishness and self-interest. Egotism is the verbalization of that egoism. That is, an egotist makes extensive reference to himself or herself when speaking or writing. They demonstrate no humility what so ever. The word "I" is foremost in their vocabulary. We think of people who are like this as self-admirers, boasters, bragging, smug, and painfully arrogant.

Criticizing themselves would be virtually impossible, and taking criticism from others would be difficult at best.

Some leaders recognize that followers don't appreciate egotists, so they have learned to speak and write appropriately, using the words "we" or "the team" profusely. Sometimes they even use these words out of context, much to the entertainment of their followers who see transparently through this attempt. The egotism displayed by a person is visible and obvious to everyone except the egotist himself or herself. Leaders who are guilty of this sin need to learn to focus less on themselves and more on others.

Yet, while egotism can be very negative to a leader's credibility and therefore their effectiveness, ego is also that part of our personality that gives us the passion and drive to *make things happen*. In the book *Insights on Leadership*, *John P. Schuster writes:*

> "One tricky part of servant/self based leadership is that ego can never be annihilated, and the juicy and energizing ego drives to compete, to win, to kick butt, to show off and strut your stuff—all these sources of passion and raw energy and creativity can't just be shut off like water coming out of the shower spout...The best servant-leaders are filled with the grace of the spirit/self, directing them to good, and are passionate warriors with strong egos that give them the drive to acquire and use power."

The key to ego is balance. A healthy amount of ego gives the Legacy Leader the confidence, stamina, and willpower to move forward and make things happen.

Leaders must realize that they will make mistakes. They may find that they indeed have some character flaw. How leaders deal with these flaws will speak encyclopedic volumes about their character, intent, and priorities. Leaders must also realize that there will be a price to be paid for character flaws. Finally, leaders should take comfort in the fact that by dealing with their flaws they will gain increased credibility, trust, and loyalty from their followers. Indeed their reputation as leaders who deal with their own shortcomings will attract and recruit new followers who want to associate with a leader of this caliber.

THIRTEEN

THE LEGACY LEADER LEARNS FROM FAILURE

There are only a few certainties in life. One of them is this: if you are a leader, you will experience some failure. At some point, you will have obstacles, setbacks, and outright disappointment. In fact, if a leader has not experienced failure, perhaps he or she has very likely not taken sufficient risk. It is also possible that despite whatever success they've experienced, they likely have not been as successful as they could have been had they experienced failures along the way. Colin Powell has this to say about leadership and failure:

> "There are no secrets to success. It is the result of preparation, hard work, and learning from failure."

That statement really does say it all.

Great leaders learn from failure. The greatest leaders are motivated by failure. The wisest leaders expect the failures, and are prepared to deal with them when they occur. In my book *Breakthrough Thinking: The Legacy Leader's Role in Driving Innovation*, I talk about the attitude of a Breakthrough Thinking Leader. I suggest that leaders need to have a "failure is not an option" mentality. I believe that is true. But let's be clear: that does not mean that there will not be failure along the way. The point is that leaders do not accept failure as the end point. They see it instead as a beginning. It's the place from which they will launch their next success.

We don't have to work hard to find example after example of leadership failures. Enron, WorldCom, AIG, Tyco, and GM are just a few examples of companies that have been in the news in recent times for failure to meet their company objectives. And failures are not reserved for Corporate America, we've seen many religious and political leaders fall from their perch.

A few years ago we witnessed the fall from grace of Larry Craig, a conservative senator from Idaho, who was arrested for soliciting sex from an undercover police officer in a men's restroom at the Minneapolis airport. Ted Stevens, a senator from Alaska, was convicted of lying on Senate financial disclosure documents to hide more than $250,000 in gifts and services on his home from the head of the now-defunct oil services company. Congressman Charles Rangel of New York has served in Congress for more than forty years. Recently he was the target of a far-ranging investigation by the House Ethics Committee. The committee considered allegations whether Rangel protected an oil company from a major tax bill and whether he paid appropriate taxes for a beach home he owns in the Dominican Republic. Former Detroit mayor Kwame Kilpatrick was convicted and sentenced to prison on multiple felony counts of perjury and obstruction of justice. He resigned in September 2008 after lying under oath about his affair with his chief of staff, Christine Beatty. Some years back, Jim Bakker, a televangelist, was convicted of fraud. Donald Trump filed for bankruptcy. Of course the ultimate in leadership failure: Nixon resigned the presidency in the midst of the Watergate break-in case.

These are of course high profile cases of leadership failures. But there are many more failures that happen in businesses every single day. They occur at all levels of the organization, and with varying levels of impact. In his article "Why Leaders Fail," Mark Sanborn writes:

> "In the recent past, we've witnessed the public downfall of leaders from almost every area of endeavor—business, politics, religion, and sports. One day they're on top of the heap, the next, the heap's on top of them. Of course, we think that such catastrophic failure could never happen to us. We've worked hard to achieve our well-deserved positions of leadership—and we won't give them up for anything! The bad news is: the distance between beloved leader and despised failure is shorter than we think."

Sanborn's insight on this point is excellent. Leaders can go from hero to zero in a blink of the eye. However, failure does not mean that a leader can't be highly successful in the long term. How the leader deals with failure and what they learn from it ultimately determines their level of success.

Perhaps the first lesson to learn from failure is to that we should try to avoid failure in the first place! If leaders are alert to the warning signs of potential failure they could short circuit some failure from happening; or at least avoid from repeating the same mistake more than once. So, perhaps a good place to begin is to consider some of the reasons why leaders fail.

Not considering their legacy

There are many cases when a leader's failure can be traced back to their personal behavior. Perhaps a decision that the leader made or some judgment they exhibited that was flawed. The simplest example of this type of self-destructive behavior is seen in the number of political leaders who have fallen as a result of having an extra-marital affair exposed. Bright and rising careers have come to a screaming halt when this kind of discovery is made public. This begs a simple question: what were they thinking? The answer is also simple: they weren't. Had that person thought carefully about their actions and the ramifications to their family, their career, and their legacy, I suspect they would have chosen a very different course of action.

It's amazing the number of times that this kind of lapse in judgment causes the downfall of a leader. Analyzing the reasons for this leads me to the conclusion that it must be the leader's arrogance that caused them to think they could "get away" with whatever they were doing. The bottom line is that if leaders would ask themselves how they would feel if their actions were made public on the front page of the New York Times before they did it, I would bet they might take a different approach.

Lack of focus

During the early days of the Obama administration, even some of his supporters voiced concern that the president may have had "too much on the agenda." One of the causes of leadership failure is the inability to bring a laser-like focus to the priorities they need their organizations to work on. There are times when leaders lose sight of what's important. The laser-like focus that propelled them to the top disappears and they become distracted by the trappings of leadership, such as wealth and notoriety.

Leaders must make sure that they are a very clear vision of where they want to go and they must always be refining their top priorities. They must have this laser-like focus while at the same time being able to keep a "big-picture" perspective. That is easier said than done.

Poor communications

One of my favorite lines from the movie *Cool Hand Luke* is, "What we have here is a failure to communicate." We dedicated an entire chapter in this book to the legacy leader's role as communicator. Clearly, the leader must keep effective communication channels open with his or her entire organization. The chasm that can exist between the corner office and the shop floor can at times dwarf the Grand Canyon.

Importantly, as we previously discussed, the leader's communication must be transparent, clear, and direct. Sanborn puts it like this:

> "Followers can't possibly understand a leader's intent when the leader him- or herself isn't sure what it is! And when leaders are unclear about their own purpose, they often hide their confusion and uncertainty in ambiguous communication."

Risk Aversion

Fear of failure. That's the number one reason why people don't take risks. When it comes to leadership, however, taking risks is a part of the game. Thus, what a leader must do is learn to balance their own personal bias and level of risk taking, with their fiduciary responsibilities for running their organizations in a responsible way. Leaders must also learn to trust their instincts. They should rely on sound, albeit imperfect, data to make decisions and move forward with relative haste. The alternative approach will create a slow and lethargic organizational culture that will likely miss trends and opportunities to lead the industry rather than follow the competition.

Ignoring character flaws

A leader needs to be constantly vigilant of their personal style and of signs of falling into character flaw trappings. It's not difficult to slip. The pressures of everyday leadership and the compounding effect of external pressures from customers, competitors, the market place, and shareholders can add up quickly.

Thus, it is very important for leaders to conduct frequent inventory of their behaviors to ensure that they are staying true to their character and integrity and that they are avoiding the five cardinal sins of character flaws: arrogance, dishonesty, disloyalty, self-centeredness, and egotism (see Chapter 12). Analyzing the root causes of many of the leadership failures in recent history yields sufficient evidence that one of these five flaws (most often arrogance) played an important and detrimental role in the leader's decision-making process.

Along the same lines of character flaws, we can consider the effect of a lapse in ethical judgment and its impact on the leader's success or failure. As we have already discussed, integrity is one of the highest principles of leadership.

Mark Sanborn captures it best this way:

> "When integrity ceases to be a leader's top priority, when a compromise of ethics is rationalized away as necessary for the "greater good," when achieving results becomes more important than the means to their achievement—that is the moment when a leader steps onto the slippery slope of failure."

Lack of passion

Passion inspires passion. The most successful leaders are passionate people who love what they do. They ooze positive energy that permeates throughout their organizations and infects everyone on their team. Leaders with passion talk a certain way, they walk a certain way, and they behave a certain way. There is simply no way that a leader without passion can inspire and motivate followers to achieve great success.

The leader's passion begins with their vision. It must be a vision that they are committed to heart and soul. They must believe in it and behave always in ways consistent with it. So in order to avoid failure, a leader will need to keep his or her vision always before them. The minute that they lose their love for that vision, their passion will fade along with their energy. When that happens, no charisma or charm, or even eloquence as a speaker will prevent the end outcome: failure.

Failure is a great educator. Failure is also the great de-railer. The difference between the two is attitude. The attitude we take towards the failure determines whether it defeats us or whether it builds us up. Many of the best leaders in history have a PhD from the University of Hard Knocks. Failure must not be viewed as the end. It is an opportunity for a new beginning, with a renewed passion and a wisdom that comes from experience. There are five important lessons that leaders can learn from failure. Let's take a look at each of them:

Move quickly to do damage control

When something fails, the quicker you move to fix it or at least stop if from getting worse, the better. If you are sick, the sooner you take medicine, the sooner you'll feel better. If there is a water leak in a pipe in your bathroom, you fix it quickly to avoid a flooded bathroom. The same is true in business. When a mistake is made, it should be dealt with quickly. That is not to say that the problem ought not be studied and understood, but there needs to be some quick action to control the damage done.

I am not suggesting that problems should all be fixed with band-aids. I am an engineer by training, so I understand the value of conducting complete failure root cause analysis and implementing long-term corrective action. That is the only way to really avoid the same failure from re-occurring. However, we have all seen the devastating effects of leaders taking far too much time to deal with failure in a timely manner. The reasons for the delays may be many. It could be that the leader is paralyzed and surprised by the failure and is not able to react quickly. Or it may be that in an abundance of caution, they want to get all the facts clear before responding. Whatever the reasons are, leaders must move quickly to respond to failures.

By responding with haste to failures, whether business or personal, leaders are more able to bring calm to a situation that may have been spinning out of control. If the leader is seen as forthright in dealing with the issue, he or she will have a greater opportunity to recover from it.

Learn from failure and communicate lessons learned

When we fail at something, our first instinct is to hide it! After all, who really enjoys failure? We want to minimize the number of people who know it. That is not an unreasonable reaction to failure. However, it would be irresponsible for leaders not to share the lessons learned from failure with their organizations. In fact, it's the leader's responsibility to help create a "learning organization."

There are number of different definitions of a Learning Organization in published literature. In their book, *The Learning Company: A Strategy for Sustainable Development*, Pedler, Burgoyne, and Boydell summarize it this way:

> "An organization that facilitates the learning of all its members and continuously transforms itself."

Peter Senge, author of *The Fifth Discipline*, has a slightly different definition for a learning organization. He defines a learning organization this way:

> "Organizations where people continually expand their capacity to create the results they truly desire, where new and expansive patterns of thinking are nurtured, where collective aspiration is set free, and where people are continually learning to learn together."

I will not attempt to improve on these expert's viewpoints on learning organizations. But I will make one observation: you cannot have a learning organization if the leader is not a learning leader. Leaders have to be willing to share the lessons of failure in order for the entire organization to benefit.

Unlearn the behaviors that caused the failure

If learning from failure is important, unlearning the behaviors that caused the failure in the first place is equally important. They say that the definition of lunacy is doing the same thing over and over again and expecting a different result. Once we analyze the causes of our failures, we must take the important step of creating new behavior habits that will drive a new and better outcome.

The best leaders are able to reinvent themselves with every new experience. However, unlearning behaviors is not always easy. For leaders who have become accustomed to acting a particular way, it may be quite difficult to suddenly change their way of being. It may even seem unnatural for them to do so. By definition, a habit is something we do often, and it's probably something we've been doing a very long time. So we should expect that changing it might also require time and effort. Leadership is a journey that is made richer and more rewarding by the lessons learned along the way.

Deal with failure appropriately

Failure is one of the toughest things for a leader to deal with. When a leader fails it's a direct attach on their ego. It leads to feelings of inadequacy, isolation, and ineffectiveness. No matter how temporary the setback may be, to a leader, failure is personal. Despite this, leaders have to remain focused and in control of their senses so that they can deal appropriately with the failure.

Here are the three actions that a leader must take to respond appropriately to failure:

1. Acknowledge the failure

2. Don't play the blame game, but do assign responsibility for the failure

3. Change direction, take action, and move forward

Leaders must resist the temptation to play the blame game. Finding someone to blame or spending time conjuring up excuses is a complete waste of time. The strong and courageous leader simply steps up, acknowledges the failure, and works quickly to determine what the best course of action is to take to overcome the problem. Moreover, most often leaders need look no further than the person in the mirror if they want to know who's responsible for the failure. Determining who is responsible is important however because dealing with the individual or individuals needs to be a part of the solution. If the leader is the one responsible, it may be that they forfeit their right to lead that organization and must resign for the greater good of the team. Similarly, it may be necessary for others to be appropriately disciplined if it is deemed necessary. Not dealing with those responsible for the failure is not an option, because of the impact on the rest of the organization and the credibility issue it creates for leadership within organization.

Successful people see failure as a "teaching moment." They seek to get feedback from individuals closest to the situation who will tell them the truth. Finally, armed with the feedback and the lessons learned from the failure, they develop an appropriate course of action and execute the plan.

Don't be defeated by failure

I love the story of the man who found himself in a deep pit. He had fallen in because of his carelessness. While he was in the pit, he had experienced a dramatic range of emotions. At first he was surprised to find himself in that situation. He asked himself, *How could I have been so stupid?* Then he became angry as he considered his predicament. After some time and with no signs of help to be able to climb out of the pit, he became desperate and impatient. Finally, he succumbed to the hopelessness of his situation and resigned himself to die in the pit.

Suddenly the man heard footsteps approaching. He called out for help. A man saw him down below and asked, "What's the problem?" The man explained that he had fallen in the pit and was stuck and pleaded for help. The other man reached into his wallet and tossed down some money, saying, "Here's some money. That should help you out," and he walked away. A while later a woman came by and seeing the man in the pit asked, "What are you doing?" Once again, the man explained his situation and asked for help. The woman said, "I will pray for you," and she walked away.

Finally, a third person came to the edge of the pit and, seeing the man, he called out to him, saying, "What are you doing down there?" The man sighed and mustered the energy to tell his story one more time, and asked for help. Without hesitation, the man jumped into the pit with him.

"What are you doing?" he asked. "Now we are both in the pit!"

"Yes," he said, "but I've been here before, and I know the way out."

Attitude determines whether we are defeated by failure or whether we become stronger as a result of it. We all have a hard time getting over large failures and we tend to remember our failures much more clearly than our successes. We revisit the events that lead to the failure and dwell on the past wishing we could go back and have a "do-over." In life there are no "do-overs," but there are "do-agains." Legacy Leaders learn, grow and build from failures; they are not defeated by them.

FOURTEEN

THE LEGACY LEADER
IS COURAGEOUS

In the first edition of this book, I did not include a chapter on the leader's courage. That was a mistake. It takes a courageous person willing to take risks and do what is often right (albeit not popular) to drive an organization to achieve great success. Leadership is not for the faint of heart. It is not for individuals who retreat into a corner when they make a mistake, rather than learn from it and get back in the game. Leadership is not for people who are arrogant and think they know it all, but rather for people who are courageous to surround themselves with people far smarter than they and inspire them to achieve great things.

Peter F. Druker once said, "Whenever you see a successful business, someone once made a courageous decision." That statement, perhaps better than most, captures the essence of how important it is for a leader to be courageous. Leaders with courage are those that when times are tough and hard decisions need to be made, step forward and make the call. While others run for cover, they are willing to do what they think is right and take responsibility for the result.

For the Greek philosophers, courage was one of the cardinal virtues, and could be divided in two subsets: physical and moral. There are many classic examples of physical courage of leaders, particularly military leaders who led their armies into battle. That certainly took physical courage. As it relates to the business context however, we want to concern ourselves with the leader's moral courage. In this chapter, we will explore the leader's courage and its impact on the organization's success or failure.

Every leader inevitably comes to a place when they face a tough decision. When that time comes, it is their personal courage that enables them to stand firm and get through difficult situations. It takes courage to make decisions that may be unpopular. It also takes courage to take risks. Yet that is precisely what a leader often faces; and they often face it alone.

In French, the word *courage* means "heart and spirit." No doubt many great leaders throughout history have acted from their hearts. Over time, the definition of courage has become synonymous with heroics. However, it means much more. It is in fact, according to Aristotle, the first human virtue because it makes all of the other virtues possible. Thus, courage begins on the inside of each of us. When we face a difficult situation, the first battle is within ourselves. We face our own biases, our own personal fears, and maybe even our own insecurities as we wrestle with the decision that needs to be made. Having courage does not mean having no fear; rather it means doing what is necessary and what is right despite our fear. It is the leader with that strength of character who, despite fear, will have the power to move forward.

The courage of true leadership is exposed in the midst of the most challenging circumstances and difficult situations. It is in those times when leaders must be able to get out of our comfort zone and move other people out of their comfort zone. This is especially true since the easiest thing to do is stay where we are comfortable and not "rock the boat." There are many limiting factors that will get in the way of a leader achieving their maximum success. One of those limiting factors is fear. The courageous leader faces up to those fears, and by taking them on, inspire others to do the same. Billy Graham once said, "Courage is contagious. When a brave man takes a stand, the spines of others are stiffened." The most courageous leaders are also the most inspirational.

John Quincy Adams once said, "If your actions inspire others to dream more, learn more, do more and become more, you are a leader." Isn't that great? And isn't that what leadership is truly all about? The greatest leaders are those who motivate others to dream big, become better, and achieve more. That takes a courageous leader. To think big, you have to take big risks. And with big risks come great rewards, but also come the possibility of huge failure.

In his article "Wanted: Leader's With Courage," Ray Weekes of the Brisbane Institute wrote:

> "It was Tom Peters, in an article in the Harvard Business Review on what makes a successful leader, who concluded that great leaders were frighteningly smart, had tons of animal energy, were blessed with monumental impatience, were able to distil a vision for their troops, recognized and resolved the big issues, maintained a healthy disgust for bureaucracy, were performance freaks, were honest, straightforward straight shooters, were rapidly decisive and were future focused, not report or past oriented. Also great leaders were rigorous in their own execution and follow-up and were highly driven. This individual leader exists largely in Tom Peters' imagination.
>
> Realistically a leader can be some of those things all of the time and all of those things some of the time. But one of the true virtues of leadership is missing from Tom Peters' rather colorful list - courage. This was recognized by Defense Force Chief, Major General Peter Cosgrove, in an address to the QUT Business Leaders' Forum in 2000 on his leadership experiences. He gave four essential elements of leadership - integrity, humility, compassion and courage."

In my book, *The Leader In The Mirror: The Legacy Leader's Critical Self Assessment*, I identified four questions that a leader must ask themselves to gauge their courage as leaders. Those four questions are:

Do I do what is right even when it's hard to do?

Do I stand firm?

Do I say what needs to be said even when it's not popular?

Do I admit and learn from my mistakes?

These four questions form the foundation of what a leader must to exhibit the courage needed to drive organizational success.

Do what is right even when it's hard to do

In September 2003, Fortune Magazine ran an article on Bill George. Mr. George, an incredibly successful captain of industry, had led Medtronic from 1989 until 2001. During his tenure, the company grew from $755 million in annual sales to more than $5.5 billion. It also grew from 4,000 employees to over 26,000. Medtronic also became a model for other companies. It dominated in its field, and still does today. After his retirement, George wrote a book entitled *Authentic Leadership*. In it, he relates the story of how he struggled with finding and listening to his inner voice, and doing what is right. He wrote:

> "Thank you, Enron and Arthur Andersen and WorldCom and HealthSouth. You woke us up. The business world has run off the rails, mistaking wealth for success and image for leadership. We're in danger of wrecking the very concept of the corporation. It's not often that a business leader (make that a recently retired business leader) gets to sound off in a major magazine, so let's not mince words: Many, many leaders in my generation have failed.
>
> It's too late to undo those failures. But it's not too late for the next generation of leaders to learn from them. Legislation

like Sarbanes-Oxley alone won't do the trick. What tomorrow's leaders need is a tough preparatory course on the pressures and temptations they'll face once they've arrived in the executive suite. Those forces are powerful enough to drag down even the most well-intentioned leaders.

I know. It almost happened to me."

George goes on to describe what he calls "the game." The rules of the game are quite simple: report quarterly earnings that rise with smooth predictability. Then as a CEO, treat yourself as a god for managing that smooth predictability, and pay yourself accordingly. If anyone suggests that a strategic blunder has been made, bury the mistake in divestitures and a series of restructuring charges. George points to Enron, Arthur Andersen, WorldCom, and HealthSouth as examples of this very game gone wrong. Had he been writing his book in 2009, he would have plenty of other examples including AIG, along with many other banks and financial institutions and the automobile companies that have recently caused the collapse of the US economy. What is interesting is the reason that George attributes to why the game is played. He goes on to write:

"My generation of CEOs, like many of today's business students, embarked on our careers with a mixture of ambition and idealism. But something happened along the way. We began listening to the wrong people: Wall Street analysts, media pundits, economists, compensation consultants, public relations staffs, hedge funds, fellow CEOs—all the players in what I call the Game. That Game has stopped today's chief executives from focusing their energies on their company's customers, employees, and—ironically, since the Game is supposed to be all about them—shareholders. That's right. The biggest losers of the shareholder-value movement have been the shareholders themselves."

George learned early on in his career that once a leader is promoted all the way to the top, the pressure to make the numbers simply goes up. Despite the fact that outside pressures to keep the share price and profits in a straight-upward line are insane, the reality is that precisely what many CEOs face every day. With that pressure, and the risk of being embarrassed or fired for lack luster earnings numbers, comes to temptation to do whatever it takes, regardless of right and wrong.

For almost twenty years, I have worked in the life science and medical device industry. The products these companies make affect people's lives. This is particularly true of the implantable devices that can, and often do, save lives. These products have to be perfect. There can be no shortcuts taken in order to "improve the bottom line" at the expense of product efficacy and quality. Period. There is no room for a leader that would not have the courage to keep that priority as paramount.

One true story, perhaps better than any other, captures the essence of the leader's courage in making difficult decisions and always doing what is right. In October 1982, seven Chicago residents died after taking cyanide-laced Tylenol capsules. Their deaths prompted a massive product recall by Johnson & Johnson, the makers of the painkiller. Thousands of bottles of Tylenol were removed from supermarket shelves and sent to laboratories for testing. Production of Tylenol was halted after every bottle of the product was removed from every store shelve in America. The company issued warnings to hospitals and distributors and discontinued all advertising. All in all, more than 31 million bottles were in circulation, with a retail value of over US$100 million. Johnson & Johnson went further and advertised in the national media for individuals not to consume any products that contained Tylenol. Even after it was determined that only capsules were tampered with, they offered to exchange all Tylenol capsules already purchased by the public with solid tablets.

What followed was an intense investigation by authorities. Soon, there were copycat incidents involving eye drops, mouthwashes, and other over-the-counter products. This prompted the government to move quickly to require makers of such products to revamp their packaging and create tamper proof packaging for over-the-counter drugs. Ultimately, those responsible were apprehended and brought to justice. But seven people were dead and the financial damage to the company was done.

Before the crisis, Tylenol was the most successful over-the-counter product in the United States with over one hundred million users. The brand was responsible for 19 percent of Johnson & Johnson's corporate profits during the first three quarters of 1982. Tylenol was the clear leader in the painkiller field accounting for nearly 40 percent market share. It outsold Bayer, Excedrin, and all the other over-the-counter pain medicine at that time. Tylenol *was* J&J as much as any other product.

Johnson & Johnson chairman, James Burke, provided clear direction to the team dealing with the crisis. He gave them two tasks to accomplish: first, protect people. Second, save the product. Everyone in J&J knew the product was good. But it would take some work to regain consumer confidence. This now-famous case is studied by most MBA students as an example of management being guided by the right compass and doing the right things. Johnson & Johnson was praised by the media for its handling of the incident. Although sales did tumble to less than 10 percent, they rebounded in less than a year. Today, Tylenol continues to be the best-selling over-the-counter painkiller world-wide.

There is no finer example that I can give as to the power of leaders doing the right thing, even when it's hard to do.

Bill George once said, "It would be another lie to say I was never tempted by all those outside voices—or by an equally dangerous inner one. Ambition, ego, call it what you will—it's a demon I've struggled with throughout my career." He was of course referring to those voices that tempt leaders to take the easy path. Leaders must have the courage not to succumb to that temptation.

Stand firm

Courage in business leadership is expressed in many ways. It can mean changing a vision or strategy. It can also mean holding an unpopular position at the risk of facing personal criticism. To stand firm does not mean to stand stubborn, however. A leader must remain flexible enough to allow for change in light of new information. Leaders ought to be ready to re-evaluate a course of action or direction if enough evidence dictates that a change is necessary. What must not be negotiated or bartered away are the moral absolutes of ethics and legal behaviors.

Say what needs to be said even when it's not popular

What is the classic definition of a lose-lose situation? The answer is: when a leader has to deliver bad news. If they deliver the news, they run the risk of being criticized because the news is negative. If they don't share the news, they are criticized for withholding important information. That is what some would call the proverbial "rock and a hard place." Nevertheless, leaders must have the courage to say what needs to be said even when it's not popular.

Over my career, like all leaders, I have had to deliver some bad news. I can think of nothing worse than when I was announcing headcount reductions in Hand Innovations, LLC, in Miami in 2007. The reductions had long been expected, and we had communicated transparently about them being necessary as part of the integration of the company after the acquisition. That did not make it any less difficult. I found the reaction of the associates as expected: emotional. It was emotional for those affected by the news directly, but also for those who were surviving the cuts. Nevertheless, the news needed to be delivered honestly and directly.

I learned, though, that it takes more than courage to deliver bad news. It takes a leader who cares and is committed to the greater good of the organization and the people in it. People want to be led by someone who has not only the courage to do what is necessary, and say what needs to be said, but who also has the emotional intelligence to do so with compassion. Moreover, they want a leader who will have the courage to be responsible for the decisions made.

As is often the case, how we say something is equally important as what we say. There is a right way and a wrong way for a leader to deliver bad news, and say what needs to be said even when it's not popular.

Leaders need to have the courage to deliver the news personally and directly. An e-mail blast to the entire corporation would not be the best way to do that! Further, leaders must choose their words carefully to ensure that they are being transparent with the information, and not appearing to be evasive. Ambiguous communications will send the wrong message to the organization about the reason why the changes are taking place or what the strategies and priorities are. It will do much more to fuel rumors rather than calm them down. Ultimately, if the leader fails in delivering the news appropriately it will lead to a loss of trust in management.

The right way to deliver the news is to do so humbly and with a healthy dose of compassion. The leader must explain why the decisions are being made and the ramifications of not making them. Also important is that leaders acknowledge the emotional impact of the decisions made, and that change can be hard for some. This is not an apology for the actions being taken rather it's an honest and complete explanation. Leaders must resist the temptation to shy away from straightforward communications. Instead they must have the courage to not "beat around the bush" and say what needs to be said.

When leaders are honest with their followers, it promotes trust. And as we already have discussed, trust leads to credibility, which is the foundation of effective leadership. Voicing an unpopular opinion, position or decision is not easy, but it's the right thing for a leader to do.

Admit and learn from mistakes

We have already dedicated an entire chapter in this book on what leaders must do to learn and grow from their mistakes. As we concluded in Chapter 12, leaders must have the courage to acknowledge when they make a mistake, accept the consequences of that mistake, learn from it and move on.

To be able to do that, the leader has to have the capacity to realistically assess him or herself and understand the personal values that truly matter. If a leader is incapable of conducting a critical self-assessment, then their ability to learn from mistakes will be handicapped. Often times it is the leader's own ego that blocks them from seeing the faults that others can plainly see.

Another potential roadblock to the leader learning from their mistakes is their resistance to change. Not organizational change. Most effective leaders are quite good at driving organizational change. The change we are referring to here is personal behavioral change. The kind of change we are indicating here requires an honest, introspective review of who we are as leaders.

Ray Weekes phrased it this way:

> "For outstanding leaders to exercise courage, it follows that courage in any context, whether it be in the business arena, political sphere or whatever, it needs to be underpinned by certain personal characteristics of the individual that are derived from an unsparing self examination."

Part of acknowledging and learning from mistakes include the courage it takes for a leader to admit and show vulnerability. It can be difficult for anyone to admit they have a weakness. That is especially true for a Type-A personality leader. While some might perceive this weakness as a flaw in the leader, it can be turned to a huge advantage. It simply takes the courage of the leader to surround themselves with talented people. The leader who does that in essence endears themselves to their followers who dedicate every waking moment to achieving the organizational success. More leaders need to learn to say, "I need help with this."

Finally, it takes a fair amount of humility as a leader to learn from our mistakes. I know for me personally, some of the mistakes I have made as a leader have been quite humbling. They have been a strong reminder that the moment we start to believe we can do no wrong we will be able to do nothing right. Some lessons can be painful. The cost can be far more than financial; they can be personal. Loss of confidence and trust, or even loss of credibility as a leader, can result when leaders are not able to take a step back, evaluate their actions and motives, and learn from them. If this sounds like the voice if experience, that's only because it is.

CONCLUSIONS

THE LEGACY LEADER
HAS PURPOSE

Never before in the history of mankind has the need for strong, ethical, moral, and purposeful leadership been more evident than today. We live in a complex world that has been made smaller by technology, but larger by sociological, economic, political, racial, and religious differences.

Leaders, whether political, industrial, educational, scientific, or religious, all share a similar burden. They all have a responsibility to the individuals they lead, to the organizations they lead, and to the community in which they live. Ultimately, they have a responsibility to the world around them to do something good. They have a duty to create value. That value can be in the form of wealth, scientific and medical progress, technological breakthroughs, or laws that protect and improve the lives of many. It can be that the value will come from driving innovations that lead to job creation and communities to flourish, developing the next generation of people to continue the work began by others, and improving the educational system for all to benefit. Maybe the value will come from creating tools that make it possible for things that were once only dreams to become a reality. The list can go on and on. Again, I say, ultimately, the purpose of leadership is to do something good and of lasting value.

Throughout this book, I have tried to illustrate how the leader's character, their integrity, their morals, their courage, and their credibility are fused, and form the foundation for the level of success that the leader will enjoy. Regardless of the industry or field that the leader is in, whether they are the leaders of a giant corporation or a small team, it is their day in and day out behavior as it relates to their people that will make them successful.

Clearly, the leader's expertise in a particular subject matter may be crucial to the ultimate achievement of the organizational vision. However, more often than not, the leader need not, and probably ought not, be the expert. Consider the President of the United States. He is the Commander-in-Chief of the Armed Forces, but even if he has served as high-ranking military officer in the past, the wise commander-in-chief relies completely on the advice and hard work of the true experts around them when making decisions about military matters.

What they must rely on is the loyalty, respect, trust, credibility, and communication that they must have with their followers who are giving the advice and suggesting courses of action. The president need not be the expert as the leader, but he had better work on being seen as a person of character who can be trusted. He must act in ways that lead his followers to believe in him and his vision. He must act in ways that gain and keep his credibility high. He must communicate with people around him in ways that make his vision clear and empowers people to get it done. He must ensure that people around him are being developed and prepared for other important jobs. He must in essence, concern himself with the people, and let the people achieve the goals that make the vision possible. He must be a leader with courage to take risks, make mistakes, evolve and learn continuously.

Leadership styles vary dramatically from person to person. Differences in educational backgrounds, religious beliefs, political affiliations, personality traits, and life experiences are among a few of the many that can be listed as contributing factors to the leader's style. Some leaders are natural communicators; others struggle to make their points clear. Some leaders are liked, while others are tolerated. There are leaders with charisma and charm, and others who are as dry as fallen autumn leaves. There are leaders who are direct, and others who are more subtle. Despite these many differences, there is one constant that will always be shared by leaders: they will have a legacy. As was mentioned at the beginning, it is inevitable that leaders will indeed have legacies. Fortunately, in most cases, they have some control over what that legacy will be.

According to Stephen Covey, to have a legacy means:

> "To be involved in ways that contribute and truly make a difference in every area of life—in our work, our communities, our churches, our neighborhoods, and most of all, in our families."

Joe Batten, in his article "Servant-Leadership: A Passion to Serve," writes:

> "Real servant-leaders are committed to the growth and renewal of all with whom they come into contact."

In these statements by these two experts lies the true purpose of leadership: making a positive difference for those around us. The leader chooses how they go about doing that and what area to do it in—but they must begin with that end in mind. They must define their personal purpose, which defines their vision, which reflects their character. Then they must set out to practice the principles of Legacy Leadership. They should challenge themselves and those around them to strive for levels of greatness not out of a sense of arrogance or ego, but with a humble spirit and a noble intent.

As you turn the last page of this book, realize that, as a leader, you affect people's lives. You're not just in charge of a business and making money, but you are accountable to the people that help you do that. You are not just responsible for the manufacturing facility that produces widgets, but for the people who sit at the bench and make them. You're not there just to make sure people work and get paid; you are there to make sure they grow and develop. Know that your words as a leader can either tear the very fabric of your followers' spirit, or serve as the wind beneath their wings to send them soaring. Know that your actions, whether personal or professional, affect your followers. Know that if you trade your integrity and compromise you credibility, you betray your followers' trust. Have no reservation over the fact that if you are not a leader of character, you will never achieve the heights of what could have been. Finally, rest assured that your legacy rests solely in your hands.

What will people say about you as a leader?

EPILOGUE

When the first edition of the Legacy Leader was published in 2003, the country was still in the early recovery days of the horrible attacks of September 11, 2001. That will be a date that will live with us forever. On that terrible day, underneath a blue and clear sky, citizens all over the world watched in horror as highjacked airliners were slammed into the World Trade Tower buildings in New York City, another crashed into the Pentagon Building in Washington, DC, and a fourth airplane crashed into a field in Pennsylvania, its true target having been missed. Thousands of lives were lost before our eyes. Our priorities were forever altered.

In one hideous act, the terrorist responsible managed to shock the majority of the people on the planet. They also managed to unite our nation in a way that it has not been since World War II. It caused our nation to go to war, has cost us billions of dollars, and more than 4000 brave American soldiers have made ultimate sacrifice for our country and our freedom. We must never forget them.

The events of 9/11 caused our country to travel a path that has, in some experts' estimation, accelerated the advent of the difficult economic times we now face in the United States. The collapse of our financial institutions, the bailout of American car manufacturers, and the record number of companies filling for bankruptcy and laying off employees are just a few of the side effects we are all feeling.

Now more than ever, we need leaders of character. We need Legacy Leaders, who will put the interest of the followers first. We must have leaders who will motivate and inspire us to align and work together for the improvement of all mankind. We must have leaders who earn and keep our trust. We need the leaders in government, industry, education, research, medicine, finance, and especially in our churches, to be men and women of the highest ethical and moral standards. We need leaders who are uncompromising in their values and unwavering in their zeal.

As Barrack Obama is sworn in as the forty-fourth President of The United States, our country is hopeful that he will be the Legacy Leader that will unite our nation once again, inspire an entire generation of people to rise up, and solve the problems our nation and our world faces. But he will not succeed alone. It will take leaders in all areas of government and industry to make it happen. History books fifty or one-hundred years hence will judge us and our success.

PART 2

BREAKTHROUGH THINKING: THE LEADER'S LEGACY ROLE IN DRIVING INNOVATION

PREFACE

Ever since man first walked on the earth he has manipulated the world around him. The earliest forms of innovation likely had to do with self-preservation such as creating tools for hunting and farming. Early inventions focused on creating better shelter and clothing to protect against the elements, and inventing treatments for medical conditions thereby extending life expectancy. Later innovations focused on more than just improving the basic needs for existence to inventing ways to provide for their comfort and entertainment. The fantastic innovative leaps that have been made in the past century alone are staggering. A short ten to fifteen years ago, the Internet was unknown to ninety percent of people in the United States. Today it is the most significant source of information, communication, and entertainment used by the vast majority of people.

Why do we innovate? We innovate because innovation is fundamental to being human. From a business point of view, innovation properly channeled creates entire industries. Just consider what the invention of plastic has meant to the world. How many new products came into existence because of that one development? Every major industry has somehow been affected by the advancements in polymer plastic technologies. From toy manufactures, to medical device companies, to the auto industry, plastic has revolutionized the design of thousands, indeed hundreds of thousands, of products.

Innovation, it seems to me, is the purpose for which we are placed on this earth, albeit for a relatively short period of time. Without innovation, and the human imaginative spirit, where would mankind be today? From the time that man discovered fire and began to understand and discover ways how to use it, all the way to the first step on the moon by Neil Armstrong, to the creation of the first super computer, and the development of robotics to help make our lives easier, man seems to have an insatiable appetite for discovery and innovation.

Breakthrough thinking is not a nice to have for innovation; it is an imperative for innovation. Without true breakthrough thinking by engineers, scientist, and leaders, we would be doomed exclusively to a "new and improved" mentality. In marketing terms, we call these products derivatives or product extensions. While from time to time, derivatives can be truly innovative and breakthrough in solving a new need, most times creating derivative products is the quickest, least complicated way for a company to launch another product to make money. That's not necessarily a bad thing.

However, it is much more challenging, and far more difficult, for a team to think of a better way to help the customer solve a need. After all, innovation is about applying technology to a real need. Innovation is about developing a completely new, different, and better solution, rather than tweak an old solution to the problem. There is nothing wrong with improving on products. Thank God that Microsoft did not stop at DOS! Otherwise, current versions of Windows would not exist. But what's next? Would we be satisfied with another version of Windows that gives only incremental improvements to the old? What we really need is a whole new way of computing; a yet-unimagined way of data transfer! This is where science fiction meets reality. This is also where breakthrough thinking is the difference between mediocre results, and revolutionary ones.

In this section of the book, we attempt to capture the essence of what is necessary to have true breakthrough thinking teams, and how to harness their power to achieve incredible, exciting, and truly innovative and revolutionary results. The leader's role in driving these breakthrough teams must not be underestimated. All projects and teams need management. However, innovative projects demand breakthrough-thinking leadership. Without strong, focused, and breakthrough thinking leadership, innovation will not occur.

Breakthrough thinking is not optional for great teams to achieve great things; and if we are to leave the world a better place than we found it, we must always strive to do great things.

FIFTEEN

THE STORY OF REDHAND

It was early November, 2001. My Outlook calendar had a one-hour meeting in the Advanced Technology Center Building, room P-208A. This would be my first AMS (Anti-Microbial Suture) Team meeting. It was also the first time I met a few new colleagues who have since become some of my very best friends. The journey this team was about to embark on would be a fantastic voyage, filled with new experiences, and ultimately, a new way of thinking; a breakthrough way of thinking. Howard Scalzo, Mark Mooney, Dr. Thomas Barbolt, Dr. Mark Storch, Dr. Stephen Rothenburger, Dennis Humphreys, and a cast of many others were gathered in this very small conference room; some attended via a conference call.

During the first team meeting, Howard, my R&D counterpart, outlined the concept idea of the AMS. He briefly discussed what R&D had been working on in the laboratory, where as far as I could tell, brilliant, albeit mad scientists, labored day and night to come-up with exciting new technologies and gadgets. It was also the place where only a few who learned the "secret password" are privileged to enter. When Howard was done with the description of the product that could be developed, I was very excited. The world of sutures is quite a mature business. Sutures have been in use for many centuries, and while there have been dramatic innovations in the polymer technologies used in these medical devices, it had been some time since we had a new product to launch in this category.

The first question I had was, "When can we have it?" Howard looked at me and said, "We can probably do it by the end of 2004."

Surely he must be kidding, I thought to myself. In marketing terms that might as well been infinity. "2004?" I repeated. "I thought we were talking months, not years."

That's when I got "the look"—come to think of it, my team would give me "the look" many times over the next twelve months. It's what I call the "what are you smoking?" look. Howard chuckled, and no doubt thought to himself, "Oh boy, here we go again with these marketing guys who don't have a clue about what it takes to make something new. Particularly something nobody has ever done before!"

I took my queue from "the look," and I said something to the effect of how I understood there would be huge hurdles ahead, and the complexities, not to mention the risks, would be daunting, but that we should set a goal to launch the product within the next twelve months. I got "the look" again. Even those on the phone gave me "the look." I could feel it. There was silence for what seemed a long time but was likely only ten or fifteen seconds. The seed of breakthrough thinking had been planted, and some in the room were considering the possibility. No doubt others were dismissing it as a crazy idea, but a few were thinking about it. That's all we needed.

If breakthrough thinking is to take place, you first need to have a breakthrough goal. A goal that not only seems unreasonable, but in fact is unreasonable!

Before the meeting was over we agreed that having a product launch within the next twelve months would be our "stretch goal." I suspect that many left the room shaking their heads thinking "no way." But a few left thinking "why not?" So the first step that we took was to gather those "why not" thinkers together, and dive deeply into what it would take to get this done. We quickly formed a team we later dubbed the "speed team." We laid out a detailed plan for what needed to happen over the next many months if we were going to have a shot at making this product launch in twelve months.

The reality that this had never been done before sunk in. Never before had our company developed a product from idea, to concept, to development, to FDA approval, to production, in that short period of time. However, I insisted that the only outcome that would be acceptable was to have the product launched before the end of 2002. That's when the team's ultimate success was determined: when we all agreed that we would make this target. As unlikely as it may seem, we were all committed to making it happen.

Our next step was to rally the team around our vision for success. On March 6, 2002, I hosted the first team Technical Summit. We gathered all functional areas including R&D, Operations, National Planning, Regulator Affairs, Quality Assurance, Marketing, Packaging and Graphics Engineering, and Medical Affairs. We included representatives from all over the globe to ensure that we had a global perspective to this product.

For two days, we followed a rigorous agenda. The end-in-mind of the work session was simple: get everyone in the team to buy-in to the vision and time frame of the product launch. To do this, we discussed all elements of the project, challenging every single aspect of the status quo, and the way we normally did things. Clearly, if we were going to be successful, we needed to create a new model for how things got done. We could not live within the same framework that had traditionally been the way things were done in the organization—that would be way too slow for us. During that meeting, I asked everyone to make a personal commitment to the project, and our goal—especially the time line.

Before the meeting began, I arrived early to set-up the large conference room we had reserved at a local hotel. I brought two cans of red paint with me, a few mixing sticks, some paint brushes and pans, as well as a large painter's canvas drop cloth that I had purchased at Home Depot for about $9.99. I had requested that the chairs and tables in the room be set up in a U-shape. I placed the cloth, paint, brushes, and the other items I brought with me, in the center of the U-Shape. Having opened the drop cloth, the room looked more like a painter's workshop than a conference room.

Once the meeting began, I opened the meeting by explaining the objectives for the workshop. Different than other typical meetings, I expressed that this would be an active working session; we were there to get stuff done! To make decisions, forge partnerships, and agree on direction, strategy, and tactics that would lead our team to its ultimate vision of launching the product in 2002. Most important, we were there to gain the commitment of every individual present to the project and its success.

While I continued to set the expectation for the meeting, I dipped a brush in the red paint and wrote "The AMS Declaration of Commitment 3/16/02" on the canvas. AMS was an acronym for Anti-Microbial Suture. I then asked that during the next two days, as each of the team members felt compelled, and completely committed to the project, they were to come to the canvas, dip their hand in paint, and put their handprint and signature on the canvas as a sign of their buy-in. By the end of the first day, the project's "holy shroud" had been born (see Figure 1).

After a long two-day meeting in which we had worked very hard, everyone was exhausted. We were coming to the end of our meeting, and I was very pleased with the results thus far. We had made excellent progress, not just on defining the strategies and tactics, and making important decisions, but also on how we were going to go about our work. We had established a new culture within our team. Our culture would be one of a continual state of challenge. Challenging each other, the ideas, and the methodologies became the norm. But it was done in the spirit of finding solutions not derailing the progress being made. We made many good decisions in those two days, and had a plan of action clearly spelled-out for the next several months to drive towards our end objective.

I began to thank the group for its hard work, and was about to close the meeting, when one of the team members called out "hold on, we still have one more job to do today. We need to give our team a name." She was right, but there was a loud collective sigh in the room as people were very tired. It was late in the afternoon, and this was the only thing standing between us and a cocktail, to be followed by dinner.

"Okay folks," I said. "Nancy is right. We need a name."

"That's easy," came a voice from one of the members of the team. "REDHAND."

There was a cheer from the rest of the team.

"REDHAND it is!" I proclaimed.

From that moment on, project REDHAND became the most recognized team name in the company. The "Shroud of REDHAND" was treated as an icon. We took it to special meetings, and even presented it at the next Executive Board meeting when we gave a complete project update and announced our breakthrough objective of launching the product that year! It became a tangible symbol of the team's commitment. Project REDHAND would not fail. Less than twelve months after this initial global kick-off meeting, Vicryl Plus Antibacterial Suture, the first Antibacterial suture cleared by the FDA, was released to the market.

I have had the pleasure of working on and leading many teams over the past twenty five years. Leading the REDHAND team has been the highlight of those years. No other team has taught me as much about what it takes to drive results. The lessons learned from the journey traveled by the REDHAND team are embodied in this book.

Figure 1. Picture of Project REDHAND canvas with team member's handprints. It became known as the "Shroud of REDHAND." I proudly display this canvas in my office as a constant reminder of what is possible.

SIXTEEN

BREAKTHROUGH THINKING STARTS WITH THE LEADER

The most significant obstacle to teams achieving breakthrough results is the inability of people to believe that achieving the breakthrough results is possible in the first place! The most significant failure of a leader is letting them get away with that attitude. That is why I believe that what Mr. Bill Weldon, CEO of Johnson & Johnson, once told me is absolutely correct. He said, "Individuals who want to make it happen will find a way to do it, while those who don't, will simply find an excuse." Leaders must have the desire to succeed and a drive to "find a way," and they must have the ability to influence others to want to do the same. That's the key to teams achieving breakthrough thinking.

I am convinced that unless the leader clearly, unequivocally, and passionately, makes the statement that the organizational culture will be one in which breakthrough thinking will be the only acceptable standard, the organization will never take on that attitude and exhibit the behaviors necessary to drive breakthrough results. Moreover, if the leader fails to get other leaders in the organization to firmly believe and support a breakthrough-thinking environment, and not just talk about it, then the concept of breakthrough will be unsuccessful.

Without the leader's relentless commitment, it will become the management "buzzword" of the month, doomed to meet the same fate that so many other management fads have. Breakthrough thinking is more than that. It is real. The results that can be achieved are real, and anyone who says it can't be done in our organization because our processes or products are "different" is simply wrong.

Breakthrough Thinking is not about products or processes. It's about leader's behaviors and the environment they create. It is also about the team member's attitudes, beliefs, and the behaviors that result from these.

Thus, part two of this book is about several things: first, it's about convincing leaders that breakthrough thinking is critical for their success as leaders, and therefore their organization's success. Second, it is about clearly identifying characteristics of breakthrough teams and the culture required to foster a breakthrough-thinking environment. Finally, it's about detailing what leaders must do to drive innovation in breakthrough teams.

What we will not do in this part of the book is put forth a formula for creating breakthrough and innovative teams. No such formula exists, as teams are dynamic, ever-evolving living organisms. Each of these teams has its unique DNA, and the successful leader understands the nature of these teams. One thing is certain however, if the team will achieve breakthrough results and be the most innovative possible, it will be the leader's responsibility to create the environment where that can take place.

More importantly, it will take consistent, persistent, and sustained leadership to maintain a Breakthrough-Thinking culture. A great team can generate great results, even breakthrough ones once, maybe even twice. But only when there is a breakthrough thinking culture established in the organization at large, will the results be sustainable over prolonged periods of time.

In early 2002, I attended a one-day training session on a new initiative being introduced in the company I worked at that time, ETHICON, Inc. a Johnson & Johnson Company. The training was called GAP. Our company president, Mr. Cliff Holland, had mandated that all members of the management staff and other key positions attend one of these day long sessions. The program was repeated numerous times over a period of several months to ensure that everyone had an opportunity to attend. Cliff considered these training events so important that he attended each of them! There were no excuses accepted for not attending one of the scheduled sessions for a full day.

The purpose of each of these meetings was to train the organization on a new way of thinking; a breakthrough way of thinking. Throughout the day, small groups were challenged to think about our business, and identify the "drift" that existed in our environment. Drift was defined as the "talk" that could be heard in the hallways, or the cafeteria, or even during meetings. It was intended to identify the organizational culture: the good, the bad, and the ugly.

Then we were asked to challenge that "drift." In essence, to choose between the status quo and creating a new drift. We opened the door to the possibility of creating—and owning—the place we would like to work at. What if we changed our environment and our organizational culture? What would it look like? What if we all changed the way we spoke on a daily basis? What if we changed the way we thought about our daily activities? What if our attitudes were different? What would our environment look and feel like then? What if? These are very empowering questions, and handled seriously, they can lead to a revolution that can only result in a more effective organization.

Towards the end of each of these sessions, each participant had an opportunity to pledge his or her support to a new culture. Indicating their ownership to creating that new culture, and more importantly, making a statement as to what they stood for! One by one, each person was given an opportunity to stand-up, and state his or her position: "I stand for ..."

Many stood for results; others stood for being accountable for personal behaviors. Yet others stood for eliminating organizational barriers and creating a new and better way of doing things. The list was as varied and diverse as the individuals involved. When it came time for the president of the company to stand and proclaim what he stood for, he got up, came almost to a position of military attention, and firmly said, "I stand for people." He said it with conviction. He said it as an absolute.

"I stand for people." I was impressed. More importantly, I was motivated. Motivated to make happen what we had all just pledged our support to doing: to change our organizational culture and drive us to a new level of achievement. We had our leader's pledge of support; what else did we need? A level of achievement that frankly, at the beginning of the session, I thought was unrealistic and unachievable.

During the opening minutes of the session, Mr. Holland had laid out his vision for our company's growth. Perhaps more importantly, he had carefully explained why we needed to go where his vision would take us. The "how" of getting there he did not know yet. But he was clear on the "what" and the "why." As a leader of a breakthrough organization, that is precisely what he needed to define.

No doubt other people in the room had very mixed emotions about the President's message. Realistically speaking, in a room full of people, many of whom are very experienced in business, and who have lived through the ups and downs of corporate fads, there is a high probability that some will look with skepticism as the leader outlines a future that looks and feels so dramatically different than their current reality.

The emotions of those in attendance at the meeting likely ranged from a controlled desire to laugh aloud at the sheer lunacy of the idea, to a fear that the leader was indeed serious. They might have thought that he would drive the organization to ruins trying to reach unattainable and unrealistic objectives. Fear of the objectives he, and the corporate management board had set for the organization: "to be the fastest growing, most inventive medical device company in the world," while at the same time doubling the revenue in just three years. What was he smoking?

How could a company really expect to grow at that alarming rate? Suddenly the term "Breakthrough Thinking" took on a whole new meaning. If we were going to have even a whisper of a prayer at achieving this objective we would need a whole lot of breakthrough thinking.

The purpose and importance of these one-day sessions came into clear focus. We were not there to learn how to think in a breakthrough way. We certainly were not there to figure out exactly how we were going to reach the $4 billion sales objective. That would become the on-going work of many cross-functional and New Business Development teams. We were there to get religion! We were there to hear the message about Breakthrough Thinking as a "way of life;" the new organizational culture. We had been gathered to have an opportunity to share in our leader's vision, and to generate some genuine excitement about our new culture and our new way of thinking. That was a pivotal period for the company.

Not long after that one-day training session—perhaps better referred to as our "indoctrination session"—the company group chairman for our company, Mr. Dennis Longstreet, spoke to the entire organization. His message, like that of Mr. Holland, was crystal clear. We all understood. They wanted $4 billion in sales by the year 2005! It was simply crazy given where we were in 2002. Yet I believed in that very moment it could be done.

In the days and months following the early part of 2002, the organizational culture underwent a transformation. The organization had a new vigor about it; and despite difficult economic and market conditions, the company continued to re-invent itself, adjusting to the changing environment and figuring out ways to remain the number one medical device company in the world, a title it has earned and held longer than most can remember.

Few people would believe that a large organization, in existence for more than seventy-five years, and who is the dominant world leader in market share in its industry, could be so agile. Few could understand the speed at which progress could be made within the same structure that once, not long before then, did not even use computers to run daily manufacturing operations.

In the early 1990s, the powerhouse consulting firm McKinsey predicted that ETHICON would either re-invent itself, or it would suffer the same fate as other giants who had succumbed to the fears of "re-engineering." ETHICON rose to that challenge, and today is a thriving, global business, stronger than ever. However, rather than rest on that success, this company chose to strive for a new level of performance. A breakthrough level!

After they began the revolution of breakthrough thinking at ETHICON, Cliff modeled the behaviors that leaders must exhibit if breakthrough teams are to flourish, and achieve impressive results. Many of the concepts put forth in this book come from observing leaders like him in action, and applying these concepts on a daily basis in my own team. The ideas of what a leader must do to create the right environment for breakthrough to occur are not incredibly sophisticated or complicated. Quite the contrary, the behaviors are elegantly simple, and natural, as we will soon see.

The change in culture was begun in ETHICON soon began to manifest itself in the way people—and therefore some teams—were behaving. Throughout 2002, I had the privilege and great fortune of leading and working with a team of high power, high energy scientist, engineers, marketers, finance experts, and clinical experts to develop a new platform product for the company (See the REDHAND Story section of this book). We embarked on inventing a new product that will ultimately become the standard of care in surgical sutures–an antibacterial suture. Many of the concepts and lessons put forth in this book are based on lessons learned from leading this team. How this team rose to the challenge of developing this product, and launching it to the market in less than one year, was impressive. The team behaved in ways completely consistent with breakthrough thinking, and accepted only success as its ultimate outcome.

No doubt, REDHAND's success is attributable to many factors. Excellent people first and foremost. Strong project and team dynamics management were two other important factors in the team's success. However, probably the overriding key to the level of achievement reached by the team was having an environment, created by breakthrough thinking leaders that allowed our team to quickly pass through the stages of breakthrough thinking.

In essence, creating and maintaining the right environment for the team to indeed breakthrough. Breakthrough what? Breakthrough the organizational barriers, real or perceived, that could stand in the way of team making progress; breakthrough the attitudes that de-motivate teams and the fear that can paralyze individuals. Breakthrough the traditional ways of doing things that lead to predictable, and ever so painfully slow, outcomes.

Thus, this part of the book is ultimately about the leader's role in creating a breakthrough environment in which their team can drive innovation and greater-than-expected results. To do this, the leader must:

1. Understand the drivers of breakthrough thinking

2. Understand the stages of breakthrough thinking, and the leader's role in moving the team members through these stages quickly

3. Understand the required composition of team members in breakthrough teams, and how to use each of them effectively

4. Understand the "Perstorming™" Team Dynamics Model

5. Understand how to harness powerful individuals to unleash powerful teams

6. Understand the true meaning of innovation

As for the breakthrough thinking revolution that Mr. Holland began in ETHICON and its eventual success? It will very much depend on the current and future leaders of the organization. They can choose to either adopt the breakthrough attitude, continuing to create and foster the environment in which the power of the people can be unleashed, or return to a more ordinary way of doing business. The latter would be easier. The former would be better. It will require a sustained commitment to the vision by the leaders, and a relentless passion for accepting no outcome other than success. It will require brave leaders who will choose the harder road.

Breakthrough leadership is an on-going process, and it must be maintained and managed daily. Otherwise, it will indeed become the next management trend to be replaced by the latest and greatest from the management consulting community.

Is leading a truly revolutionary, breakthrough team easy? No, it's not. It takes hard work. It requires a tireless commitment and passion for the vision you are trying to achieve. It thrives only when the leader is able to communicate that passion and vision effectively, and when he or she does their job in creating the right environment as will be discussed in the chapters to follow. However, while applying the ideas put forth in this book may require some hard work, the concepts themselves are not hard, or complex. So don't shy away from the challenge of creating a breakthrough environment and leading breakthrough teams. And never let anyone tell you, it can't be done. They are wrong.

SEVENTEEN

BREAKTHROUGH THINKING DRIVERS

To begin the process of breakthrough thinking in an organization or team, the leader has to first understand six simple, but profound drivers of breakthrough. They are:

- Diversity of Thought
- Awakening
- Learning to partner effectively
- Having a "failure is not an option" attitude
- Ask for the Impossible. Settle for the Improbable
- "Don't sweat the small stuff"
- Use the "third eye"

Let's begin by looking at these individually.

Diversity of Thought

The concept of diversity has been a part of the corporate organizational culture and landscape for more than a decade now. In the early 1990s, many companies began to embrace diversity as a necessary, albeit painful, business process. The overall objective was to drive personal behavioral change that would make the workplace more effective, and therefore a more productive environment. There was a time when managing diversity was the subject of many executive board meetings of the largest and most successful corporations.

I can point to the Office of Diversity and Inclusion at Johnson & Johnson as an example of the commitment made by the J&J Executive Board to the diversity process. They understand that managing diversity is a tool they can use to fuel business growth for the corporation. My good friend Anthony Carter, VP for Diversity & Inclusion at J&J, certainly understands that. So does my friend Raymond Arroyo, who, as the VP of Diversity for Aetna, works to ensure that diversity is not only understood and appreciated, but leveraged as a competitive advantage.

Some would be tempted to point to such commitment by corporations that apply a great deal of resources to managing the process of diversity as trying to avoid legal liability and criticism for not offering equal opportunity to people of different backgrounds, sexual orientation, race, or other differences. I suppose there could be an element of truth to that. However, this author would argue that the benefits to the corporation, and to the individuals, would be positive just for having an emphasis on the process of diversity.

Therefore, rather than look too deeply into the reasons why the corporation is embracing such a process, we ought to look with investigative eyes into the positive outcomes that result. The fact is that companies that embrace diversity in all of its dimensions outperform companies that don't. The data supporting this are clear and readily available.

There are many dimensions of diversity. The obvious ones are race and gender. By far, these two get the most play with our contemporary media and literature when the subject of diversity is discussed. However, clearly, there are other dimensions of diversity such as age, education, religion, sexual orientation, physical handicaps, language, and appearance to name just a few.

Not surprisingly, most of the dimensions of diversity have a negative connotation associated with them. We think of diversity in terms of race, and we may first consider that someone is being discriminated against because of his or her background. When the gender issue is raised, we may first lean towards thinking that women are paid less for similar work, or they don't get the same promotional opportunities as their male counterparts. Similarly, with sexual orientation, age, religion, and physical disabilities, we often associate these dimensions of diversity first with some form of discrimination that an individual may face day in and day out.

This is not a bad thing. After all, it is this level of heightened awareness to the issues, and increased sensitivities that have moved congress to pass laws protecting people against many of the different forms of discrimination based on these differences. It is this level of sensitivity to the business repercussions of not dealing with the issues surrounding diversity that has propelled companies to learn how to manage diversity, rather than ignore it, and use it to benefit their business.

There is one additional dimension of diversity that has nothing but a positive connotation: Diversity of thought! This is a concept that, at its roots, has an overwhelming quality of common sense to it. Think about it for a moment. Doesn't it just make sense to take advantage of the diversity of thought process that is a natural outcome of having people of diverse backgrounds? Isn't it painfully obvious to all that two or three well-developed, thorough, and well thought-out opinions coming from individuals with different backgrounds would be better than to have one opinion shared by all who are of similar thinking? The answer must clearly be yes!

That is what Diversity of Thought is all about. It's about harnessing the power of creative ideas and problem solutions, by managing the process of creating an environment where diverse ideas are sought, recognized, valued, and equally considered. For a breakthrough team, this diversity of thought is a lifeline. Only teams that embrace diversity of thought can ever hope to reach the highest levels of performance and resulting achievement.

What must a leader do in order to create the nurturing environment for diversity of thought to take place? There are several important considerations:

1. Leaders must clearly articulate the need for diversity of thought to the organization or team

2. They must make it clear that all opinions, ideas, and experiences are to be valued and considered by other members of the team

3. They must recruit a diverse team. Ensuring that there is a cross-section of technical expertise and functional areas. The leader must look at other elements of diversity as well, and try as best as possible to increase the mix of people without compromising the integrity of the expertise needed for the job to be successfully completed

4. They must monitor team dynamics during meetings, and look at other forms of communications (such as voice mails and e-mails) to ensure that all team members are participating and included in the process

5. They must reward diversity of thought. Leaders should praise those who recognize it, and reward the team when it reaches a milestone

6. Finally, the leader must re-state the need for and value of diversity of thought

Diversity of thought will not happen by accident. It will flourish when nurtured, encouraged, and expected by the leader of the team.

Awakening

An "awakening" takes place when the leader, through words, actions, or both, inspires his or her followers to action. It offers a vision that, until then, the followers could not see or feel a part of. It is a rally cry to motivate a group of people to do something great. It is a moment, almost frozen in time, when a leader's abstract, and maybe even unrealistic idea, becomes attainable.

Perhaps because of his position in history more than for any other reason, President John F. Kennedy, in his short tenure as president, was able to ignite the fuel in several important moments in our history. In 1960, then-Senator John F. Kennedy challenged students at the University of Michigan to serve their country in the cause for peace by living and working in developing countries.

From that "awakening" came an agency sponsored by the federal government devoted to world peace and friendship. Since then, more than 170,000 volunteers have served in more than 130 nations to work on a variety of issues and projects ranging from health care, education, information technology, government, and environmental preservation. On March 1, 1961, President Kennedy established the Peace Corps, and supported his "awakening" call with action. Today, more than forty years later, the Peace Corps remain a vital and vibrant organization.

A few months later, in a special message to Congress on urgent national needs, delivered on May 25, 1961, President Kennedy said:

> "I therefore ask the Congress, above and beyond the increases I have earlier requested for space activities, to provide the funds which are needed to meet the following national goals: First, I believe that this nation should commit itself to achieving the goal, before the decade is out, of landing a man

on the moon and returning him safely to earth. No single space project in this period will be more impressive to mankind, or more important for the long-range exploration; and none will be so difficult or expensive to accomplish. We propose to accelerate the development of the appropriate lunar spacecraft. We propose to develop alternate liquid and solid fuel boosters, much larger than any now being developed, until certain explorations that are particularly important for one purpose that this nation will never overlook; the survival of the man who first makes this daring flight. But in a very real sense, it will not be one man going to the moon; if we make this judgment affirmatively, it will be an entire nation. For all of us must work to put him there."

Think about that for a moment. In 1960, technology that we now take for granted was not even an imaginary thought in the mind of leading scientists. The laptop computer on which these words are being written, likely has more memory, power and speed than most of the computers that were used in 1969 to accomplish that incredible feat of landing the man on the moon and returning him safely home. The Blackberry phones, which we now take for granted, have more communication capacity than all the computers in NASA had in 1963!

Consider how implausible, not to mention improbable, that idea must have seemed to the engineers and scientists of the day when the words were first uttered by Kennedy. The complexities, the number of unknowns, and the precision required was baffling. They still are today! In the early 1960s we did not have the necessary facilities and people, the plastics and combustible fuel technologies required, and computers where in the infancy stages of development. All of these would have to be "invented" before we could put a man on the moon.

Yet by his words, Kennedy ignited the fuse that would ultimately lead Neil Armstrong on July 20, 1969 to utter the words that a nation had waited almost a decade to hear: "That's one small step for man, one giant leap for mankind."

Breakthrough thinking requires leaders to drive an "awakening." Leaders must first have a clear vision. Next they must forcefully believe in it, be passionate about it, and be committed to its outcome. Finally, they must communicate it in an invigorating way, making the possibility of that vision seem not only attainable, but also worthy of the effort to pursue it. This country was first, and the only one to land a man on the moon because one man dared to challenge a nation to make it happen. Breakthrough leaders have the courage to imagine a future and a result that make others shudder at the thought.

There is an old Chinese proverb that goes like this:

> "Let the man that says it can't be done be silent, less he disturbs the man that is already doing it."

That's the way breakthrough leaders think, and they passionately communicate their vision in a way that creates "the awakening."

"Failure is not an option"

On April 11, 1970, at 2:13 p.m., under clear blue skies, Apollo 13 was launched under the command of James Lovell. Jack Swigert and Fred Haise were the other two astronauts onboard the spaceship. Liftoff was flawless. They entered earth's orbit at 2:25 p.m. and set a course towards the moon shortly thereafter.

The first two days of the journey were uneventful, until April 13 at 10:07:53 p.m., when Swigert gave the Oxygen tanks "a stir" according to directions he had received from the control center in Houston, Texas. There was a large bang, and in a matter of seconds things went from being routine to being a life and death emergency.

The loud blast the astronauts heard was the explosion of liquid oxygen tank number two in the service module. This tank provided the vital oxygen used by fuel cells that were Apollo's primary source of power. It was then when Commander Lovell spoke those now famous words:

"Houston we had a problem." (In the movie *Apollo 13*, Hollywood changed the word "had" to "have," I suppose for dramatic effect.)

With the space ship more than 200,000 nautical miles away from earth and a service module without its main propulsion engine, the crew was certainly in a dire situation. The explosion had disabled the module's main supply of life-sustaining oxygen and power. The crew would have to rely on the lunar module, a spaceship designed to separate from the control module, land two astronauts on the moon, then carry them back to the ship which would be waiting in lunar orbit. It was not designed to be used by three astronauts as a lifeboat. But that's what it was quickly turning into. Now, the mother ship was a wreck, drifting aimlessly. For the next three days (eighty-six hours and fifty seven minutes to be precise), this crew, and the scientist and engineers on earth, would work to bring them back alive.

As if the problems that had been caused by the explosion of the oxygen tank were not enough, there were several other problems that occurred during those eighty plus hours that only decreased the chances that these three men would survive. In fact, some of the problems started even before the launch, when one of the prime crewmembers, Lt. Commander Ken Mattingly was exposed to German measles a few days before the launch. Swigert replaced him. One of the most significant problems facing the crew as they worked to return safely to Earth was how to get them back before they ran out of the oxygen they had remaining. They also needed to worry about their trajectory and firing their engines in order to make minor course corrections that would normally be done by the computer rather than manually.

The accident was surely keeping Mission Control, and all the experts on the ground, working in simulators and on their computers for most of those three days. The astronauts were forced to shut down the systems in the Control Module in order to conserve energy that would be needed during the last stages of the return flight home. So, the Control Module was set to 38 degrees Fahrenheit. This cold made it difficult for the crew to rest, and surely added to their fatigue.

Each of these, and countless of other problems, gave the crew and the folks in mission control sufficient work to keep them awake for three days. The solution that was invented when one particular problem surfaced, probably better than any other, indicated the level of breakthrough thinking that was going on with this NASA team.

As carbon dioxide levels were rising in the control module, the atmosphere in the closed space was slowly becoming toxic, and left unchecked would have surely led to the astronauts' death. Under normal circumstances, the carbon dioxide was scrubbed by a lithium hydroxide filter. The Lunar Module's canister system overloaded and the carbon dioxide in the small space was rising quickly. The lunar module that the astronauts were using as a lifeboat was not designed to host three men for an extended period of time. Thus the carbon dioxide filter began to fail. Ironically, there was another filter available. It was the filter used in the service module. However, one had been designed to be round, the other was square!

Mission control engineers studied the problem, and instructed the astronauts to create an adapter that would attach a hose to the lithium hydroxide canister in the Control Module so they could purify the air. The rigged filter in essence made a round peg fit a square hole. Within an hour of installing the make-shift filter, the carbon dioxide levels had dropped sharply, and the men cheated death again. Ingenuity and breakthrough thinking at its best!

In his book, *Where No One Has Gone Before: A History of Apollo Lunar Exploration Missions*, W. David Compton wrote:

"By a matchless display of tenacity, resourcefulness, ingenuity, and courage, a determined group of men at Mission Control working closely with a cool, expert crew averted catastrophe and brought the astronauts through a brush with death.

As an aborted mission, Apollo 13 must officially be classified as a failure, the first in 22 manned flights. But, in another sense, as a brilliant demonstration of the human spirit triumphing under almost unbearable stress, it is the most successful failure in the annals of space flight."

What can this "successful failure" be attributed to? The answer is: to many things! It can be attributed to the ingenuity of the engineers and scientist who solved problem after problem to give the crew a fighting chance to return unharmed. It can be attributed to the ship's designers who built a spacecraft that was able to survive this ordeal. Credit surely goes to the astronauts, their expertise, their level-headed actions, and their courage. But there is one other action, a leader's action that in my opinion had everything to do with making this safe return to earth possible. It happened shortly after the emergency began, when the engineers were assembled together by Gene Kranse, the Director of Flight Operations.

As the team began to brainstorm ideas on how to return the crew safely, there was a great deal of disagreement among the team members. No doubt the arguments that ensued must have been heated. But during a critical moment when the team seemed to be concluding that the situation was hopeless, and that bringing the crew back alive was a long shot at best, Gene Kranse uttered what may be the most important words he has ever spoken during his entire life. He told the team "failure is not an option."

With those five words, Kranse sealed the fate of Jim Lovell, Jack Swigert, and Fred Haise. They were coming home. Period. No choice. No arguments. Just make it happen! After all, if failure is not an option, what is the only possible outcome? Success! He took away every excuse that individuals could come-up with. As the leader, he set the bar for what would be acceptable. He would accept nothing less.

Imagine what would have happened if he had said, "Well guys, let's give it the best try we can," or "Give it your best shot." Words such as those allow for the possibility of failure, and in this case failure meant death for three people, and perhaps for the entire space program.

It was Gene Kranse's attitude, and the expectation he set for the team early on during the crisis that set the tone for this group of people to achieve what surely must have seemed impossible.

"Failure is not an option." That is the attitude of a Breakthrough Thinking leader.

Ask For the Impossible...Settle for the Improbable

We don't always know what we are capable of until someone demands something great from us. At times, the best comes out when we are under pressure, or we feel that we must deliver what has been demanded of us. That's why coaches push their players so hard. It's that push that motivates the team players to strive to achieve more than they ever thought possible.

I recall one day, during one of the REDHAND Team meetings, I set out an objective that got "the look." I am not sure what I was asking for, but no doubt it must have been outlandish! There was a short silence in the room, and then Dr. Tom Barbolt said, "Tony, the improbable we can do right away. The impossible is going to take a little time."

I smiled at Tom and said, "Tom, I ask for the impossible, but I'll settle for the improbable."

It became our team's motto: "Ask for the impossible, but settle for the improbable."

The story of United States Navy Master Chief Carl Brashear is a fantastic example of what a person can achieve when motivated by high demands placed on them. In his case, it was Master Chief Brashear's father's high expectations of him that drove Brashear to achieve all he did.

Carl Brashear grew up on a farm in Kentucky, a member of a poor sharecropper's family. He was educated in a small segregated school. He enlisted in the Navy in 1948. After his initial duty as a steward, he began handling aircraft for a squadron in Key West, Florida. As time went on he became interested in deep-sea salvage diving. He applied and graduated from the Navy's Deep Sea Diving School, despite significant hardship stemming primarily from the fact that he was a black man.

While serving on the USS Hoist in 1966, during a recovery operation searching for a nuclear weapon off the coast of Spain, Brashear was badly injured and surgeons amputated his left leg below the knee. He refused to retire, insisting on serving after he was able to demonstrate that he could still dive and perform his additional duties. In 1970, he qualified as the first black master diver in the history of the U.S. Navy. Master Chief Brashear overcame many obstacles throughout his life to achieve numerous significant accomplishments. He asked for the impossible and settled for the improbable!

Breakthrough Team Leaders need to ask their teams for the impossible, realizing that they may need to settle for the improbable. The improbable is always more than anyone would have thought possible in the first place!

"Don't sweat the small stuff"

One of the biggest thieves of energy, motivation, and time for any team is spending too much time worrying about the "small stuff." We can define this small stuff as certain details, tasks, or situations that, when put in the context of the "big picture," would be rather insignificant.

Perhaps one of the best analogies that I can think of as it relates to dealing with the "small stuff" is how maintenance issues are dealt with in aircrafts. My father spent many years as a crew chief in aircraft maintenance. I asked him to define for me how maintenance items on aircrafts were categorized and resolved.

As you would expect, there is a manual for everything in aircraft maintenance, a book that explains how to deal with every indicator light that may come-on in the cockpit. A white light is usually used just to relay some information. A green light indicates the system is working properly. An amber light indicates a problem that needs to be looked into, but does not require immediate attention. It can also represent something that is transient. That is, an amber light may indicate a system that is cycling either on its way to green, or on its way to red. A red light, as one would expect, indicates a system failure. A red indicator light requires immediate attention and action. There are other indicators such as horns, computer generated voices that provide the pilots mission critical information to keep the aircraft flying safely. These systems are often redundant.

There are also systems on the aircraft that do not warrant an indication light. The coffee maker may be one example of this. Not having an operational coffee maker on-board the aircraft, while devastating to those of us who must have a cup of java in order to function in the morning, is not mission critical to the safe operation of the aircraft. Moreover, not having a functioning coffee maker would certainly not ground the airplane. In fact, the maintenance crew chief would put his or her team's resources to address any and all other mission critical maintenance items before expending any of the team's time addressing the coffee maker. That's because they are not "sweating the small stuff." It's simply not important enough!

The coffee maker, like a passenger seat that does not recline, or an in-operational lavatory (if there are others on-board working, or if the flight is relatively short in duration), an in-operational audiovisual system (stereo or TV), or other aircraft creature comforts, would all be considered "small stuff."

The small stuff can have an urgent feeling about it. This is especially true if the leader reacts in a way that sends the signal that something is not quite right. It could be the leader's excitement, tone of voice, or body language that sends the message, but the team perceives the urgency of the matter, and they jump to action to try to overcome whatever the issue is. Often, they do this at the expense of focusing on what is truly important. As the leader sets the tone for the team, how he or she reacts to a situation will either keep the team focused, or send them into a tailspin chasing solutions that may not be critical at that moment. Therefore, it is important for leaders to be very discerning as to what really requires a heightened level of energetic response from them to move the team to action.

The reality that every breakthrough team will face is that "stuff will happen"; and it will not always be good stuff. I recall a period of a few months while we were working on project REDHAND when nothing was going wrong. Everything, and I do mean everything, was going our way. Every experiment was giving us great results, the clinical papers were being written, the regulatory issues were all being properly addressed, manufacturing plans were in place, and validations were progressing on schedule. The team was making huge leaps forward against the Gantt chart.

It was an uncomfortable feeling for me as the team leader. What were we missing? How could everything be perfect? I have been involved in enough projects, particularly engineering projects, throughout my career to know that when you least expect it, something unexpected will happen.

Murphy's Law states that "whatever can go wrong will go wrong at the worst possible time." It's not myth; just ask any engineer and they will tell you they have been the victim of Murphy's Law at some point in their career! It gives us a healthy dose of reality to keep that in mind. So, Howard Scalzo, my R&D counterpart, and I sat one morning and tried to come up with a list of what we could be missing. We did this quietly. We did not call a team meeting, or involve anyone else. There was no need to alarm the team. They were focusing on all the right things, and nothing was more important than that.

Howard and I looked for the proverbial monkey holding the wrench just waiting to toss it into the works. We brainstormed several scenarios of what could go wrong, and what we would do about it if it did. We figured that while we could not think of every possible scenario, we would likely catch most of them. And if they did not make it to our list, it was probably because they were too "small to worry about." This proactive activity gave us a sense of security and a contingency plan that would help us manage situations that would arise without falling into the trap of sweating the "small stuff."

One final thing about the "small stuff": just because it may be considered "small stuff" does not mean that it may not be important. After all, breakthrough teams should only be working on things that are important. However, small stuff must be properly managed and delegated to the right persons in the team because unattended "small things" can grow into attention getting monsters.

Use the "third eye"

There are three important things the leader of a breakthrough team must keep a close eye on: the team's vision, process, and people.

First, the leader must keep an eagle eye on his or her vision. In the absence of that focus, it will be profoundly difficult for the leader to act in ways consistent with the vision, and even harder to keep the team focused on it. Second, the leader must keep an eye on the team's process. How effectively is the team dealing with all the stages that teams naturally go through? Keep in mind that every team goes through team stages and that stages repeat as dynamics and circumstances, milestones, and other issues are faced by the team. Therefore, the leader must be on guard to ensure that the team is healthy as it runs through the normal life cycle. Finally, the leader must use their "third eye" to watch over his or her people. The leader must make sure that every member of the team is engaged, motivated, energized, and feeling like they are valued members of the team. Too often leaders overlook this very important task.

EIGHTEEN

STAGES OF BREAKTHROUGH THINKING

It has often been said that the limit of what we can accomplish is our imagination. Yet, considering the billions of people who have lived since time began, the number of truly innovative and revolutionary ideas that have led to a new technology or a new way of doing something are remarkably few. That may be because the number of people who are natural breakthrough thinkers is equally remarkably few. It is simply not the way most people think. Rather, most people live in a world of limitations.

Many of these limitations are self-imposed. Our society, families, friends, or other socio-economic factors ingrain some of these limitations in us. Despite these limitations, individuals manage to transcend them, and go on to achieve great things; people like Albert Einstein, Thomas Edison, Henry Ford, Marie Currie, Benjamin Franklin, Dean Kamen, Michael Dell, and Bill Gates, just to name a few.

The challenge is to get ordinary people to realize that they have untapped extraordinary talent, lurking just beneath their limiting skepticism. If a leader could tap into the imagination of his or her followers, and inspire them to believe that what they currently believe is impossible can indeed become possible, then success is inevitable. I believe that there is a natural process that most people go through on their way to becoming breakthrough thinkers. The leader of breakthrough teams should be aware of these, and work hard to move his or her people quickly through them.

Disbelief: "What are you smoking?"

The first reaction of most people when they are exposed to what at first seems like a crazy idea is disbelief. First, people may have a hard time believing that the leader is even suggesting the possibility of something that crazy. They may think to themselves that this is evidence of just how disconnected this leader is with reality. Such was the case when the CEO of a major corporation suggested that the company was going to double in revenue in just three years, from $2 to $4 billion. The first thing many of us thought was "what is this guy smoking?" Surely he must be crazy! Immediately we start to think about everything that could prevent that from happening. Everything from organizational culture, shortage of resources, and the existing market conditions just to name a few.

Using the example of President Kennedy, and his challenge that we land a man on the moon, imagine the reaction of many experts who heard him make his remarks for the first time. What might have been their reaction? Some, no doubt, immediately dismissed the idea as political rhetoric by a young, inexperienced president. After all, the technology and the precision required to pull off such a stunt didn't even exist at the time. In light of all that would need to be overcome, those same skeptics likely did the mental math to compute what they thought the probabilities of actually doing it could be. Certainly, the odds would have seemed to be stacked against the possibility of making this dream a reality.

Not believing that something is possible is the easiest of alternatives. When a person thinks something is impossible, they don't even try to make it happen. Why would they? After all, it's impossible! Rather than spending any energy in trying to figure out the best way to make something happen, these individuals spend their mental energy convincing themselves, and others, that "it" can't be done.

There are several important aspects of this stage in breakthrough thinking that a leader must be aware of.

First, it is natural for people to, at first, have a feeling of disbelief. Thus as leaders we should expect that people are going to have this reaction to our vision. In fact if there is no reaction of disbelief it may be that our vision is not enough of a stretch or a challenge for the team to achieve.

Second, the leader must understand that of all of the stages of breakthrough thinking that we will describe in this chapter, this is the most debilitating for their vision to be accomplished in a timely fashion. As long as those who will follow believe that the vision is impossible, nothing will happen. In fact, the longer some have this feeling of disbelief, the longer they will share that with others, and perhaps poison the thought process of others who would have been more willing to move forward faster.

Thus, the leader's most important task is to move individuals quickly from this stage of disbelief to the next one. In order to do this, the leader should:

1. Have a very clear vision and be able to articulate it without hesitation

2. Remain on message each and every time that there is an opportunity to speak to the followers about the vision

3. Recruit individuals who are "early adopters" or risk takers. These are individuals who like a challenge, and who will help the leader recruit and convince others

4. Spend as much time as possible, one-on-one, with key

stakeholders in the process. These are individuals who would play a key role in moving the leader's agenda forward

Consideration: "Okay, I'll keep an open mind"

Once the leader is able to overcome the initial shock and disbelief of those he or she is trying to influence and solicit to join in on their vision, they have entered the "consideration" stage. This is where individuals, having heard a well-articulated and detailed vision, and having heard some compelling reasons why this vision would be a good objective to accomplish, decide that they are going to "keep an open mind" about what is being proposed.

This is an important victory for the leader. They have managed to move the person, or persons, from a position of disbelief where no progress could ever be made, to a place where at least they are willing to consider the possibility. Here's what the leader must now do to move them to the next step:

1. Continue to communicate the vision clearly

2. Remain focused on message

3. Encourage them to think about what it would be like when the goal is successfully completed

4. Be ready for the person or persons to conclude that their first instinct was indeed correct and that they really don't believe what the leader is asking can be achieved

Skepticism: "You are smoking … this will not work!"

Even after the leader has done a good job of communicating the vision, and even after some of the team members have initially, albeit cautiously, bought into the idea, they may have a moment of regression. It may be that after carefully considering the leader's challenge to the team and goal he or she has set, they shake their head and sincerely believe that the leader must be completely disconnected with reality. This is a critical stage in a breakthrough team. The leader will either successfully navigate the followers through this or risk a self-defeating attitude that will permeate from one team member to the next.

To successful move the team through the Skepticism phase, a leader should:

1. Remain firm in their conviction about the goal and vision

2. Ensure that the team has outlined a top-level plan of action that will provide a strategic road map. This will add a frame around what may otherwise be a vague concept or idea

3. Challenge key members of the team, especially those who may be most skeptics, to imagine the possibility. Have them outline what they think would be the necessary plan of action to make it happen. The idea here is simple: if they can devise a plan of action to accomplish the vision, regardless of the plan that they come-up with, they will be developing a road map for something that they just before thought was impossible. The very plan they develop may disprove their belief and help them overcome their skepticism

4. Finally, the leader must not allow the team to dwell on this stage and move them forward via assignments and action driven milestones. It is entirely possible that the small victories that the team will win by doing that will provide the very evidence they need to really move past this stage and move into the next: Illumination

Illumination = Gut Feeling + Data

Most people have a sixth sense that they use from time to time. It's that ability to simply "feel" something intangible. We call it a "gut feeling." We use our gut feelings to make decisions about everything from which way to go when we reach a fork in the road, to trying to predict the next upturn in the stock market. But, taken in a vacuum, gut feelings can be unreliable. However, when they are supported by some data or experience in similar situations, the accuracy of actions taken as a result of gut feelings can be dramatically improved.

The breakthrough leader relies heavily on his or her gut feeling, and the gut feeling of his or her team members. The leader will want to call on that gut feeling and encourage others to do the same, to help them crystallize the possibility of success as it relates to the vision set for the team. Combined with supporting evidence, even if it is only preliminary in nature, it will lead to a moment of illumination; the very instant during which some of the mystery over the outcome is unveiled.

Consider the fork in the road again. If you reach the fork in the road and are uncertain what to do, your gut may tell you to go left. Just then, your passenger says, "I recognize that church on the corner. I think we need to go left." That bit of data, combined with your gut feeling, convinces you on the course of action to take. The illumination stage leaves the team with that "maybe this is possible after all" feeling.

The light goes on

This next stage in breakthrough thinking teams may be one of the most rewarding. It is the moment when people come to the conclusion that, "Wow, this will work!" We've all had that feeling of revelation, when something we did not understand before suddenly becomes clear. You can see it in the face of a child when they first understand that pressing a certain button—not just any button—in the remote control makes the television set come on. You can also see it in the expression of a student when they first grasp the application, not just the concept, of what, until then, was only a complex mathematical theory in a textbook. That sense of discovery fascinates and motivates people.

The breakthrough-thinking leader strives to get his or her team to truly understand the vision. Not just in theory, but in application. What will the world look like when the goal is accomplished? How will the team member's environment be different from what it is now once they achieve the expected outcome? Why is this important? When these questions are answered for the team members, the "light will go on," and they will not only understand, but they will become committed believers!

Buy-In: "I believe! I'm in. I am committed"

As a leader, you will have no trouble knowing if your people have reached this stage. You will see it in their eyes, you will hear it in their voices, and you will certainly see it in their actions. Celebrate when you get there, but until then, the leader must recognize his or her role to convince the team that the direction they have charted, and the course they want to navigate, is the right one. Communication and consistent behavior indicating belief in the vision is the key to the leader's success in getting the team and individuals to "buy in."

Fear

Franklin Roosevelt once said, "We have nothing to fear, but fear itself." How true that statement is! As a leader, he understood the paralyzing effects that fear could have on a nation. At some point, probably sooner rather than later, all leaders will have to deal with the fear factor. That's when individuals in the team will focus on the possibility of failure, and the repercussions to them individually and collectively in the event of that failure.

Fear has a detrimental effect on teams, and the leader must confront the issue directly and swiftly. Fear will also lead people to become risk adverse. Frederick Wilcox's quote says it best: "Progress always involves risk; you can't steal second base and keep your foot on first base." Indulging the baseball analogy, this quote captures the nature of risk. If you do some research, you will find that some of the greatest base stealers in the history of baseball also share another interesting statistic. They have all been thrown out trying to steal a base more often than most other players. That's the price for trying to steal second base often.

Similarly, if you look at the greatest home run hitters like Babe Ruth, Hank Aaron, Ken Griffey, Jr., and Sammy Sosa, you will note that they share the distinction of also being among players who have struck out most often while at bat. You simply cannot swing that hard all the time without missing some of the time! That's the penalty for the risk they take. Risk has rewards but it also has a downside. That downside is what people are afraid of experiencing. And it is that downside that breakthrough leaders must help their teams overcome.

To overcome the fear factor leaders must:

1. Reassure the team that they (the leader) will be accountable for the team's results. Committing to them that he or she will be concerned with the best interest of each individual and of the team as a whole

2. Let them know that they will fight for necessary resources to ensure the team's success

3. Pledge to them that they will communicate openly and proactively as to how the team is doing, how it is being perceived, and what can be done to improve areas that may need to be improved

4. Instill a "you go, we go attitude." That is, remind them

that the team's success is dependent on all members working together to drive the desired results

5. Remind them of your "failure is not an option" mentality

6. Finally, the leader, now more than ever, must remain firm in their commitment to the vision. They must portray an unwavering confidence that will overwhelm the fear factor

One more thing on fear: it can happen often through the life cycle of the team. New milestones or upcoming deadlines can renew a sense of fear in individuals in the team. Interim or short-term failures along the way can also have that effect.

On the REDHAND team, we had a saying that we used very often: "If you are not scared, you don't understand." To those of us on the team that meant that there was always a certain element of healthy fear. In fact, if you really understood the number of activities on-going at any one moment in the project and if you had a good idea of the risks that we were taking on a daily basis, you had to be a bit scared. Fear is a natural emotion and one that, with continued support from the leader, can be overcome relatively quickly.

The stages of breakthrough thinking are nothing more than the normal range of emotions that most people will go through on their way to greatness. The leader's role during this critical phase of creating a breakthrough-thinking team is to move team members—and to a certain extent, those around the team who will need to support it—through these stages as quickly as possible.

How should a leader do this? First, and always, have a crystal clear, non-wavering vision and purpose. Second, be like a broken record repeating your message often and being consistent and persistent in the message. Third, accept no naysayers. Fourth, encourage people to consider the possibility and visualize what success would look and feel like. Finally, challenge them to "make it happen."

NINETEEN

CAST OF CHARACTERS IN BREAKTHROUGH TEAMS

The cast of characters needed to have true breakthrough teams is a diverse one. As will be described next, the personalities, likes and dislikes, and work styles are uniquely different. The leader must clearly understand each of the styles in the cast so that they can best manage the team, and so that he or she can bring out the best in each of the individuals.

Moreover, the leader will want to ensure that they have the proper number of each style of personality on the team to ensure balance and to effectively move the team forward towards the stated breakthrough objective. This is likely one of the most important roles the leader will play throughout the life of the team. Effectively aligning, directing, and motivating each member individually (and collectively as a team) will no doubt play a pivotal part in whatever success the team will enjoy.

While individual's styles in teams will tend to align more closely to one type over another, it is entirely possible—likely in fact—that some members will at times play more than one role in the team. It can depend on the stage in which the team finds itself at the time, the tasks at hand, and several other internal and external pressures that can change the dynamics within a team. For instance, a person who has one dominant personality style under normal, non-stressful times may become easily agitated and frustrated when under stress. Another person may exhibit the opposite reaction to stress—becoming subdued or very calm during times when others are panicking around them.

While leading the REDHAND Team, several important patterns and team member styles became evident. Over time, what also became clear were the behaviors that each of these team members exhibited, and what the pros and cons of these behaviors were. If the leader understands and utilizes these people effectively, their chances of driving breakthrough results are enormously increased.

The "Gentle Rottweiler"

Rottweilers have a reputation for being somewhat vicious and extremely persistent dogs. It is said that once they bite down on something, getting them to release it takes a Herculean effort. Their powerful jaws can do some major damage to whatever they clamp down on. In a Breakthrough Team, you need to have at least one "Gentle Rottweiler."

A Gentle Rottweiler is someone who is extremely persistent. Once they are aligned and motivated on a task, they pursue all necessary steps until the job is done to their very high standard. Some may refer to these individuals as somewhat anal-retentive. If they understand what needs to be done, you can count on this individual to keep true to whatever process is defined for completing the task.

A prime example of a Gentle Rottweiler is the project manager of a team. What you need most in a person in that role are the following traits:

- Persistent
- Focused
- Organized
- Logical thinker
- Very process oriented
- Clear and single-minded about what the objective is

In the REDHAND team, we had a fantastic Gentle Rottweiler. He was our Gantt Chart Guru. Mark ran our meetings, and kept each team member on task every time. He was forceful about our process. He ran a tight ship! He ensured that our team lived by what we fondly referred to as "Mark's Critical Path." One thing was sure, no team member wanted to be in the "critical path." Whoever that person was could rest assured that they would be at the receiving end of persistent e-mails, voice mails, and even personal visits from Mark, asking for updates on the deliverable that would take that particular task off the critical path. Once Mark bit down, he would not let go. In all of his persistence and with all of the fervor that Mark pursued his intended target, he never drew blood when he bit down. He simply hung on until the job was done. We used this approach effectively, and even with humor, in our team to move the project forward. Without our Gentle Rottweiler, our team would not have been successful.

In summary, the "Gentle Rottweiler":

- Bites down but does not draw blood
- Will not let go
- Project management is "their thing"
- To this person "no" is an insult

Pros of a the "Gentle Rottweiler":

- Keeps the team on track
- Strong process and facilitation skills

Cons of a "Gentle Rottweiler":

- Can drive some team members crazy
- Can be a bit stubborn and overzealous

Every Breakthrough Team needs to have a very strong, proactive, and effective Gentle Rottweiler. And every team leader needs to understand how to utilize them effectively.

To utilize the "Gentle Rottweiler" effectively the leader must:

- Support them by keeping the team on process
- Run interference for them when they are unable to get another team member to deliver on the critical path item on a timely manner
- Work closely with them, and get them to back-off when necessary

The Logical Skeptic

A healthy dose of skepticism is a good thing. Like the old saying goes "if something sounds too good to be true, it probably is." In other words, a reasonable person makes judgments as to how reasonable an idea or proposition is or isn't. Only the most gullible persons would not exhibit a bit of skepticism. Well managed, that skepticism will help to create just enough doubt to cause most people to reassess their current thinking.

In a breakthrough team, having one or two "logical skeptics" is very important. These are individuals that have more skeptic bones in their bodies than most other team members. It may be simply in their nature to question things more than usual. Sometimes, those more skeptical are individuals with greater experience. Perhaps they've been around long enough to see many projects come and go, and have learned what has worked in the past and what has not. This experience may have given them a certain discernment that their less experience colleagues on the team may not yet have. But this same discernment may prove to be a roadblock for these individuals to consider a new approach as the team's next course of action.

Logical skeptics are not obstructionist! In fact, they are no less dedicated to the team's mission than anyone else; perhaps even more so. Their intentions are positive, even though their skepticism may lead them to often question ideas and predicted outcomes. They may especially question the more aggressive short-term objectives that the team has set. One important trait about the "Logical Skeptic" is that they are not stubborn and they are open to discussing logical and well thought out approaches to solve problems.

In summary, the "Logical Skeptic":

- Usually questions predicted outcomes
- Is open to being convinced (they are not stubborn)
- Is firmly committed to the team's goals
- Is cautious about team promises made

Pros of a the "Logical Skeptic":

- Keeps the team honest with decisions and approaches taken
- They usually have a great deal of experience

Cons of a "Logical Skeptic":

- Can slow the process if not managed well
- May use lessons learned from previous work as reasons not try something, as opposed to using that experience to develop alternative course of action

To utilize the "Logical Skeptic" effectively the leader must:

- Allow the person to air their thoughts
- Ask them to provide alternatives that would alleviate whatever concerns they have
- Continue to challenge them with the team's overall mission and objectives
- Solicit their support and appeal to their experience
- Ensure that they don't become a roadblock to the team's progress

The Persistent Tackler

When I was first considering what to call this next cast member, the name "Radar" came to mind. In the syndicated show *Mash*, Radar O'Reilly was the name of the company clerk who could scrounge anything that was needed. Not only could he find anything that the unit needed, he had all the necessary contacts with other units, and even the local farmers, to barter for what was required.

Radar also had an uncanny ability to know what those around him needed even before they did. One of the most lovable qualities of this character was his ability to finish his Company Commander Lieutenant Colonel Blake's sentences for him. Once again indicating that he was always ahead of what was needed. These qualities are only some of what is needed in a breakthrough team.

In a breakthrough team, the Persistent Tackler is someone that does much more than simply helps "find" resources required by the team. They go after obstacles with a passion, removing them from the team's path. They can identify those obstacles, and more importantly have the networks necessary to work behind the scenes to overcome these.

The Persistent Tackler is zealous about his or her team, and is firmly committed to the objectives. This person is unfamiliar with the term can't. They define what we all mean by "can-do attitude." The most effective tacklers are those who are so in-tune with the team's day-to-day activities that they can predict needs before they occur. Every breakthrough team needs at least one good Persistent Tackler!

In summary, the "Persistent Tackler":

- Removes obstacles
- Not just a "go to person," but a definite "go at" person
- Has a "don't mess with my team" mentality
- Can scrounge anything
- Is firmly committed to the team's goals

Pros of the "Persistent Tackler":

- Clears the way for the team to make quick progress
- Has a strong organizational network
- Is usually well-respected and liked by others in the organization

Cons of a "Persistent Tackler":

- Can be perceived as overbearing

To utilize "Persistent Tackler" effectively the leader must:

- Make sure that they are very clear on the team's short-term and long-term objectives
- Keep them informed of changes happening on the critical path of the project
- Ensure that they do not violate company procedures and policies in their zeal to get the job done
- Thank them often for their creativity and proactive work

The Intellectual Doer

In every organization there are some people about whom everyone says, "I wish I had ten more like them!" These are individuals who know what they are doing, are self-motivated, usually have a strong network within the organization, and have a positive can-do attitude. We refer to these individuals as "Intellectual Doers." Breakthrough teams need to have a bunch of Intellectual Doers. In fact, everyone on the team needs to be an Intellectual Doer! The difference between an Intellectual Doer and just a doer is initiative.

A doer is someone who does what he or she is told. Once they accomplish the task or tasks assigned, they wait until further instructions are received before doing anything else. Whether they are uncertain as to what they need to do, or because they rather not take the initiative to take the next step, they will simply wait for the next task to be assigned.

I am reminded of an observation I made during a hot summer day some years ago when a crew of six people were working on a landscape project in my home. One man was clearly in charge. He gave the orders and the others executed them. One afternoon, I was looking out the window and noticed that all the men were standing around it seemed to me, looking rather aimless. I wondered if all was okay so I went out to the deck and asked if anything was wrong. One of the men looked up, squinted as the bright sun light hit his eyes, and casually said, "Nah, we're just waiting for the boss to tell us what to do next." All I could do was think to myself: thank God I was not paying by the hour.

Ironically, pinned beneath one of about twenty-five boulders that were to be a part of the landscape design was a detailed, color-coded landscape drawing that clearly spelled out what the design of the area was to look like. The crew could have simply followed the drawing, moved every boulder and every plant that was to be planted to its proper place in anticipation of their boss arriving to tell them exactly what to do. When the foreman arrived, he lifted the boulder pinning the design drawing, studied it for a few moments, and began to instruct each of the other men in the crew on what to do with each plant and rock.

Why not take the initiative and do it? I wondered. One obvious reason would be they did not want to run the risk of moving the heavy rocks to the wrong place and then having to move them again. Another reason could be that the boss's style was very dictatorial and they had learned not to move a muscle without being instructed. Whatever the case, they were taking no chances! The job got done, but no doubt it took longer than it needed to. I may not have been paying by the hour but that foreman was. Either because of his poor leadership style or his crew's unwillingness to take a risk (or both) it cost him time. Time in the landscape business, as in any other business, is money.

Taking initiative means taking some risks. The risk is that whatever action they take will be the wrong one. Too many people are unwilling to take on that risk. "It's not my job" is their motto. But for a breakthrough team to be successful, it needs to have team members who are not only willing to take risks but are happy to do so. Intellectual doers, once they understand and have bought into the leader's vision, use their best judgment and expertise to make things happen. Going above and beyond what is expected of them, they anticipate what needs to happen next, determine how they can best tackle a task, and go to it. Going back to my landscape crew for a moment, what the foreman needed was a few intellectual doers; a few guys willing to pick-up that drawing (i.e. the vision!), understand it, and execute the plan.

In summary, the "Intellectual Doer":

- They just don't do stuff... they think of the right stuff to do and do it too!
- Are keenly aware of the team's vision and how they can support it
- Are self directed and motivated
- Are willing to take a risk

Pros of a the "Intellectual Doer":

- Can do attitude
- Decisive
- Creative problem solvers

Cons of a "Intellectual Doer":

- None!

To utilize the "Intellectual Doer" effectively the leader must:

- Make sure that they (the intellectual doer) understand the team's vision
- Ensure that they are well tuned to the tactical objectives and milestones that need to be accomplished
- After that, you may ask them if they take cream and sugar with their coffee as you fetch it for them, but other than that stay out of their way!

The Committed Critic

Often times the role of "Committed Critic" falls to the Quality Assurance Engineer (QAE). This is particularly true in projects governed by FDA regulations. The QAE often plays the role of cop for the team. Making sure that every necessary test is conducted, that the proper validations are planned and executed, that the data is interpreted and justified in such a way that it can pass the scrutiny of even the most discerning inspector.

QAEs have a tough job! Generally, they are not the most popular people in an organization. As a former Director of Engineering, and having once managed a large manufacturing business unit in an FDA-regulated industry, I for one am a huge fan of these individuals. I saw their job as paramount to keeping our teams on the straight and narrow path of compliance with all regulations and requirements.

Having lived through a number of FDA audits, it can be a pleasant experience when you have all your documentation in order, your validations and equipment records are immaculate, and you can demonstrate beyond any doubt the efficacy of your processes to manufacture a medical device. Others less fortunate have discovered the pain of the converse being the case.

I expect my QAE to be anal about his or her job. I want them to be picky with all aspects of what the team is doing. I need them to make sure that what is being done is reflective of good developmental and engineering practices. But left to their whims, the QAE can at times become a roadblock to progress. Others in the team can perceive them as always negative and trying to find fault in everything. They can seem unreasonable and unyielding; stubborn in fact. However, their role cannot be underestimated. It is one of the keys to the success of the team. Like the old saying goes: "You never have time to do it right the first time, but you always have time to do it again."

A good QAE can help a team not have to repeat activities over and over again. Every team needs a great QAE. Anyone reading this who does not work in the engineering or manufacturing areas, where there may be no QAEs, would be tempted to think that this section does not apply to their world. Think again!

Every industry, and every team, needs a person who fills the role of police officer. An independent observer of sorts, whose mission in life is to make sure that the team is working according to whatever rules govern the industry or area that the group is working in. This person sees their job as helping the team to avoid catastrophic and costly mistakes. If there is no one filling that role, get one.

There is one important difference between a "committed critic" and just a "critic." The word *committed* indicates that the person is not only a member of the team, but they are committed to the team's success. They win when the team wins.

In summary, the "Committed Critic":

- Is a tough critic on team's approach, decisions, and actions
- Sees their job as poking holes in the team's strategies and approach
- May be an ad hoc member of the team
- Stays close enough to know what's up, but may not be involved in the details

Pros of a the "Committed Critic":

- Helps team avoid catastrophic misses

Cons of a "Committed Critic":

- Can shut down (or slow down) the team's creative process

To utilize the "Committed Critic" effectively the leader must:

- Help them understand the team's vision and why it is important to achieve the objectives

- Engage them early in the team's life and keep them engaged throughout the entire process

- Help their remarks and input come across as constructive and positive

- Challenge them to think of creative solutions to issues that may surface

- Publicly and privately encourage the team to consider the committed critic's feedback

- Challenge them to focus on the big picture

The Creative Conductor

It may seem absurdly obvious to state that leading a breakthrough-thinking team you need a breakthrough-thinking leader. This person possesses all the qualities we've come to expect and demand of our leaders: they must be visionaries, excellent communicators, and they must be passionate about the vision they are pursuing. They must also be good motivators, change agents, and have the capacity to direct a group of people to achieve results.

However, the breakthrough leader is unique in a few ways from the ordinary, albeit effective, leader. They have decided that the reality of what currently is will in no way be an obstacle to what they intend to create. Rather than accept reality as a barrier and a "zone" to be worked around or through to get to a given objective, they are inclined to create a "new zone."

The creative conductor envisions a place that may indeed only exist in the imaginary world and they are convinced that through their creativity—and the creativity of a dedicated team of qualified people—they can achieve whatever objective they set. Only a person that has that quality—an almost unrealistic optimism—can generate sufficient energy to get a team to consider the impossible! That's the Creative Conductor.

A breakthrough team needs a Creative Conductor to set the bar high enough to be a Herculean effort to achieve, yet stands ready to ignite the fuse of the rocket that will propel the team over the hurdles they will face. The Creative Conductor is very much a hands-on leader. They stay close to the action, without being in the way. They are constantly thinking of creative ways to challenge the team members, but are careful not to frustrate them with too many ideas that may seem overly aloof. Finally, the Creative Conductor is a student of team dynamics and understands how to use them to facilitate the team through its natural stages. We will cover more on team stages and a new team performance model later in the text.

In summary, the "Creative Conductor":

- Is the team leader
- Sets tone and culture for team
- Must have the vision and be able to articulate consistently and repeatedly
- Acts as cheerleader, motivator, caretaker, and communicator
- Harnesses the strengths of each of the members of the cast. Uses each cast member effectively to keep the team moving forward

Pros of a the "Creative Conductor":

- Team members rally behind them
- Teams will want to achieve the objectives set by the Creative Conductor

Cons of a "Creative Conductor":

- Can be seen as disconnected with reality

To be an effective "Creative Conductor" the leader must:

- Remain faithful to his or her vision
- Stay connected to the team
- Be where the action is
- Remove barriers that the team may encounter
- Challenge the team to accomplish the impossible

TWENTY

THE PERSTORMING™ MODEL

There are many models and theories surrounding the stages that teams go through in their life cycles. The simple idea that teams go through forming, norming, storming and performing stages makes sense. It follows human nature and mimics the way people behave in a variety of situations. In each of these stages, there are some interpersonal dynamics that occur between the people involved.

Anytime you have two or more people together, there are going to be some interpersonal issues to deal with. As it relates to team dynamics, with each of the stages in the life cycle of a team there will also be group behavioral patterns to deal with, in addition to the interpersonal issues between individuals. For the leader of the team, the work begins immediately as the team is being formed to deal with these individual and group issues. There are tasks that the leader will need to do in each of the stages to move the team along to the next stage.

Figure 2 illustrates the relationship between the team stages, the interpersonal issues, the group behavior issues, the group task issues, and the leadership issues that occur in each of the stages. Starting with the Team Stages and moving clockwise, each stage has a corresponding interpersonal issue, group behavior pattern, group task issue, and leadership issue. The goal is to move through the stages as quickly as possible and achieve group synergy in a high performing team.

Figure 2: Team Stages Model

With the clear objective of getting the team to the performing stage, the leader needs to keep a few things in mind: first, every team will go through these stages. Second, each stage has its own set of dynamics that will require a different response from the leader. Third, the stages while sequential in nature (that is a team forms, norms, storms, and then performs), stages can, and often do, repeat. So let us take these stages in order and explore them individually.

Forming

As the name implies, the forming stage is simply when the team first comes together. Think back for a moment when you entered a conference room to meet as a team for the first time. The thoughts that may have crossed your mind may have been things like: do I know anyone else in the room? Who's who in the room? What level are they in the organization? Who's in charge? What should be my role in this first meeting? Why am I even here? What's the objective for this team? If you were lucky, you found a familiar face in the group and you immediately gravitated towards them and, if possible, you sat next to them.

It is therefore no surprise that when a group first comes together, you will find clusters of people sitting together. All the operations folks will be sitting near each other, the marketing gang will be clustered, the R&D gurus will huddle together, engineers will sit with engineers, and the managers will be alone—because no one wants to sit with the managers.

The interpersonal dynamic that occurs in the forming stage of a team is referred to as inclusion. That is, people are looking to figure out how they fit into the group. That leads to the group behavior of people moving to similarities (i.e. people of like backgrounds or who know each other sit close together). In essence, people are looking to define the membership. What's the leader's role at this point? Clearly the group is completely dependent on the leader. They are looking for the leader to answer all of these questions, and give the team its initial identity. This is precisely what the leader must be prepared to do; and the faster he or she can do it, the faster the team can move to the next stage in the team's life cycle.

Norming

The term *norming* obviously has its roots in the word *normal*. In the world of political foreign affairs, oftentimes there is reference to the "normalization" of relationships between two or more nations. That is, diplomats from two or more countries are said to have reached agreement on an issue or issues, and a normal relationship can be resumed from that point on. Perhaps that means that there can be trade again between the nations or that citizens from the countries can travel from one place to the next. In the norming stage of the team's life cycle, members of the team agree on a variety of issues. These can include who's in control, when meetings will take place, what the rules for the team will be, the roles that each person will play in the team, how decisions will be made, and what will be acceptable behaviors from team members.

Referring back to the Team Stages Model, the interpersonal issues in the norming stage are those of control. That is, each individual is trying to determine who the most influential members of the team are, and specifically, they are trying to determine what their own personal level of influence is. At the same time, the group is moving to a consensus and establishing its operating principles. As a group the most important task at this point is likely establishing how decisions will be reached. From the leader's perspective, at this stage, the team is equally dependent on them to help the group navigate through. The leader is depending on the team to work through the issues.

What the leader must do at this point is facilitate the discussions. In fact, they must incite the discussions to take place. Often times the simplest way for the leader to move the team through this stage is to start with the simple exercise of brainstorming the individual member's expectations about what behaviors they expect other members to exhibit in meetings. Making a list of these will likely lead to discussion of what is important to each of the members, and can easily lead to productive talks about other issues such as what decision making process the team will use.

Storming

While a team is in the "normalization process," storms can break out. Invariably, when you put two or more people together, ask them to agree on a number of things, and force them to work on achieving one common result, there will be disagreement as to how, when and why things should be done. These "discussions" can span the spectrum from civil and completely polite discussions, to all out loud verbal brawls as individuals voice their disagreements.

Several things can be said about these "storms": first, they will happen. Second, they are necessary for the team to grow and mature as a team. Third, properly managed, they can, and often do, lead to much better performing teams. On the other hand, ill-managed, these storms can lead to the complete breakdown of the relationship between team members, and therefore the team.

How do you know that the team is in the storming stage? There are several indicators. The more obvious ones are things such as: how aggressive is the tone of the discussion that is taking place? What's the tone of voice people are using? How many people are speaking at once during a discussion? Are people listening to one another? Is there a clear disagreement between two or more members of the team? Have individual members of the team shut down and are they no longer contributing to the discussions? Not to mention the clearest of all signals: has an individual stormed out of the room in anger?

The less obvious indicators that teams are in the storming stages can be found in the body language of each individual. Are they sitting with arms crossed across their chest? Are they reacting to comments made by other members of the team by rolling their eyes in disbelief in obvious disagreement with what is being said? Are they engaged in the meeting, or are they doodling on a note pad? Perhaps they are checking e-mail messages on their remote wireless hand-held computer, or voice mail on their cellular phones. These are all signs that there is not agreement among members.

The leader's role in this stage is critical. First, if a storm is not taking place and it needs to, start one! By making a challenge, asking a question, or making an observation, the leader can strategically plant the seed that will generate a healthy storm. A healthy storm is one that is managed and facilitated. It has a clear beginning, a discussion period, a move towards similarities and conclusions, and a decision point.

The second role of the leader in this stage is to make sure that the storm moves through these phases, and most importantly that, after an appropriate discussion period, a conclusion is reached and a decision is made. This is when the leader will most rely on what the team agreed to be the standards of behaviors between members, and what the group agreed would be the decision-making process. Whether decisions were to be made by majority vote or when necessary by a unilateral decision from the leader, the process must be followed and a decision made to move the group ahead. Third, the leader will want to make sure that through the facilitation of the storm, members are heard, ideas are captured and fully explored when possible, and that the group dynamics are such that people feel okay with the debating process that is taking place.

I recall one particular meeting that the REDHAND team had, where a stormy argument erupted. There was a very "lively debate" taking place. Some team members even became angry. The discussion went on for what seemed a very long time, although it was probably only five or six minutes. Then suddenly, there was silence. People looked around waiting for someone to speak. I waited a bit longer, and then said, "Do you feel it?" I got a puzzled look back from the team members. "Feel the friction?" I asked. I went on to assure the team that it was okay to feel that way.

I thanked the team members for their willingness to be passionate about their beliefs and for debating their positions openly. I explained that it was a necessary process for us to go through and that each time we did, we got better at managing through them. More importantly, I explained, each time we debated, we ended up with a better solution to whatever the issue was we were dealing with. Finally, I reminded them of the decision-making process we had agreed to use, and how it was important that once a decision was reached by the team, we all must be one hundred percent supportive of it. The meeting continued, the team grew closer, and we were better off because of it.

The storming stage can be a time consuming stage. If the arguments go on long past their productive period or if the personal dynamics between individuals are left unchecked, the debates can deteriorate quickly to unproductive fights. These can lead to resentment among team members, and ultimately to disruptions in the ability of the team to perform effectively.

One of the key mistakes a team leader can make is to ignore the storms, or assume that there is no need to deal with the interpersonal and group behavioral issues that these storms create. To do so assures the team's failure. Instead, the leader should welcome these storms, learn to manage through them effectively, insist on open communication of all ideas, ensure that there is a productive exchange between individuals, monitor individual behaviors, and ensure that they are conforming to the standards that the team agreed to in the norming stage. Finally, the leader needs to be fully engaged to step in as necessary to focus the discussion, move the group to a conclusion on the issue, and if necessary make a decision to get the group re-engaged on its primary objective.

In the storming stage there is a struggle going on between team members. The group uses whatever skills they have to negotiate, and ideally to try to collaborate, toward a resolution to the issue. The leader takes on a significant facilitation role. Ultimately, well managed, this stage will lead to a high performance breakthrough thinking team.

Performing

There are clear signs that are indicative of a team being in the "Performing" stage. The results and milestones being accomplished are evidence of this stage. When a team is in the performing stage, good things are happening. Progress towards the stated objective is clearly visible. At this point in the team's life cycle, there is often a genuine affection between members. If nothing else, there is certainly a mutual and personal respect between team members. The result is a team that is collaborating to productively achieve results.

At this stage, there is an interdependent relationship between the leader, and the team. The leader depends on the team to execute the plan, but can do little to help them do it.

Consider the example of an all-star basketball team. During the forming, norming, and storming stages of the team's life cycle, the coache's role is significant. It is during these stages that the coach must instill what he wants from his team. It is during each of the team practice sessions that he or she can deal with the storms between players, the difference in playing styles, and the strengths and weaknesses of each team member. It is then that the coach practices the plays over and over again, while having the flexibility to stop play at any point to make corrections. However, once the real game begins and the team is on the court, it is up to the players to execute on the team's strategies. The coach is reduced to a cheerleader. It is only during specific breaks in the action through time-outs or by swapping players in and out of the game at times, that the coach can more directly influence the game and its outcome.

So the leader's role during the performing stage is to be a strong supporter of the team. They must use this time to monitor the results being achieved and make any corrections needed to keep the team on track.

Team stages are dynamic

Often times when teaching a seminar on team dynamics, I have the participants engage in a game I like to call "Win As Much As You Can." The rules are simple. We break up into small groups, trying to have at least four separate teams. I explain that there will be eight to ten rounds in the game. Each team will decide whether to cast an "X" or "Y" vote based on the following rules:

1. If all four teams cast an "X" vote, each team loses 100 points

2. If three teams cast "X," and one team casts a "Y," the

teams casting the "X" each get 100 points, and the team casting the "Y" loses 300 points

3. If two teams vote "X," and the other two vote "Y," the teams casting the "X" each get 200 points, and the teams casting the "Y" each lose 200 points

4. If one team votes "X" and the other three vote "Y," the team casting the "X" gets 300 points and the teams casting the "Y" each lose 100 points

5. If all four teams cast a "Y," each team wins 150 points

The game goes like this: I give the teams a few minutes to study the rules, and ask me any questions they have about them. I let them know that on my count, I will ask each team to flash either their "X" or "Y" card. All teams will cast their vote at the exact time. I will record the scores for each round. I also inform them that there will be negotiation sessions between rounds three, five, and seven. Each team will have the opportunity to send one representative to the negotiation table to discuss strategy with the other teams. They are not required to participate in the negotiations. That's it! No other rules are given.

As soon as the game begins, you can begin to witness the groups going through each of the team stages. Since I have them under a time pressure to get started, they quickly move through the forming stage, and a leader emerges. Soon the teams find themselves bypassing the norming stage and deeply entrenched in the storming phase, trying to decide whether to cast an "X" or a "Y" vote. Some members of the team struggle to get any attention to have their opinions heard, others study the rules carefully trying to find some trick. There is no trick.

Finally, I interrupt the growing banter in the room, and I announce, "Okay, on my count each team will cast their vote. Ready? One, two, and three."

Each team holds up a card. I record the cards thrown by each team. I have conducted this experimental game more than a dozen times with different groups, and there is no set pattern as to how the votes are cast. Except for one thing: it is never four "Y"s. So, I record the scores, and inevitably, at least one team gets some points, and at least one team loses some points.

Each team goes back to their brainstorming trying to determine what their strategy should be for their next vote in round two. Quickly they are back in their isolated group trying hard to be secretive about what they are talking about, less the other teams hear their strategy. Again, the team stages and dynamics can be observed.

Throughout the exercise, some team members are highly engaged, while others sit quietly and don't contribute to the team's effort, especially those who have tried to speak before but where shut out by one or two other members of the team. There is always someone holding the cards, in an attempt to control the team's actions. Usually, a question or two may be directed at me seeking some clarification on the rules. Questions such as: "What will the winner get?" or "Can we talk to the other teams?" I usually answer the same way, by repeating the few rules that I outlined at the beginning of the game. I never tell them that they can't speak to the other teams.

We move on to voting for round two. I record the scores and give the teams three to four minutes to get ready for the next round. At the end of round three, each team picks their negotiator and these individuals meet in another room for five minutes or so. It's fun to watch this process take place. The negotiators come back to their teams, share the results of their meeting with the other negotiators, and help the team decide how to vote next. At that time I remind all teams about the purpose of the game: "Win As Much as You Can."

Next, I call for the vote for round four. When the "X"s and "Y"s are cast, what follows is always a huge surprise to me. Without exception, one or more of the negotiators scream out in disgust as they discover that they have been betrayed by some of the other negotiators. That is, they vote a particular way as was agreed to by all negotiators, and find that the others have taken advantage of knowing how someone would vote to maximize their winnings. It happens every time! That's when the real fun begins.

Now the dynamics in the group change dramatically. Usually, any communications that existed between the teams is gone, and at times the negotiator is verbally punished by his or her team mates for selling them on the idea of trusting the other team's negotiator, or for having made a poor deal. The teams revert back to their strategy of trying to outwit the other teams and maximize their winnings.

This goes on for several more rounds and through two more negotiation sessions. Usually, everyone has a good time, and at the end the result is about the same. Most of the time, there is no winner. All teams end up with a negative score. There are some exceptions, and from time to time one or two teams will have positive numbers on the scorecard. However, never have I facilitated this team dynamic simulation where teams have optimized their winning. The only possible way to do that given the voting rules would have been for all teams to always vote "Y" in every single round. That would maximize every team's score. The objective was to "Win As Much As You Can." It wasn't "Win As Much As You Can At The Expense Of Everyone Else!" Yet that's exactly what every team was trying to do: beat everyone else.

At the end of the game, we spend some time processing what took place in the teams. We discuss the team dynamics, the communication process that each team used, the roles that each individual played, and what could have improved their performance as a team. This fun exercise helps to quickly demonstrate each of the team stages, the dynamics that play out between team members in each of the stages, and the results that are often achieved by teams that are not quite aligned and directed to one common goal.

The exercise also clearly demonstrates how dynamic team stages are, as each of the teams goes through the norming, storming, and performing stages adjusting to new data, new inputs, or even to external factors such as the behavior of other team members in other teams. This lesson became very clear to me one day as I played this game with my staff for the second time.

In 1997, I was in living in Puerto Rico, managing a Manufacturing Business unit for a large Johnson & Johnson company. A year earlier, when I first took over the group, I played the game with my staff. I had a team of fifteen direct reports: two middle management supervisors, eleven manufacturing supervisors, and two manufacturing planners. We split the group into four teams, and played the game. The result the first time we played the game was the same as it always had been with any other group that I played the game with. The scores were all negative as each team try to out-do the other. We had a fun time playing the game, but then got to the important work of making the point: we are all one team, and we have to work together to achieve the goal.

We agreed that we would watch our team dynamics, manage our decision-making process, and keep open lines of communication between the team members. We vowed to vote "Y" on a daily basis and make the team a winning team. I was pleased. In fact, I was even proud of myself. That is until we played the game a second time six months later.

Six months after I had first played the game with my staff, I decided to try it again, during one of the off-site meetings we held quarterly. I outlined the same exact rules, and I figured, surely they would cast all "Y"s right from the get-go, and there would be no point in going past the first two or three rounds to make the point. Much to my dismay, the very first round had three "Y"s and one "X" as the votes where cast! I was shocked. How was this possible? Surely they remembered the game from six months ago. And no doubt they remembered the results. What was the problem?

The answer was so simple it was painful to have it highlighted in this manner. In the past six months, we had added one new member to the team. He was in the team that cast the "X." When that team threw up the "X," the other teams shouted disbelief! They immediately started accusing members of that team of having violated their trust. In their defense, they offered-up the new guy as the sacrificial lamb, and made him the guilty party for "having forced them to do it."

The next few rounds were no better, as other teams started to forgo the "Y"s. Then, after round three, there was an immediate impromptu negotiation that took place, and fortunately, the teams got back in alignment, and the "Y"s ruled once again. All teams voted "Y"s for the remaining rounds. The damage however, had been done. The final score would not be an optimal score for the team, as they had stormed their way through the first three rounds and cost themselves some negative scores that detracted from their final totals.

Again, we had fun with the exercise. As before, we pledged as a team to focus on the objective, communicate clearly and consistently, and watch our team dynamics. This time, we also agreed that next time a new member of the team is added, we were going to do a better job of integrating them into our team's culture.

As the leader of the group, the failure of the team to optimize their score the second time we played this game, was mine. I underestimated the impact to the team's dynamics with the addition of a new team member. I will never do that again!

Leaders must always keep in mind that team stages can, and often, repeat. Each time that a new member is added to the team, the group is back to the forming stage. It's the leader's job to make sure that they navigate through this stage quickly so that there is no time loss by the team in integrating the new member. They must also ensure that the new team member clearly understands the team's vision, the established norms, and how they fit into the team.

Additionally, anytime a disagreement ensues between two or more members of the team, the team may find itself back in the storming stage. Navigating through that stage to reach a conclusion, and to make a decision, is of paramount importance. Finally, the leader must keep in mind that team stages are not static. They are dynamic, and evolve with the team. Thus, understanding the Team Stage Model is important for the breakthrough team leader to effectively lead the group and achieve the desired results.

Time is at a premium for Breakthrough Teams

There is one element of team stages that warrants further discussion. Time, or the lack thereof, may be a breakthrough team's most significant hurdle to overcome. Each of the team stages takes time to maneuver. The longer the team spends trying to get to the performing stage, the longer it will take for the team's objectives to be achieved.

The leader's role is to get the team performing as quickly as possible. Their aim should be to minimize the time spent in each of the other team stages. There are a few ways a leader can do this. One way is to work feverishly to be effective in moving their team through the stages. Another way would be to find a way to combine two stages into one, thereby minimizing the time spent in each stage. Usually the most time consuming of all stages is the storming stage. What if there was a way to combine this stage with the performing stage? There is. We call this the "Perstorming™" Stage.

The Perstorming™ Stage

Figure 3 is a graphical depiction of the Perstorming™ Stage. The idea is a simple one. Consider a pipe that has valves for inputs and temperature controls. The speed of a liquid passed through a pipe can be controlled by narrowing sections of the pipe. Narrowing the pipe leads to increased speed of the fluid. Widening the pipe of course leads to a speed decrease in the fluid. Another way that the speed can be controlled is with external factors such as temperature, mechanical accelerators such as a fan, and filters. This short thermodynamics lesson may be of interest but the obvious question is: how does this apply to a team model?

When the team is in the performing stage, things are relatively calm. The team is making good progress towards the objective. Over time, the team can slow down as things get a bit too comfortable. Given that speed is a key element to breakthrough teams, the leader needs to be observant for signs of slow-down and they need to be ready to inject a bit of energy to change, influence the team, and speed things along.

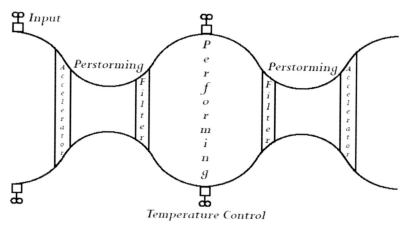

Figure 3. The Perstorming™ Stage Model

Often times the best way to accelerate a team is to "create" an issue. This can be done by asking certain questions, making a challenge to a given process, or throwing out an idea for the team to consider. Of course, these must all be done at the appropriate time, but the idea is to generate some discussion. Essentially, the leader starts a "mini-storm." Using the input valve and an "accelerator question or challenge," the leader narrows the pipe and increases the rate of speed through the pipe. The leader in essence is controlling the temperature gauge for the team, setting the thermostat at the appropriate level to get the group just a bit uncomfortable, and moving towards problem resolution.

Once the leader is satisfied that the team has taken the challenge and that they are dealing with it, he or she must be ready to apply the filter that will help the team re-align - in essence dealing with the mini-storm as they ordinarily would in the storming phases of the team—and move the group back to the performing stage.

The leader repeats this process as appropriate to ensure a constant flow in the pipeline, and to make sure that time is not wasted during the performing stage. This must not be interpreted as simply trying to derail the team's efforts just to generate a storm. It is a process that should be carefully calculated and timed appropriately. This requires a good sense of the team's dynamics and the team players. Most importantly, it requires that the leader be quite connected to the team and their daily progress. Otherwise, the risk is that the leader will be increasing the temperature at the wrong time, using the wrong accelerators, and not putting filters in place to align the team.

To use the Perstorming Stage, the Breakthrough Thinking Leader must:

- Keep an eye out for appropriate accelerators and inject them at the right time
- Control the team's "temperature" and set the thermostat appropriately
- Manage the ensuing "mini-storm"
- Have an alignment filter ready to apply
- Know when to repeat the process

TWENTY-ONE

UNLEASHING
POWERFUL PEOPLE

The recipe for creating a powerful breakthrough-thinking team starts with a healthy dose of team building. This can be done in a variety of ways. One of the finest examples that I have ever personally witnessed and was privileged to be a part of, was a meeting held in Sun City, South Africa.

On May 12, 2003, I started my trek to Sun City to attend a meeting of what was then referred to as the company's European Marketing Organization (EMO). I was one of two invited guest from the United States to attend this important training and strategic planning meeting for the EMO. More than fifty European Franchise Directors and Marketing and Sales Managers would be in attendance. The agenda for the meeting included various important subjects, product training, and a pre-launch meeting for the European launch of Vicryl Plus (the world's first antibacterial suture). However, one of the most important unspoken agenda items for this meeting was to do some serious team building: to strengthen personal relationships between these individuals.

Each one of the people present were extremely competent, knowledgeable, and quite capable of driving business results in their respective regions of Europe. However, together the power that could be generated by this team would be phenomenal. This was more than a training meeting. This was to be a bonding experience. My good friend and colleague Anthony Bishop, the Communications Director, set out on a mission. Anthony was the brain behind the meeting. His strategy, start to finish, was brilliant.

First, he chose an exotic, far-away place. While at first this may have seemed inconvenient to those attending, no doubt the experience of the trip will be unforgettable and those attending will forever be closer as friends rather than simply colleagues. This alone would be worth the investment cost of the meeting. Second, he chose a theme for the meeting that was right on target for what he wanted to accomplish. To most people it was initially difficult to see the link of the theme to what the purpose of the meeting was, and how it would relate back to our business in medical devices and sutures. However, in the end, it was all tied together brilliantly.

Next, Anthony began to send e-mail postcards to those attending the meeting. He prepared the postcards as if addressed from Sun City, South Africa, with motivational messages introducing the theme of the meeting, and its purpose. Every few weeks another e-mail postcard would arrive with a few more details about the meeting, and the expectations for the meeting. He was building excitement and anticipation for the gathering weeks in advance of the actual date.

Once we arrived in Sun City, the safari theme of the meeting was clearly evident. During the opening session of the meeting, participants walked in to an elegant ballroom, decorated with banners that complimented the safari theme and depicted the strategic objectives of the organization. The meeting opened with a video that used the beauty of the African landscape and its wild animals to create an environment of passion, high energy, and power.

As the meeting continued, the theme began to take on a personality of its own and was brought to life when Ian Thomas took the stage. Ian is the author of *The Power of the Pride* and was our guest speaker at the meeting. Ian used his experience as a student of lions and the pride to relate it back to the business world. Once again, even those who might have been skeptical as to whether there was a connection between this theme and the reality of our day-to-day business must have been convinced once they heard Ian speak. The unique correlation between how the pride behaves as it fights for survival, and what we can learn and apply to teams in the business world, soon became obvious.

During his talk that day, Ian Thomas described numerous aspects of the way in which lions survive in the wild. I was amazed at how many important team lessons can be learned from the pride. Three of these lessons struck me as most important.

First, Ian described the physical characteristics of a lioness and how these make her an incredible and powerful hunter. He described the strength in her legs and the amazing night vision. He talked about her sharp, razor-like claws, and the incredibly strong jaw and sharp teeth. The lioness is an impressive hunter! However, the true strength of the hunting lioness is the team she is in and how all the lionesses hunt together, following a specific strategy, delivering the same result every time. While individuals can be powerful, there is nothing more powerful than a team made-up of powerful individuals!

Next, Ian described a zebra hunt that he had witnessed. He went into fascinating detail as to how the lionesses work together to ambush the herd of zebra. In this particular case, the zebra, a powerful animal itself, can cause serious harm to its aggressor with its hind legs. As the lioness chases the zebra, it uses it powerful legs to try to kick the lioness chasing it. Should the zebra land a blow, it can be deadly to its predator.

The lioness persists and keeps on the chase. When she finally is able to bring down the zebra, it moves quickly to take a tight hold on its prey. The zebra frantically spins its powerful legs in a circle, trying desperately to escape the grip of its attacker; but the lioness, being careful to evade the zebra's hoofs, avoiding a potentially bone crushing blow, holds on for dear life.

Why does the lioness do that? Because she knows that in just another second or two, her team of lioness will be there to back her up. She is certain that all she needs to do is hold on for just a few moments longer and she will have all the help she needs to finish-off the zebra. That confidence in her teammates motivates her to press on. It is fascinating that all the lionesses have been chasing the same animal; the one chosen by the lead hunter. They did not go off on their own chasing their own prey. They teamed up, followed the leader, and worked together to bring down one animal that would feed them all. Team members must trust each other implicitly if they are to be a powerful team!

The third part of Ian's presentation that struck me the most was his description of how the pride lionesses train and protect the generation behind them. One could be fooled into thinking that this is simply motherly instinct. However, lionesses are veracious protectors of the next generation because the future survival of the pride rests on those individuals. They are continuously training the next generation of hunters. Whether they do it during playtime or during an actual hunt, the training goes on in perpetuity. The next generation is carefully protected and developed.

Imagine what power could be harnessed and stored for future use if the next generation of leaders and powerful people were truly mentored, coached, and developed by the powerful people of today! We would ensure not just our success today, but tomorrow's, next week's, and next year's as well. Powerful teams nurture and develop powerful people!

Ian's message was profound and it was very much on target. The theme of the EMO meeting was crystallizing before our eyes! It was building from "power of the individual," the "power of speed," and the "power of innovative thought," to the "power of the team."

Later that day, the team participated in a true African safari. We drove deep into a natural park in South Africa, and together saw some of the powerful wildlife up close. As the meeting progressed, you could see and feel the group becoming close and more cohesive. Friendships were being forged.

Late evening of day two of the meeting, the team sat in a beautiful amphitheater. It had the feel of an ancient and solemn place. The night was beautiful, and one could not help but to marvel at the brilliant stars in the African skies. Each person there had a drum in front of them, and for the next hour or so, a native South African woman taught the group the basics about this ancient communicational tool used by the natives: the drum. Before long, she had all fifty of us drumming in unison and in complete rhythm with each other. The sound filled the theater and no doubt carried far away from that place as well. Several things became very clear as we experienced this wonderful evening.

First, while one drum can be very loud, fifty drums can be much louder! Second, the music we were making sounded best when we worked together, in unison. Third, if just one person out of the fifty was out of synchronization, it was evident to all because it plainly stood out. Fourth, even when some individuals were out of synchronization, the leader could make minor adjustments through the use of signals or other gestures, to signal a change needed to fix the problem.

And so it goes with a powerful team:

1. Fifty are stronger than one

2. Results are best when all work in unison toward the same goal

3. Those not contributing to the same goal are easy to identify

4. With strong, quick acting leadership, the team can be harmonized back to the goal

That night, the team drummed to one beat. No doubt they will be able to do it again!

Later that same evening, I watched as this group of people from diverse backgrounds, who spoke different languages, danced and laughed together. Probably the funniest thing was watching this group of Europeans sing and dance to Rocky Roads like they had been born in West Virginia, USA.

Finally, on day three, the meeting came to an end and we all headed back home. Through the use of video, music, adult-learning techniques, a mix of classroom and main-stage presentations, as well as a healthy dose of exposing team members to the sights and smells of the savannah, Anthony had made this experience a tremendous learning experience. He understood well that you must communicate with the mind, but stimulate and stir the heart. No doubt all were changed by the experience. No doubt we left there a more powerful team than when we first arrived. The Pride was ready for the hunt!

TWENTY-TWO

INNOVATION UNCOVERED

"Innovation is about how to apply technology to a real need."
—Dean Kamen

In January 2004, I had the pleasure of listening to Dean Kamen speak on the subject of innovation. Dean is the president of DEKA Research and Development Corporation. He is an inventor and a brilliant man. Among his most famous inventions is the iBot wheelchair and the Segway™ people mover. He is also the founder of "First," an incredible program geared towards helping teenagers gain a love for science and engineering.

In his presentation, Mr. Kamen outlined seven "rude realities" of innovation. His approach made a sound impression in me, and got me thinking about what true innovation really is.

What Constitutes Innovation?

T.S. Elliot once said, "Between the idea and the reality falls the shadow." Having a great widget or the latest technology is of little value if there is no problem that it addresses. According to Dean

Kamen, innovation "is about how to apply technology to a real need." So the first step is to clearly understand the need.

As it relates to breakthrough teams, it is important that they have a clear understanding of the need that they are trying to fill. The leader's vision is so very important in not only helping to identify it, but in driving the team to fully describe that need. Only then, after a clear definition of the problem has been established, can solutions—innovative ones—be developed to meet that need.

Critics and Fear are Innovation's Worst Enemy

It never ceases to amaze me how negative our society and culture can be. We focus on the negative. We look for it. We thrive on it. You can see this in almost any facet of our culture. Politicians running for office can expect that every speck of dirt that can possibly be unearthed about them will be, and will be highlighted in the national media, while their strong points will be largely unmentioned. When the space shuttle disasters occurred (the first in 1986, the most recent in 2001), there was no shortage of critics of the NASA space program. Suddenly the countless of other flawless missions flown by the shuttle seemed unimportant. When projects fail to deliver on time or budget within a company, there is the tendency to punish the offenders, rather than shake it off and get back in the game.

The key is not to surrender to the critics or worst yet to your own vision. When Thomas Edison was questioned about how he felt having failed at more than 700 attempts at inventing the light bulb he replied, "I did not fail more than 700 times; I know 700 ways of how not to do it." Edison understood that failure is part of the innovation game. He expected it and he used it to learn from it. In breakthrough teams, working at the speed of light, there will be failure. Some of that failure would have been predictable, most of it not. Learning to deal with failure effectively will in large part determine the team's ability to achieve breakthrough results.

In the REDHAND team we had a saying: "If you are not afraid, you don't understand." We laughed each time someone said this. But it was true. We were trying to do things so dramatically different from the way other teams had done things, and we knew there was significant risk that we were undertaking. Naturally with that risk, always comes the fear of failure. So, those who truly understood what we were trying to accomplish always had a healthy amount of fear.

Failure is a natural part of the innovation process. "Fail often, fail early." Not bad advice for Breakthrough Teams.

"New & Improved" vs. "Truly Revolutionary"

"New and Improved!" These words adorn bottles of detergents, dishwashing soaps, and all sorts of other consumer products. In marketing terms, we call these products derivatives or product extensions. While from time to time, derivatives can be truly innovative and breakthrough in solving a new need, most times creating derivative products is the quickest, least complicated way for a company to launch another product to make money. That's a good thing.

However, it is much more challenging, and far more difficult, for a team to think of a whole better way to help the customer solve a need. It is tougher to develop a completely new, different, and innovative solution, rather than tweak an old solution to the problem. There is nothing wrong with improving on products. Thank God that Microsoft did not stop at DOS! Otherwise, current versions of Windows would not exist. But what's next? Should we be satisfied with another version of Windows that gives only incremental improvements to the old version? Would it not be better to invent a whole new way of computing instead? A yet unimagined way of data transfer? This is where science fiction meets reality.

If a team is truly going to come up with a breakthrough solution, the first step is to have a well-defined unmet need. Second, they must be challenged with the task of creating a solution that redefines the current state-of-the-art. Otherwise, you will end up with another product extension. The automobile industry is a master at product extensions. Each year, Mercedes-Benz uncovers, under a great deal of fanfare, the latest model of their E-320 sedan. Somehow, through the magic of marketing, they make us feel like this is the hottest, newest, and coolest car they've ever created. And there is always some new gadget or feature that makes us think that. Sometimes, they even change the body type of the car to add to the illusion of "new and improved." But strip away the new bells and whistles, and you still have the same car that they sold some years ago.

I'm not trying to diminish the progress made by the automobile industry in engine efficiency, safety, and creature comforts. I think they are great, and I for one am a big fan of Mercedes-Benz as a company. However, we need a company that will re-define what cars are, how they are operated, and the fuel type they use before there will be true breakthrough results in automobile design. To take it to a true breakthrough level, what we really need is a team that will revolutionize the way we travel!

Consider the Ford Model T. Invented in the early 1900s, it revolutionized the way we traveled. We went from the horse and buggy to a motorized vehicle; it was a whole new way of getting from point "a" to point "b." More than one hundred years later we have cars that today have the equivalent power of hundreds of horses. We get from point "a" to point "b" with greater speed, more comfort, and much more safely than we did then. However, boiled down to their basic function and how they do their job, the 1905 Ford Model T is not very different from the 2009 Ford Mustang. They both use fossil fuel; both have four tires, and a steering column. The Mustang may be faster, safer, and have more comfortable features for the rider, but essentially both cars do the same job; they transport us from point "a" to point "b." You want breakthrough in transportation? Invent the Star Trek Transporter System! That would be breakthrough in transportation. Help me get from my home to Paris for that one day meeting in a matter of seconds. For frequently business travelers such as me, that would be true breakthrough in transportation. It's a whole new way of thinking about travel!

Innovation Can Scare Some People

The reality that innovation can scare some people smacked me right in the face recently in a way that brought it to life. A team had developed a very innovative design for a medical implant, and was set to launch it in a big way. There was one problem, however: it was too good! Surgeons had been accustomed to using a surgical hammer to literally pound in the earlier designs of the implant to ensure that it was secured in the body. Many implants from several leading manufacturers behaved similarly, and they had been that way for decades.

Our team had found a better way. Imagine developing a device that would not only improve on the expected outcomes from the old design, but the device would be easier to install. Imagine that you had all the data to support and validate that fact. Yet because of a preconceived notion of how the implant was supposed to behave, some surgeons struggled to accept the new design because it did not conform to how they had come to expect the implant would behave. Even though the data was clear, the surgeon's skepticism, and their past experience, made it difficult for them to accept a new reality. They eventually did and the product did well, but it took a long time and lots of training and marketing efforts to make that happen.

Breakthrough teams develop solutions that truly revolutionize the way things are thought of and done. These solutions may sometimes take a while to be adopted by a skeptic or stubborn market. Rather than allow this to discourage the creative process of the team, the breakthrough leader stays true to his or her course, and reaffirms that their vision is the correct one without hesitation.

According to Dean Kamen, "Innovation is about accepting a new truth." If a team is going to achieve breakthrough thinking and breakthrough results, all members of the team are going to have to believe in the possibility of creating a "new truth."

Innovation Demands Leadership

All projects and teams need management. But innovative projects demand leadership. Breakthrough Teams are not exempted from this rule. In fact, without strong leadership and aggressive project management, innovation will not occur. Some would argue that managing a breakthrough team too closely would stifle the innovative process. No doubt, that can indeed occur. Left unattended, however, creative genius types will keep creating. Sometimes creating solutions to non-problems, or veering off the path leading to the intended solution. Thus, to achieve the solution of an identified need, the team must remain focused.

Clearly there is a place for what we could refer to as "pure research." Somewhat aimless, its purpose is to simply see where a particular course of action will lead. Some of finest examples of innovative designs have occurred by accident. The invention of the post-it note comes to mind. I am not sure that someone set out to invent a glue that was just sticky enough, but not too sticky. More than likely, the inventor was out to make the strongest glue compound possible, and he ran into this unexpected outcome. Was that real innovation? Or was the real innovation in finding or creating a problem that this solved? In essence, creating a new market place for an accidental invention? A debate can be made on both ends of this argument no doubt.

Suffice it to say that, from a business perspective, the company was able to capitalize on the "accidental finding." However, it would be foolish for the company to spend all of its resources funding and supporting this undefined research with the hope of having a successful accidental finding. Certainly spending some of its resources in this area is wise; which is why almost every company has a Research and Development organization. For the purposes of our discussion on breakthrough teams, trying to accomplish a particular vision and an innovative solution to a defined need, a specific team structure, management, and strong leadership are required.

Mistakes Happen

There will be times in the lifecycle of a breakthrough team when individuals will make mistakes. In most cases, these mistakes are not of significant impact to the overall progress of the team, and are easily corrected. In extreme cases, a mistake can derail the team completely and cause the team's failure. That is a risk that breakthrough teams will face. Given the speed at which they must move to accomplish their objectives, the odds are increased that mistakes will occur. There can be no doubt that how the leader—and the organization at large—reacts to these mistakes will define the level of risks that individuals will be willing to take.

One thing is certain: the penalty for failure cannot be greater that the reward for success!

Innovation Takes Work

In the opening chapter of this section of the book, we answered the question "why innovate?" Part of the reason is that properly developed innovation creates entire industries. Just consider what the invention of plastic has meant to the world. How many new products came into existence because of that one development? Every major industry has somehow been affected by the advancements in polymer plastic technologies. From toy manufacturers and medical device companies to the auto industry, plastic has revolutionized the design of thousands, indeed hundreds of thousands, of products.

From a business perspective, the answer to "why innovate?" is painfully obvious. The companies that are best at innovation win. Perhaps not so obvious is the question of when we should innovate? The answer is before the need becomes a crisis. The hard part is determining what the right need is that should be addressed. That's the breakthrough leader's job: to figure out where we need to go before we need to go there. So, the when is now!

Kindle Merrill once said, "Every remarkable event begins with a crazy idea, and ends with a courageous lunatic."

The courageous lunatic is the breakthrough legacy leader. He or she must be willing to initiate and embrace change in order to jump-start the process of innovation. Then, with passion for their vision, a relentless purpose of seeing it become a reality, and applying all the lessons learned earlier in this text for driving breakthrough teams, the leader goes about influencing their team to achieve something extraordinary.

The only question remaining, then, is who should innovate? The answer is everybody! Harnessing the mental energy of all members of the team is the only way that breakthrough results can be achieved. Whether they are optimist or pessimist, they have something to offer. It's all a matter of reference point. Consider the Wright brothers, who were optimistic about their ability to invent airplanes. They were driven by that passion. Their focus was to build the best flying machine possible. That great innovation led to another great invention, albeit from a pessimist: the parachute.

Finally, sometimes the hardest thing for a leader to do is let go. But they must know when to do just that. Leaders create the vision, motivate the team to not only accept, but also to adopt the vision, direct and support the team, and then stand back, and let the team do the impossible!

TWENTY-THREE

THE MOUSE TRAP

"The Breakthrough Thinking Legacy Leader builds organizations that constantly reinvent and refresh themselves, making customer loyalty and long-term success unavoidable."
—A. Lopez

It was going to be a sunny, hot summer day in Orlando, Florida. I found myself with ten hours or so before I was scheduled to take a flight home. I had been in Florida for a few weeks attending an Air Force training course. The class ended earlier than expected on that final day, about 10 a.m. that morning. Not wanting to miss a great opportunity, I rented a car, and, still dressed in my cadet summer uniform, I headed off to Disney World.

It was 1983, and it was going to be my very first trip to the park. I had never had a chance to visit Disney as a child, so my excitement built with every mile I traveled. I was traveling alone so I knew I could move quickly through the parks and see most of what they had to offer.

As soon as I got to Disney I purchased my ticket, took a good look at the park map, and carefully but quickly charted the route I would take to see the attractions. Luckily for me, the parks were not very busy that day, so the crowds were not going to be a hindrance to my master plan. Although I moved quickly, I took it all in. My first stop was the Magic Kingdom. *Where else would you go but the Magic Kingdom?* I thought to myself. I can still remember the feeling of walking on "Main Street USA" for the very first time. It was indeed magical.

The child in me was screaming to get out, and he did. However, the young adult in me made several observations that were not lost in the excitement. First, the park was immaculate. To say that it was clean would be an understatement. Second, entering the park was like stepping into Emerald City in the *Wizard of Oz*. It was a rainbow of lively and vibrant colors. The bright colors that massaged every sense in my brain would bring an automatic smile to a person of any age.

As I strolled through the park, and got on every possible ride, the same experience was reinforced. Every ride was colorful, exciting, and fun. Third, employees in the park who interacted with me were sincerely friendly. My short discussion with each of them, usually a quick stop to ask a question, ended the same way. They always said, "Have a magical day here at Disney."

Having lived and attended high school and college in New York City, this level of politeness was almost uncomfortable for me. I quickly grew to like it. The last ride I got on in the Magic Kingdom was the Carousel of Progress. It was my introduction to animatronics, and I knew the future was going to be great.

I left the Magic Kingdom energized, with a big smile, and soon made my way over to EPCOT. I can still remember the feeling of seeing the EPCOT "ball" for the first time. Space Ship Earth was the first ride I ever enjoyed in EPCOT Center. I was amazed. It was state of the art all the way for that time period.

As I had done before, I charted my path with the park map, and made sure to walk at a furious pace from ride to ride to enjoy everything this wonderland had to offer. I made sure not to miss the details however. I noticed the landscape. It was spectacular. I noticed the paint job—pristine! I noticed how clean the park was—not a cigarette butt anywhere to be seen. All the employee's uniforms were pressed and neat.

When my day was done at Disney World, I was overwhelmed. I don't remember what I paid for the ticket, but no doubt I must have thought it was expensive when I first bought it. I did not feel that way as I made my way past the gates out to the parking lot looking for my car. I don't remember what I paid for the hamburger, Coke, and fries I ate, but no doubt the thought must have occurred to me that it was a lot more expensive than McDonalds or Burger King. Nevertheless, I left there feeling like I had gotten much more than I paid for. I was a believer; a bona fide adult Mousketeer! Hence began my study of Disney World. For the next twenty plus years I would read about them, boast about them, write about them, and whenever I taught a class on customer service, I toasted Disney as the model for all to follow.

That was then. Sadly, now there is a very different story to tell. Since my first visit to Disney all those years ago, I have returned to the parks in Orlando at least twenty times. I went with friends before I was married. I went with my wife after we were married. I took my first daughter, Cristina, when she was barely eight years old, and again when she was nine, and her sister was barely five; and yet again when they were both a bit older. Each time, the story remained the same—a great, magical place to visit where dreams did indeed come true. That is, until about five years ago.

We were living in Fort Lauderdale at the time, and I was scheduled to make another corporate move with Johnson & Johnson back to ETHICON's corporate headquarters in New Jersey. We decided to make one last trip to the great universe of Disney World. Except this time, the universe we discovered was Universal Studios, Disney's newest competition for the almighty dollar of the vacationing family in Orlando.

We arrived at Disney World and checked into one of the resort parks; after all we were loyal park goers who always stayed within Disney property. We purchased our Park Hopper tickets as usual and off to the Magic Kingdom we went. The park was crowded as usual, although this time it seemed a bit more than before. As we walked around the park, I began to realize why the park felt more crowded. There were four attractions (rides) out of service, all at the same time! That meant much longer lines in the operational rides. Then, as if a filter was lifted from my eyes, I saw it. The park looked a bit different.

I started to look around, and suddenly I noticed paint chipping off some of the walls in the rides. I was surprised to see some garbage on the ground; not much, just a few cups here and there, some sandwich wrappers getting pushed around by the air, rather than the usual friendly broom handler. Much to my dismay, I even saw a few cigarette butts on the ground! *How could this be?* I asked myself.

The next day, we decided to head over to Universal Studios. My family had never visited that park before. I had been there many years earlier when the big hit ride was "Back To The Future—The Ride." (It has now been replaced by the *Men In Black* ride, which I highly recommend!) When we got there, the contrast to Disney was immediately evident. Even my daughter Cristina commented, "Wow look at the colors," although I doubt she remembers. I do. The park was immaculate. The rides all working, the energy of the employees contagious, and with new rides being added since my last visit, it was a new experience for me as well as my family. We had a great day. I'm sure I thought the tickets were expensive. I have no doubt I probably grumbled to myself about the price of a simple lunch for my girls, and I would bet that I complained about the cost of bottled water. However, we all left there feeling like we had a great day, and would gladly do it again! I remembered that feeling; it was the same one I had for Disney just a few years before.

The contrast between the two parks became engraved in my mind the next day when we visited EPCOT Center. Again, we found some rides closed for repair, and even the rides that we got on suddenly felt old and out of date. It was the technology of the past! And worse yet, there was no sign of the future being built. Oh, there was a new ride here or there, but by and large, the majority of rides had not been updated in many years. One thing did get upgraded though, and that was the price of admission and the dollars spent on a burger; those were certainly keeping up with modern days.

After a few days, we headed home from our vacation. My children were satisfied and happy. My wife and I were tired from all the running around, and overall feeling like we had a good vacation. The businessman in me—the consultant that stresses customer service and making sure that your business is stronger than the competition—left feeling like I was witnessing the beginning of the end for Disney. I left in fact feeling like I had been a victim of the "Mouse Trap."

In 2004, during our family summer vacation, after much coaxing from my daughters, we decided to make a stop at both Universal Studios and Disney in Orlando. We first went to Universal for two days. Once again, our experience was fantastic. The rides were all up and running, the park was meticulously clean and everywhere you look it was a rainbow of bright colors, it seemed freshly painted on, although it probably wasn't.

The most significant discovery we made during this visit to the Universal was the "fast pass." This is a special ticket you can buy that allows you to enter almost any ride and get on a special line that is always shorter than the regular line. There were some lines that had eighty-minute wait times, and we managed to use the "fast pass" to get on the ride within fifteen minutes! Universal sells only a limited number of "fast passes" each day to ensure that the lines don't become too long for those willing to pay the extra thirty dollars per ticket. That extra fee makes an already expensive ticket of admission really expensive; close to ninety dollars per ticket for an adult. But to put it simply: on a hot summer day, when lines are usually sixty minutes or longer, you would pay it gladly, and Universal Studios understands that. Here's the best part: if you stay at one of the park resorts as a guest when you are in Orlando visiting the park, your room key becomes a fast pass for free!

As my family and I casually strolled through Universal Studio for two days, getting on every ride at will, and never suffering the agony of a long line, or the disappointment of a ride down for maintenance, we left there, many hundreds of dollars poorer, but feeling like we had a great time.

And now, as the famous radio commentator Paul Harvey would say, "The rest of the story." Now, it was on to Disney. We stayed at a Disney Resort hotel, purchased tickets to the parks, and headed to the Magic Kingdom. When we arrived, the park was overcrowded like we had never seen it before. I decided to head back to the hotel rather than fight the crowds, but my wife and two daughters, all braver souls than I, forged on, and soon melted into the crowds as I waved goodbye to them from the transportation center.

When my family returned to the hotel that evening, there were no smiles, no happy stories to tell. There was just the look of three tired people. They told me the story of their day. Five rides down for maintenance! The lines in the remaining operational rides were no less than eighty minutes each. Rather than admit fewer people to the park because of unavailable rides, the park filled to its maximum legal capacity. However, the most interesting part was understanding Disney's idea of the "fast pass."

At Disney, they don't sell extra tickets for a "fast pass." They give all comers an equal shot at getting "fast pass" tickets for each ride. Here's how it works: you go to a ride, and insert your park admission pass into a machine. The machine then spits out a ticket back to you that gives you a time range when you can return to that ride and go to the front of the line. Sounds pretty good? After all, with some planning and coordination, you figure you can go to several rides in advance, get a "fast pass" for each of those, and then make your way back to them at the appointed hour. Well, unfortunately you can't do that, because Disney imposes a limit on the time in between fast passes that you can get. So much for that idea!

Figure 4 is a copy of a fast pass that my daughter Cristina received for one of the rides that day. Notice that it invites the person holding the ticket to return between the hours of 7:55 p.m. and 8:55 p.m. Also notice that it points out that another fast pass ticket can be obtained after 4:15 p.m. The most significant observation one can make when looking at the ticket is the time at which my daughter got the ticket. It was 2:46 p.m. She was to come back to that ride four hours and nine minutes later to get on a three-minute ride! This is supposed to be a "fast pass?" What happened you ask? Cristina did go back four hours and nine minutes later. The ride was down for maintenance. True Story!

The next day, my wife looked at me and said "Your turn. I am not going back to the park with the girls. So, I loaded my girls on the Disney Bus, and we were off to EPCOT Center. Surely it had to be better than the experience that they had at the Magic Kingdom the day before. I was wrong.

Disney's idea of a fast pass and Universal's true fast pass are separated by one thing: Breakthrough Thinking! What lessons can the breakthrough leader take away from this story? There are several.

Figure 4: A copy of the Disney Fast Pass (front and back of the ticket stub) for Space Mountain ride, July 4, 2004.

Don't take your eye of the ball

Disney has taken their eye off the ball. In doing so, they have fallen behind in what they once were the absolute best at: customer service. In a place where once imaginative thinking and breakthrough thinking could be seen at all levels of the organization, from senior management, engineers, designers, to the person sweeping the floor at the parks, it is now painfully obvious that this is missing.

Stop investing in your team and they will stop investing in themselves

Disney was not investing appropriately in the up-keep of their parks. EPCOT Center, once the place that defined the future, is now a relic of past technology. It is in serious need of a complete overhaul. That takes big dollars, and Disney's attempt to indicate that they are building the future with small signs posted at the park are not enough to actually make it happen. What's interesting is that if a company stops investing, the employees know it, and act accordingly.

Your competition lives to kill you

Any questions?

Breakthrough thinking is not a fad

Breakthrough-thinking teams require breakthrough-thinking leaders who do their jobs with renewed emphasis every single day. If leaders work on creating a culture where this type of behavior is the norm, and they live that culture each day, only then will the culture be sustainable over time.

If current management team isn't doing the job, hire one that will

As described earlier in the text, having the appropriate team in place to make breakthrough thinking happen in an organization takes a special group of people. It's the leader's job to make sure he or she has them in place.

Grumbling paying customers are not as good as happy paying customers

As I walked through the Disney Park this last time in the summer of 2004, I asked myself, "Why don't they get it?" and, "How could they let this place get this way?" I was referring to how far in disrepair I thought the grounds looked at EPCOT Center. Then I looked around, and realized that the park was full of paying customers. Suddenly, I understood. The hardest thing for any organization to do is change when the money is still coming in.

This, however, is indicative of a very short-term business outlook. The question is how many of those people will come back next year? And how many will choose to go to Universal instead? Both are great questions. So, I decided to ask a few folks.

In a non-scientific survey, conducted over a period of several hours toward the end of my day at EPCOT, the answer to both of these questions was clear to me. I asked people in the park if they had been to Universal while in Orlando this last trip. It was not hard to find people who had visited Universal the day before coming to Disney. Thousands of people, including ourselves, do it each day. The answer all had a similar theme: "I preferred Universal Islands of Adventure," "Universal is much nicer and much newer," "I did not mind paying there, but I don't feel the same about paying today," or "Universal has much cooler rides."

The one quote that most resonated with me was from a woman in her early thirties who had brought her daughter to the park for the first time. She said, "This is sad for me, the park looks sad. Not the way I remember it." She was going to Universal the next day. She'd never been there. I wonder what she thought of it? I suspect I know the answer.

A setback does not mean you can't make a strong comeback

I have been a die-hard fan of Disney since I was a cadet in the Air Force. I believe that with a renewed sense of breakthrough thinking and leadership, they can make a strong comeback. Unfortunately, many companies have to go through rough times to get the message. Some, like Chrysler and IBM, make it through their difficult times, reinvent themselves and become top in their industries again. Others, like giant airline companies Pan Am and Eastern, die leaving reminders and warning signs for other to avoid. Disney is at the crossroad. With the right balance of investment, breakthrough thinking culture and leadership, the Mouse can be back on top!

TWENTY-FOUR

BEGINNING WITH THE END

Hangar 4B: The Myth Is Real

Hangar Rats. That was the nickname given to those of us who worked in Hangar 4B. From the exterior, this building looks no different than it has for more than sixty years when it was first built in Wright-Patterson Air Force Base, Ohio. Initially built as an aircraft maintenance hangar, it eventually became a high-tech, sophisticated maze of laboratories. The very first time I entered through the vaulted door of this top-secret place, I thought I had just entered the surreal world of James Bond, complete with secret codes and key pads to gain access to even more secured places within the already secured Hangar.

Within the massive space of Hangar 4B, we enjoyed the luxury of the most sophisticated computers, lasers, solar simulators, electron microscopes, and other electronic equipment. There was even an enormous radar range to simulate flight conditions and test the latest avionics, and electro-optics weapons and countermeasures equipment. Every space had its own special combination lock. Every office at least one safe to keep the highly confidential and top secret materials, documents, and test reports generated. Electronic gadgets abounded.

Procedures were strict in terms of protecting the integrity of the secrets being kept in this facility. And while there always seemed to be an easy going way among the people who worked in Hangar 4B, the seriousness of the work done, and the supreme need to protect the information, was never lost or underestimated. It was a serious place, where people were doing serious work.

In 1985, I reported to Wright-Patterson Air Force Base for my first assignment as a military officer. I was fortunate to be assigned to Hangar 4B. At the time, Dan Murray was the in charge of this Avionics Laboratory Branch. Dan was on his second career having retired from the Air Force as a Lieutenant Colonel, he was now civil servant with the government. The crew consisted of approximately fifty people. Some, like myself, were military officers, others civilian Department Of Defense employees, and yet others were civilian contractors working for a company that supported the research and development activities within the Hangar.

Hangar 4B came to fame when an episode of the program called NOVA aired and highlighted it as the place were "aliens" supposedly recovered after their space ships crashed here on earth, were being kept and studied. Having worked there for several years, I think I can safely say without compromising any secrets, that I never saw aliens in the Hangar. Although there was one particular area of the Hangar that very few people had access. I always wondered what lie beyond the huge vaulted door. But I am fairly certain that the only strange thing going in and out of that place were the engineers and scientist conducting top-secret work. That was certainly one-way of describing most of the people who worked in Hangar 4B. They were brilliant, albeit a bit off-center, engineers and scientists. They were the envy of people working in other branches of the Avionics Laboratory. We were set apart. Also known as the Taj Majal, because so few people were privileged to enter, Hangar 4B was reserved for us Hangar Rats. It was a name we wore proudly.

This group of people was unique in many ways. Equally unique were the results achieved by this band of renegades and unconventional individuals. They were usually breakthrough in nature. The work going on in Hangar 4B was happening nowhere else in the world. Discoveries about infra-red systems, laser warning receivers, and advanced radar technologies, have greatly contributed to the state-of-the-art in our sophisticated avionics on-board the most advanced fighter jets of today.

Looking back now nearly twenty-five years when I worked in this magical place of innovation, I've tried to understand what made it so special. How do I know it was special? Because since leaving Hangar 4B in 1988, I have worked in many different organizations, across different industries, and I have only found this spirit of creativity, this level of innovation, teamwork, and passion for results, in very few places.

What was it about Hangar 4B that made it so special? The answer no doubt is multi-factorial. However, one thing, above all others factors, made this a place of breakthrough results. It was the fact that we had a great leader in Colonel Murray. Dan Murray had a vision for his organization, and no one was ever unclear about what that mission was. Dan was a leader who clearly cared more about us than he did about himself. He could be tough, but was never without compassion. He valued diversity of all dimensions before it became a corporate fad, or it was even understood by executives in Corporate America. He created an environment where creative minds were fostered, encouraged, and challenged to take risks, make mistakes, and invent a new way of doing things. The only possible outcome given the environment Dan created, and the talented people he recruited into the organization, was discovery, innovation, and breakthrough results.

Dan Murray understood his people. He had an uncanny ability to draw out the very best in all of us and unleash our collective creative spirits. He never let us forget how special we were as a team. He was our most zealous advocate and our loudest cheerleader. His vision was our vision. His success, while unimportant to him, was a direct result of ours as a team, and as individuals. He celebrated our success!

Hangar 4B is not a myth as the NOVA program seemed to imply. It is a very real place, doing very real work. And for the many lessons I learned while working among this incredible bunch of people, the most important was this: breakthrough thinking and breakthrough results achieved by the Hangar Rats started with Dan. He was our leader; and breakthrough thinking starts and ends with the leader.

EPILOGUE

In the first chapter of this section of the book, we began with the premise that Breakthrough Thinking starts with the leader. The leader's attitude determines their actions; and it is these actions that subsequently impact the followers.

Breakthrough thinking leaders have an innate ability to dream big, see things that don't yet exist, and then somehow motivate others to achieve something that they thought impossible before. Breakthrough thinking leaders create entire new markets simply because of the way they think!

Not too many people would recognize the name Mike Yurosek. Mr. Yurosek is responsible for creating the booming business of baby carrots. Baby carrots have overtaken the nation, making their way onto dinner plates and lunch boxes all over America. They have even become one of the nation's favorite snack foods. They are now available in single-serving packs as well as large bags at groceries stores. They are offered in airplanes as snacks, and even have begun to replace French fries in some fast food places.

Baby carrots are not really babies. They are full-grown carrots that have been cut into standard two-inch sections, tumbled through a manufacturing process, and whittled down to the bite size Americans have come to love.

How did baby carrots come about? More than twenty-five years ago, Mr. Yurosek, a California farmer, became tired of trashing imperfect vegetables. He was discarding more that 400 tons of carrots each day down the cull chute at his packing plant in Bakersfield. At times, this waste could be as much as seventy percent of the total harvest for the day. Yurosek decided to create a new kind of carrot, and began cutting these misshapen carrots into the small pieces we know today. He invested in equipment necessary to achieve the result he wanted. He worked with local grocers to create a demand for this new form of freshly packed carrot.

Baby carrots have redefined the carrot. In the 1960s, the average American ate about six pounds of carrots each year. Today, that number is almost eleven pounds per year—a dramatic increase, especially in light of the overall unhealthy eating habits of Americans. Not only are we eating more of them, we are paying a significant premium for these mini-carrots. Business is booming. All because one man saw something no one else did, and worked to create a new reality. In the end, that is what breakthrough leaders do: they create new realities.

Breakthrough Thinking Legacy Leaders are individuals who visualize a new possibility, harness and use the power of individuals around them, and create new realities. The world we live in is a much better place because of breakthrough thinking leaders of the past, and it will be a better place tomorrow because of future breakthrough thinking leaders.

BIBLIOGRAPHY

AMBROSE, Stephen E., Undaunted Courage. New York, Touchstone, 96

BILLICK & PETERSON, Competitive Leadership–Twelve Principles for Success. Chicago, Triumph Books. 2001

BLISS, W. G. 2006. Costs of Employee Turnover. William G. Bliss, President of Bliss & Associates Inc., Wayne, NJ.

BRACEY, ROSENBLUM, SANDFORD, TRUEBLOOD, Managing from the Heart. New York, Delacorte Press, 1990

CLAVEL, James, The Art of War SunTzu. New York, Dell Publishing, 83

COVEY, Stephen R., The 7 Habits of Highly Effective People. New York, Fireside, 1989

DONNITHORNE, Col. Larry R., The West Point Way of Leadership. New York, Currency Doubleday, 1993

GARCIA, Charles P., Leadership Lessons Of the White House Fellows. McGraw Hill, 2009

GISCOMBE, K. & Mattis M.C. (2004) Leveling the Playing Field for Women of Color in Corporate Management: Is the Business Case Enough? Journal of Business Ethics, Volume 37, Number 1, April 2002 , pp. 103–119(17).

HERSEY, Paul, The Situational Leader. NY, Warner Books, 1984

HESSELBEIN, GOLDSMITH, BECKHARD, The Druker Foundation: The Leader of the Future. New York, Jossey-Bass, 1996

KOTTER, John, A Force for Change. New York, Free Press, 1990

LOMBARDI, Vince, Jr., What it takes to be #1. New York, McGraw Hill, 2001

MAXWELL, John C., Developing The Leaders Around You, Nashville, Thomas Nelson, 1995

MAXWELL, John C., The 21 Irrefutable Laws of Leadership, Nashville, Thomas Nelson, 1998

PEDLER, M., BURGOYNE, J. AND BOYDELL, T. 1997. *The Learning Company: A strategy for sustainable development*. 2nd Ed. London; McGraw-Hill.

SPEARS, Larry C., Insights on Leadership. Service, Stewardship, Spirit, and Servant Leadership. New York, Wiley, 1998.

SCHWARTZ, Peter, The Art of the Long View. New York, Doubleday Currency, 1991.

HispanTelligence, US Hispanic Purchasing Power 1978–2010.

Key Facts, Race, Ethnicity and Medical care. A report from the Henry J. Kaiser Family Foundation, 1997.

ABOUT THE AUTHOR

Anthony López is the author of "The Legacy Leader: Leadership With A Purpose," "Breakthrough Thinking: The Legacy Leader's Role In Driving Innovation" and "The Leader's Lobotomy: The Legacy Leader Avoid Promotion Induced Amnesia" He is also the author of two Christian books titled: "See You At The Wake: Healing Relationships Before It's Too Late" and "Jag: Christian Lessons From My Golden Retriever." Tony is a sought after motivational speaker, and is a recognized expert on leadership and management. He began his career as a US Air Force Officer where he served as a Flight Test Director and Program Manager. Tony later served as a Human Resources Officer in the Air Force Reserves. He joined Johnson & Johnson in 1991 and held leadership positions in Corporate Engineering, Manufacturing, Marketing, Communications, and General Management. Later he was Global Vice President for Marketing in ConMed. Tony is currently Senior Vice President and General Manager in CareFusion, a California based medical device company. Tony is President of L&L Associates, a leadership and management consulting group he founded in 2000.

He was also an Adjunct Professor at the Richard T. Dormer School of Business and Management Sciences at Indiana Purdue University. Tony holds a BS in Electrical Engineering, an MS in Engineering Management with Business Concentration, and is a graduate of the Department of Defense Equal Opportunity Management Institute. You can contact Tony at ablopez85@yahoo.com or tony@thelegacyleader.net. You can also visit www.thelegacyleader.net.

listen|imagine|view|experience

AUDIO BOOK DOWNLOAD INCLUDED WITH THIS BOOK!

In your hands you hold a complete digital entertainment package. Besides purchasing the paper version of this book, this book includes a free download of the audio version of this book. Simply use the code listed below when visiting our website. Once downloaded to your computer, you can listen to the book through your computer's speakers, burn it to an audio CD or save the file to your portable music device (such as Apple's popular iPod) and listen on the go!

How to get your free audio book digital download:

1. Visit www.tatepublishing.com and click on the e|LIVE logo on the home page.
2. Enter the following coupon code:
   c8d8-560f-545f-46fb-64ff-8cfd-7022-aafe
3. Download the audio book from your e|LIVE digital locker and begin enjoying your new digital entertainment package today!